Praise for

A Wealth of Family

"Thomas Brooks' moving and candid account invites everyone into his life and creates a sense of kinship from his family to your own. His intricate story of discovery empowers us all."

—Michelle Gipson, book editor, *Atlanta Daily World*

"Thomas Brooks has provided a very brave and honest account of not only his personal journey to reconnect with his biological family but also his values that support the one humanity that our world order desperately needs to understand. Brooks demonstrates how one can simultaneously pursue the very best in personal and collective identity without, in the process, building walls to others. His narrative of heritage and reunion should be read widely by adopted children and their parents."

—Dr. Jack L. Daniel, former Vice Provost and Dean at the University of Pittsburgh, current Professor of Communication, and co-author of *We Fish: The Journey to Fatherhood* with his son Dr. Omari C. Daniel

"This refreshing and thought-provoking book shows people how to cross cultural barriers."

—Brandon Massey, award-winning author of *The Other Brother*

"The author's journey to discover his diverse heritage gives us a compelling and vivid illustration of the interdependence of Africa and the USA. Brooks does a fantastic job of showing the fruits of this win-win international relationship at the family unit level."

—Mark Thaiya, Chairperson, Association of Kenyan Professionals in Atlanta

"Thomas Brooks reminds us of how essential it is to explore and know our history."

—Natasha Munson, author of *Life Lessons for My Sisters*

"The real-life journey of Thomas Brooks to embrace his diverse biological family, while holding fast to his adoptive one, warmed my soul. If you have loved ones whose lives have been touched by either side of adoption, you will want to share this story with them."

—C. Kelly Robinson, best-selling author of *Between Brothers* and *The One That Got Away*

A Wealth of Family

An Adopted Son's International Quest for Heritage, Reunion, and Enrichment

Thomas Brooks

Alpha
Multimedia, Inc.
— Houston, Texas —

First printing 2006

ISBN-13: 978-0-9774629-3-3
ISBN-10: 0-9774629-3-5
LCCN: 2006900057

ATTENTION CORPORATIONS, UNIVERSITIES, COLLEGES, AND PROFESSIONAL ORGANIZATIONS: Quantity discounts are available on bulk purchases of this book for educational, gift purposes, or as premiums for increasing magazine subscriptions or renewals. Special books or book excerpts can also be created to fit specific needs. For information, please contact Alpha Multimedia, Inc., P.O. Box 722034, Houston, TX 77272-2034, USA; +1 (281) 217-1960.

Contents

1   INTRODUCTION

5   CHAPTER ONE
The Decision to Search

11   CHAPTER TWO
A Bundle of Joy

17   CHAPTER THREE
Growing Up Lowry

25   CHAPTER FOUR
The North Side of Pittsburgh, USA

33   CHAPTER FIVE
The Shocking News

41   CHAPTER SIX
Once a Lion, Always a Lion

51   CHAPTER SEVEN
Inroads for Success

57   CHAPTER EIGHT
Pitt Is It

79   CHAPTER NINE
Survive and Advance

95   CHAPTER TEN
Two Bouquets for Mother's Day

113   CHAPTER ELEVEN
From Europe to Haight-Ashbury and Back

139   CHAPTER TWELVE
Roots and Reunion

171   CHAPTER THIRTEEN
A Piece of Africa

189   CHAPTER FOURTEEN
Enriching Relationships

215   CHAPTER FIFTEEN
Come Together

231   EPILOGUE

247   BE FEATURED IN OUR NEXT BOOK

250   ABOUT THE AUTHOR

Introduction

I wrote this book because I am proud of the heritage of my three diverse families. It is an inclusive pride, one that I believe others can identify with and celebrate.

It is my hope that you will be moved by this true story of adoption, reunion, and heritage. I have endeavored to provide a perspective on multicultural families and insights on overcoming poverty and racism.

In spite of the ups and downs I have experienced in my life, I have an optimistic view on race relations in the world. Although there will always be some prejudice, I believe that things will definitely get better with each generation. I have noticed a marked improvement in the last twenty years in the United States. To paraphrase my great Alpha Phi Alpha fraternity brother, Dr. Martin Luther King, we have prejudice and hate because we fear each other. We fear each other because we don't know each other. We don't know each other because we are so often separated from each other. Even so-called "good Christian people" have to agree that one of the most segregated times in America is Sunday morning at 11 A.M. when Blacks and Whites typically go into different buildings to worship the same God using the same Bible. We should, individually, build relationships with people who do not look like us, think like us, worship like us, or act like us.

More education and diverse experiences can eradicate racism and create world citizens. I am proud of my heritage as an African-American, and I have learned to also view myself as a world citizen. I am no longer limited by race, religion, nationality, or political ideology. During my travels to six continents, I learned to embrace diverse cultures, ideas, and ethnic groups. With this perspective, it is easy to see that the two-way racism between Blacks and Whites in America is the result of ignorance. Furthermore, discord within the African-American community between light-skinned and dark-skinned people is stupid. Ethnic group conflicts over politics like those in Kenya are misguided, tragic, and self-defeating. Ethnic group conflicts that lead to war, like those in Bosnia are even more irrational. Japanese have fought Koreans, Indians have fought with Pakistanis, and the list goes on. When we realize that all people are citizens of the world and then begin to truly value diverse cultures, ideas, and backgrounds the world becomes less dangerous and people suffer less.

We can initiate firm inroads against racism, tribalism, and infighting through education and awareness. For example, education about our own history now allows African-Americans to take pride in our great inventors, writers, physicians, and statesmen. I want to encourage Black Americans, often oppressed for almost four hundred years but now more educated than ever on our own history, to take pride in our influence on world culture.

Rightly or wrongly, the United States has more influence than any other country on the world's popular culture, including music, dance, fashion, and movies. I have personally seen this in Africa, Asia, Australia, Europe, and South America. In my opinion, African-Americans do the most to set the overall tempo for pop culture in the United States. African-Americans have given the world jazz, blues, gospel, funk, rap, and hip-hop. Elements of African-American culture are assimilated into "America's culture," and then American culture propagates across the world. Thus, in my view, African-Americans, more than any other group, set the tone for pop culture across the world. This phenomenon is monumental and African-Americans often receive little credit for it.

This book is the product of more than six years of research and writing. I am grateful for the support of my African-American mother, Joan Lowry-Brooks; my white biological mother, Dorothy Blazier-

Wallstein; and my Kenyan biological father, Mboga Mageka Omwenga, in this project.

I also acknowledge the content and advice of many friends and several other family members, including my great-uncle Bill Blazier who has put years of effort into uncovering the Blazier family heritage, tracing the family back to Europe in the 1700s. Charles Lowry, Joan's first cousin, has been of great assistance as I have collected information on the Lowry family heritage. In the end, my editor Sue Collier diligently guided my efforts to create a polished final product.

Some stories I was told and letters written to me are paraphrased within the dialogue. As much as possible, I attempted to keep the meaning and context of the original communication intact. Of course, some of the memories of my sources have faded. Some accounts conflict. It's seldom easy to write about the personal lives of others, but it was very interesting to pull together stories across generations, cultures, and continents. A few names of nonfamily members not central to the story were changed (denoted by *) to protect their privacy.

Writing about one's own family life is hard. Having a large, multicultural family increases the challenge. History, especially one's personal history, can be subjective. Even two siblings will have radically different views and memories of their shared childhood. By nature, the human mind has a way of retelling and reordering events and communications between people not so much to deceive as to make the remembrance not only bearable but also memorable. I have done my best to present an accurate story, taking advantage of detailed notes and videotapes of key trips and events. The content is my perspective, my memories. It is objectively factual to me but not necessarily objective.

I have discovered that there is a great deal in my heritage of which to be proud. There is the courage and integrity of my Kenyan father. The odyssey of my ancestors on my biological mother's side, who escaped the murderous persecution of the Orthodox Russians against Lithuanian Jews, is impressive and compelling. There is my individual piece in the large and grand African-American experience, growing up in a dynamic family in Pittsburgh. I hope this book will inspire you to explore your life, culture, and relationships and to discover something in which you can find meaning.

Thomas Brooks
January 2006

CHAPTER ONE

The Decision
to Search

As a young adopted child, I had been challenged by the question of which heritage an African-American should embrace. For example, could an African-American embrace a French heritage because of his or her affection for the French language and culture learned in high school? Does the answer change if his or her ancestors are from the French-speaking Caribbean island of Guadeloupe? Or should an African-American seek to embrace African culture? That seems obvious, but in Kenya alone there are more than seventy ethnic groups, most with their own languages and cultures. What about all the other countries in the Africa of today? Few African-Americans have any idea whether their ancestors hail from the lands known today as Nigeria, Ghana, or Angola, to name just a few. Many can live without that ancestral knowledge but, as it turns out, I was not one of them.

I was twenty-five years old when, after a few months of thought, I decided to search for my biological parents. It was 1992, during the last semester of my MBA studies at the University of Maryland. Even though I had known of my adoption since I was eleven years old and had a very good relationship with my adoptive family, I had a growing need to know more about my biological background. Because I knew nothing of my biological parents and their heritage, I felt somehow that my own human identity was partially lacking. I had this sentiment in common with many African-Americans whose family heritages were erased by centuries of slavery, but in my case even the previous generation was a mystery.

In February 1992 I spoke with my adoptive mother about my feelings. "Mom, I am proud of my place in the Lowry family and its heritage. I love you and am delighted to be your son. You are my real mother. I also want the additional knowledge of the heritage of my biological parents." I explained to her that I wanted to know their ethnic origins as well as their physical makeup and family medical histories. Additional information about their interests and accomplishments would be a bonus.

"I was told only that your biological parents were a mixed-race couple," she said quietly.

"I'd kind of concluded I was multiracial from a few comments made by you and other people over the years," I slowly said. "But it never really mattered much back then since I was viewed as a 'Black' boy in a Black family, as opposed to 'multiracial.' I remember that you would never let me tease multiracial people like the other kids did. You would never let me refer to them as 'half-breeds,' for example."

"Race doesn't matter," she said emphatically. "We are all the same in God's sight."

She paused, looking a bit uncomfortable. I added, "Mom, I want to make sure you understand that I am not looking for a new mother. You are the only mother I will ever have, in the truest sense of the word. You raised me. You cared for me when I was sick. You went hungry so I could eat. You are my *real* mother."

"Thomas, I understand," she said. "I am okay with you finding your biological parents. I wouldn't want to try to stop you, if that is what you want to do."

And that was it.

Although I am generally an optimistic person, I went into the search with low expectations. I didn't expect to actually find my biological parents. I assumed they were dead or terrible people I would not want to befriend. Or, I imagined, if I found them, they might deny they had anything to do with me. They might not want any contact with me, perhaps because they would not want their lives with their current families interrupted.

As stated, I was busy finishing my last semester of my MBA and I was working full-time as an engineer for a major defense contractor. I was also having trouble finding a new and better job at this time because of the recession that gripped the United States in the early 1990s. Many companies, especially Maryland and Virginia defense contractors, were laying off engineers and eliminating middle management positions. Consequently, there was a glut of MBAs and technical professionals. Since I was busy studying to graduate and looking to find a new career, searching for my biological parents took a decidedly low priority. This was partially because I assumed the search would be a monumental task and involve months, or even years, of research. Where would I find the money and time that might be needed to travel to find these people? Not having a ready answer, I decided to wait until after completing my MBA to begin investing a lot of resources in the search.

However, I was able to identify the agency that handled the adoption, Family Services of Western Pennsylvania, with only a few inquiring phone calls. I gathered information on state and federal laws relating to adoption and adoption information, which I thought would be essential to my search. I contacted different adoption support groups such as the Adoptees' Liberty Movement Association (ALMA), the National Adoption Information Clearinghouse (NAIC), the Adoption Support Institute, the Black Adoption Consortium, the Black Adoption Placement Center, and the National Adoption Center.

I figured that an important task before starting the search process would be to get the adoption agency to answer as many questions as possible. All it cost me was a postage stamp and the time to write a letter. Judy Scott, post-adoption clinician, was my helpful contact at

Family Services of Western Pennsylvania, which had been known as Family and Children's Service when I was born back in 1966.

On July 1, 1992, Judy mailed me my background history. The accompanying cover letter said that the information "was obtained from the agency record" and "was provided by the birth mother" at the time of my birth. Since the agency had no further contact with my biological mother, no current information was available. Judy could not answer many of my questions because of Pennsylvania laws as of 1992 regarding confidentiality. Judy provided all available nonidentifying information in the four-page document.

I was taken aback to receive any information at all. It was incredibly fulfilling to add additional pieces to the puzzle of my own identity. I felt like I had the majority of what I wanted after getting the document provided by the agency. My biological mother was a White American who gave birth to me at the age of nineteen. My biological father was Kenyan and about twenty-six years old at the time of my birth. I was indeed multiracial. I learned that both of my parents attended college. This was more information than I had ever expected to find. It gave me a good feeling about the contribution of both of my parents to my heritage.

As I read the July 1992 report, I noted the statement that my biological mother provided the source material for all of the information. For whatever reason, my biological father was not there to be interviewed by the adoption agency. Thus, the information about him and the paternal grandparents in Kenya was second- if not thirdhand.

Discovering in the report that some of my natural mother's ancestors were Lithuanians who practiced Judaism was positive. I vaguely viewed both Lithuanians and Jews as tough and determined, both groups having survived numerous conflicts over the centuries. As an athlete and a sports fan, I also knew that Lithuania had a great national basketball team for such a small nation. Of course, Kenyans have long been a dominant force in international middle- and long-distance running. I was happy to know that I had a Kenyan biological father, a tangible link to my African heritage.

My white maternal grandmother was forty-three years old at the time of my birth—quite young for a grandmother. She was described as "brilliant" in the document, which made me think that there might be some reason for my academic success.

My white maternal grandfather was described as a five-foot ten-inch truck driver of mostly German descent with a high school education.

Because she had given me up while she was a college freshman, I wondered where my biological mother attended college. I wondered about the pressure on her at the time to make a decision about what to do with me. Of course, I was happy that she did not have an abortion, though the July 1992 report stated that she had considered that option. The document stated that she had become a reservation agent with an airline by 1967, so I assumed that my birth might have caused her to leave college, at least for a period.

My nineteen-year-old biological mother had given me up for adoption as soon as I entered the world in December 1966. I was then placed in foster care. The identity of the foster care family was not revealed to me until 2006. I have learned that they were an African-American family in the community of Clairton, just south of Pittsburgh, Pennsylvania.

CHAPTER TWO

A Bundle of Joy

Jimmie Brooks and Joan Lowry-Brooks, an attractive African-American couple in Pittsburgh, had been hoping to give birth to a child during the mid-1960s. Joan had tried three times to carry a baby to term, but each pregnancy ended in a miscarriage. One miscarriage happened as late as the seventh month. That child was a boy. Joan was disconsolate.

The story of my life with the Brooks family started after her third miscarriage in 1964. The doctors told her that she could not have a child because of problems with her reproductive organs. At that point, this beautiful woman in her late twenties, who made men stop and turn on the streets of Pittsburgh, believed she would never get the child for which she so desperately longed. Off from work on a Tuesday, while at home ironing, Joan heard a voice speak to her heart: "You can adopt."

A devout Christian, Joan believed that this voice was the Holy Spirit. Never dismissing the omnipotence and peacefulness of this extraordinary presence, she seriously began to think about raising a child she and Jimmie did not conceive together.

Later that week over dinner in their small, well-kept kitchen, Joan removed her apron and began thinking out loud. "I would really like for us to have a child."

"I know," replied Jimmie solemnly, "but it seems like that is not possible."

"We can adopt."

There was a long pause. After gathering his thoughts, Jimmie responded, "I don't know."

"I would love to be a mother to a child, and you would enjoy having a son. Adoption would even allow us to be sure of the child's gender."

"I don't know about this idea," Jimmie confessed as he straightened his tall frame into a standing position. "Adoption is something we had discussed previously." As he walked away and mounted the stairs, the question remained in limbo.

Subsequently, because Joan was so passionate about the idea, Jimmie enthusiastically agreed to adopt a son.

Jimmie's mother, Emily, was thrilled with the idea, and so were Jimmie's siblings, Louise and Raymond. It seemed settled. Some lucky infant was to have an excited grandmother, uncle, and aunt on the child's adoptive father's side. On the infant's equally excited mother's side there would be a grandmother, a grandfather, four aunts, and five uncles.

Joan went to the adoption agency, taking a bus ride to its offices located in downtown Pittsburgh, and completed the necessary paperwork. She carried with her both Jimmie's and her medical and family history, and employment background. What Joan did not know was how long the adoption process would take. She was not prepared to wait more than two years.

The agency required old pictures of different family members to see the range of skin colors in the family to ensure that the adopted child would have what they viewed as the right home in terms of a perceived racial fit. There were many times when Joan would get her hopes up when she was told about a child that "might be available," only to have those hopes dashed for some reason. However, because of the societal taboo associated with interracial relationships and babies born to unwed mothers in the 1960s, there were many multiracial children available for adoption.

Early in the process, the woman at the agency asked Joan if she would mind adopting a multiracial child. Joan answered without missing a beat, "No. A child is a child. All children are God's creation. It doesn't make any difference."

One wet spring day in March 1967, the agency called Joan. Its message came through as if it were a biblical annunciation. The agency had a little boy for her. The child was in foster care at the time.

Joan was ecstatic. She didn't care about the race of the baby. All she knew was that she had a lot of love to give a child. She wanted an infant badly. She longed to raise and teach a child as her own. She knew she would make a great parent.

Although Joan and Jimmie's social milieu was clearly African-American, both had an interracial ancestral gene pool, like many Blacks in America. This, quite likely, influenced the agency to place me, a multiracial child directly descended from one African and one White parent, with them even though American society overtly viewed Joan, Jimmie, and me as "Black."

On an overcast day in May 1967, Joan traveled about an hour with a social worker, Ms. Peterson, to pick me up in Clairton from my foster care family. Joan was so excited during the drive to Clairton that it made the good-natured Ms. Peterson nervous. "When I came back outside with the baby in my arms, the sun broke through the clouds," related Joan. "I could see a bright new world through the torrent of my tears."

When Joan's sister Delores heard that the baby had arrived in the Brooks home, she immediately boarded a bus in Indianapolis and traveled roughly four hundred miles to Pittsburgh, eager to see her new nephew. My new aunts, uncles, and grandparents celebrated the news with showers of love, presents, and parties. Joan and Jimmie named me Thomas. It was as if Joan had given birth to me herself. Joan and Jimmie's house on Banfield Street in Pittsburgh became a focal gathering place for the extended family.

"How did it feel to adopt a child?" asked Delores, who had already given birth to seven children by that time.

"It was the thrill of a lifetime," Joan told her, "especially the moment when the agency put that chubby little boy in my arms."

"I know this has to make you feel good after everything you've been through."

"Yes, I just wanted a child. This child could not be any more my own than if I myself had given birth to him. God worked it out," Joan reflected. "He worked it out. I waited two years. Two years with disappointments of thinking 'Oh, maybe this is the right child.' But God had a plan. God worked it out so that the adopted child even looks like some of our brothers."

"That's so incredible. Does it feel right for you?"

"I believe that adopted children are extremely special because God picks them out and makes the match with the adoptive family. Everything has turned out just right."

The adoption was finalized legally in January 1968 when I was thirteen months old.

From that wintry day, Joan raised me to appreciate the power of God. Without even hinting that I was adopted, she consistently told me, "Tommie, God gave you to me."

One day, when I was three, I responded, "And God gave you to me, Mommy." Joan has always cherished this short verbal exchange. My response was just a function of childhood innocence. At the time, I had no idea I was adopted.

Joan took meticulous care of me and protected me. No one could harm me, unless they went through her first, she vowed, knowing that she would protect me with her life if necessary. Like most toddlers, I craved my mother's attention as a playmate. She gladly and warmly complied. I especially enjoyed playing "horsey," which involved me riding on her back as she crawled around the room on all fours. We both laughed the whole time.

But the family of three was not meant to be as Joan and Jimmie separated in 1970. They divorced in 1971. My mom never remarried.

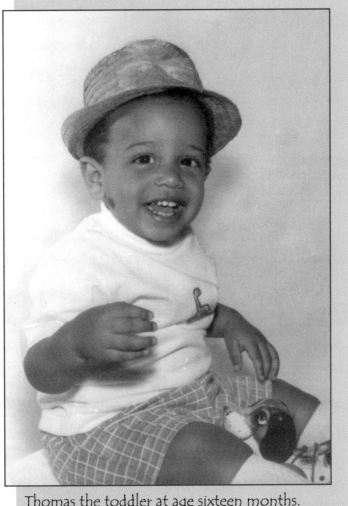

Thomas the toddler at age sixteen months.
April 1968.

From the day the divorce was final, it was basically just Joan and me. Joan reasons that Jimmie missed out, that it was his loss he was not closely involved with my growth into manhood.

I can only remember seeing Jimmie Brooks on two occasions after the divorce. Once I spent a full Saturday with Jimmie when I was five, and then again when I was eight. I remember Jimmie as a nice guy. I had a good time on both days.

During my day with Jimmie when I was eight, we made a brief stop at his workplace, a juvenile detention center. I thought I was tough for an eight-year-old, having won many fights on the North Side schoolyards around Pittsburgh. However, while I sat in the cafeteria waiting for Jimmie to grab some things from his office, I was surrounded by many delinquent teenagers. They had committed real crimes, including vandalism, knife fights, and gunpoint robberies. I was "scared straight" at the age of eight. I knew right then that I did not want to end up in a juvenile detention center. Today I believe Jimmie may have left me there purposely for those fifteen minutes to scare out of me any thought of committing crimes.

Although Jimmie otherwise did not play a significant role in my overall development, I have never harbored resentment against him. In my few interactions with him, he treated me well. I didn't miss what I never had. Whether it was with my birth mother or my adoptive mother, in retrospect I suppose I was destined to be raised by a single mother. I accepted it.

Jimmie's extended family did not forget about me after the divorce. They showed me a lot of love, in spite of the fact that I was not biologically related to them. It meant the world to me then, and it still does. Grandma Emily remained a guiding force in my life for years. Jimmie's sister, my Aunt Louise, who went by the nickname of "Cookie," was also actively involved in my life for a number of years. Aunt Cookie had a significantly large birthmark on her cheek, just like mine. Ironically, until I found out I was adopted, I assumed the birthmark was a genetic link.

After the separation of my adoptive parents in 1970, Joan and I moved in with her father, William Reed Lowry, Sr. I called him Grandpa Bill. He was a powerful and compassionate man, and we lived with him from the time I was three years old until I turned five. I continued to spend a lot of time with him after we got our own place. He had a profound influence on my development.

CHAPTER THREE

Growing Up Lowry

B orn in August 1908, one of the thirteen children of Marshall Ellsworth Lowry and Mary Elizabeth Taliafero-Lowry, Grandpa Bill Lowry came from a dynamic family. His father Marshall was originally from the Carolinas. When Marshall moved to Pittsburgh, he met his wife. The thirteen Lowry children that resulted from their union were to become well known on the North Side of Pittsburgh.

Just months before the October 1929 stock market crash, at the start of the Great Depression, Grandpa Bill and the former Vivian Warfield were married. They became the parents of five boys and five girls, including my mother Joan. These ten children raised more than forty grandchildren.

Vivian was described as the supportive housewife who loved to take care of her children. It is told that she was always in the kitchen cooking, cleaning, or pausing briefly at the kitchen table for a cup of coffee. She wore a band around her head to ease the pain from the migraine headaches she continually suffered. She died of lung cancer in 1968 when I was still a baby.

Grandpa Bill was an outspoken man, and by his actions, he showed me how to be honest and responsible. Grandpa was a lifelong member of Avery Memorial A.M.E. Zion Church on California Avenue on the North Side. He served faithfully on the Trustee Board and Steward Board. He shaped my character and helped mold my destiny during our frequent discussions. When I was in high school, I often visited Grandpa Bill with my mother. My favorite Aunt Bessie, Joan's sister, often came along, and the two sisters would cook and clean for him as he grew older. Other times, when I went by myself, Grandpa would take me to a nearby greasy spoon where we ate hot dogs and talked about life.

During and after my college years, I continued to visit him on my own. I asked him questions about his early life, and encouraged him to reminisce. Grandpa Bill would pull out photo albums, and occasionally, we would share a single shot of whiskey together. By then, he was interacting with me as a man, not just as his grandchild.

Grandpa's words became bridges to understanding the trials and adventures of a Black man growing up in the early part of the twentieth century. He once said, "Although our family was viewed as 'Negro' during the early part of the century, there was definitely Italian, Native American, Irish, and German blood in our family. We also had family from Trinidad.

"Details of the family's heritage and racial makeup were rarely discussed in the 1920s and 1930s," Grandpa continued uneasily. "No one cared about the details of our heritage at the time, partly because American society viewed the family simply as 'Negro.' It was as if everyone subconsciously kept matters of racial heritage a secret."

"Grandpa, did Black and White people get along back then?" I asked.

"Race was not a day-to-day issue among the different ethnic groups living side-by-side in our particular neighborhood, in spite of the fact that racism remained strong in the country as a whole," Grandpa responded.

"What was the North Side of Pittsburgh like back in the 1920s?" I pressed further.

"Our neighborhood was highly integrated. There were a lot of Blacks, Italians, Irish, and other ethnic groups, but to a lesser degree. The common bond everyone shared was that they were either lower middle class or poor. Race was just not a big issue on the block for most," he affirmed with a surprising air of firmness and formality.

"Did that change over the years?" I asked, anticipating what he might add to my growing treasure trove of knowledge of my heritage.

"Not for the most part," Grandpa sighed. Looking up from the photo album lying open in his lap, his withered fingers traced the edges of a dimmed photograph. Grandpa Bill continued, "As a matter of fact, my nephew Charles, your mother's cousin, did not face significant discrimination when he volunteered for the Air Force in 1949. He fought for the United States in the Korean War. Your mother, however, faced prejudice in school from other kids. The prejudice came not only from White students, but also equally from dark-skinned Blacks who did not like her light skin. Black-on-Black discrimination was typically more direct and challenging to navigate." He paused before continuing. "I hadn't thought very much about Black-on-Black discrimination before your mother had problems with it."

Changing the subject, my grandfather said to me, "Tommie, you've got to remember that the Lowry family has a legacy on the North Side.

Eight of Marshall Lowry's thirteen children. Standing: William Reed Lowry (my Grandpa Bill); and some of my great aunts and uncles: Pauline, Tootie, and Charles "Nook." Sitting: Helen, Augie, Gladys, and Bessie. June 1961.

By the time I bought the house on North Franklin Street in 1942, we were already well known. Remember that my father Marshall had thirteen children and their kids all lived around Manchester and the other North Side neighborhoods. Holidays in the 1930s and 1940s drew quite a crowd of children, grandchildren, and friends to Marshall's home on Hazelton Avenue for Mrs. Lowry's soup beans and dumplings." Grandpa smiled at the memory and paused to sip his drink.

Looking out the window, the old man picked up the threads of his story. "During the 1950s and 1960s holidays were big at my house. Thanksgiving, especially, became the de facto family reunion when all ten of my children, and all of the growing number of grandchildren were present. The large living room was filled with happiness and love. Eventually, you grandchildren would be sent upstairs, while the adults celebrated in clouds of cigarette smoke warmed by the heat of glasses filled with holiday cheer. But the holidays were never the same after your grandmother passed in 1968. You were about eighteen months old. It's too bad you were too young to remember her. She really loved you."

Seeing Grandpa's eyes mist over, I tried to change the topic. "Where were you working when you bought your house?"

Grandpa accepted the diversion and continued his oral history. "In the 1940s and 1950s," he reminisced, "good jobs were not easy to find for a Black man. At one time, I worked for a small business owner. I liked the job, and I was a friend of the owner, but there was a problem. The owner's wife kept trying to get me into bed. Of course, I rejected her repeated advances, but I didn't know how to discuss the situation with my friend, the owner. So to avoid a confrontation, I just quit. Forced to find a new position to put bread on the table, I was very lucky to land a job at Westinghouse."

Grandpa Bill had retired from Westinghouse Electric in 1971 when I was four years old. I was living in his house at that time. He was happy and proud when he came home that day, retiring as a storeroom clerk. He had started at Westinghouse as a janitor and was one of the first Blacks employed at Westinghouse, a company that, over time, came to be known by many as being progressive about hiring Blacks. Regarding his onsite retirement celebration, Grandpa Bill had boasted that the White general manager of his Westinghouse Division had a drink with him at work that day. When he had started he never would have thought that such socializing between races would occur or be permitted.

While my mother and I were living with him, he was sometimes disappointed with my behavior. Growing up as a smart-mouthed kid was not easy in Grandpa Bill's house. Grandpa was determined to correct me, even though he'd had a stroke that affected the right side of his body. However, he still had a great deal of strength in the left side and he used his left hand on me frequently. The hollow of that hand across my young rear end not only left its mark but as it came swiftly through the air it played a single shrill note that was not at all musical.

After administering the discipline, Grandpa would tell me, "I only do this because I love you. I don't want you to take this butt whipping personally."

I remember receiving my most severe whippings from Grandpa Bill for calling my cousin an obscenity, and on another occasion, for calling Grandpa Bill "bald-headed." He thought I was crazy for bringing this wrath upon myself. Joan condoned the whippings, but she cautioned her father not to hurt me severely. Today I am thankful for the tough love I received.

In my early childhood, I spent a lot of time with my four aunts and five uncles. During my first ten years, I observed that while my aunts were generally calm and reserved, a few of my uncles seemed to be wild and into partying back then. Some of my uncles and a bunch of other men sometimes spent time hanging on the corner on Liverpool Street. There always seemed to be plenty of Thunderbird, Mad Dog, and beer for them to drink while they stood on the corner.

Out of my strict mother's sight, I also sometimes "hung out" on the corner because my young cousins would be out there too. During this period, my cousins were my main playmates on the North Side. One of my most vivid memories is an occasion when we were playing touch football on the street. My cousin Billy and I, both five years old, had a disagreement.

"Tommie, you know you were out-of-bounds way back there," Billy lectured sternly.

I quickly countered, "No, I wasn't, Billy."

"Yes you were," came his heated response, realizing that a tit-for-tat war of words loomed. "You were past the car!"

"Shut up, Billy. You wasn't even lookin'." I felt the anger swell in me.

It was all pretty harmless. We both rejoined our respective huddles and prepared to start the next play. Then, the men on the corner chimed in.

"Check out Joan's boy, acting all tough," an uncle shouted. Laughter erupted.

"Billy, don't let him punk you down like that," chortled a strange man as part of a garbled string of words.

Another uncle decided to test the waters and see if he could get me to fight. "So, Tommie, are you really bad, or is it all talk?"

We gave in to their goading. Before I knew it, Billy and I were fighting. I knew that I didn't want to fight him, but I felt the pressure to perform.

Most of the men on the corner seemed to be rooting for Billy. My uncles and the other intoxicated men on the corner seemed to enjoy the entertainment. The sight and sound of young clenched fists pounding against one another seemed to bring out animal instincts in the spectators.

I don't think there was a clear winner before the men ultimately broke up the altercation; however, I do remember feeling that all of the men respected Billy and me for not backing down from each other. Although this vague feeling of respect was nice, I remember feeling bad for years about fighting my own cousin.

The next week, my uncles explained their perspective: "A Lowry can fight another Lowry, and then forget about it the next day. But a Lowry will never let anyone else lay a hand on another Lowry. If someone touches one of your cousins, you had better take a brick upside their head." I do not condone violence, but the view of my uncles was consistent with the culture of our neighborhood.

My uncles caused Grandpa Bill a lot more stress than his daughters did. His sons, products of the mean streets of the North Side, were wilder than Grandpa Bill wanted to tolerate in his later years.

Grandpa would reprimand his sons, and later all of his grandsons, about having facial hair. He believed it was unkempt. Grandpa was from a different generation. His sons, like many Blacks in the early 1970s, had some combination of an Afro, a beard, or long wavy hair. They were not sporting the clean-cut conservative professional look Grandpa preferred. Maybe because they were his boys he had different expectations of them than he did of his daughters.

My mother Joan and my four aunts spent a lot of time together. My five uncles spent a lot of time together. However, it was rare for my aunts and uncles to get together collectively during the 1970s and 1980s. Still, all ten siblings shared a common bond.

No one messed with the Lowry girls. Once, when my Aunt Bessie had some problems with neighbors, two of my uncles rode up to her Mount Washington neighborhood brandishing sawed-off shotguns. After a few threatening words, there were no further problems.

There were so many stories to be told of those years on the North Side. In one of my subsequent visits with Grandpa Bill, I reengaged his active mind. "Grandpa, what happened to the house you had on Franklin Street? I mean, it was kind of a family monument. All of your kids and grandchildren seemed to move back in for extended periods at one time or another."

"Yeah, it was kind of like 'Lowry Arms' sometimes," he joked and then sighed. His eyes looked longingly into his past. "With the three levels including the finished attic, it seemed like there was a different small family or two living on every level in the early 1970s. But I didn't mind. It gave me more time with my children and grandchildren. You know, eventually the North Side went through redevelopment, so I sold the house and moved into this senior citizens' high-rise apartment building."

"I understand," I replied. A lot of my cousins and I hated to see that house sold because so many of us had spent significant parts of our childhood there.

Referring to the house, Grandpa looked me in the eyes and told me, "Tommie, make sure as you go through college that you learn to be thankful for what you've got, because you may not always have it."

In the late 1970s and early 1980s, the elderly women in the high-rise apartment building always tried to date my widowed grandfather. This gave him an opportunity to remind me not to let any woman derail me from my career goals. He was proud of my accomplishments. As a result, Grandpa bragged about me to anyone who would listen.

"Myrtle, have you met my grandson? He is studying engineering in college." Or, "Mary, have you met my grandson? He already has a summer internship in engineering."

Although I have more than forty first cousins that might disagree, I believe I was his favorite grandchild, partially because I had spent a lot time with him in his later years, just sitting and talking. Each month, I would ask Grandpa more questions about his life. I also merited his favor as I excelled academically. He was intensely proud of me, as I was the first in his family tree to complete a four-year university education. His bragging about me embarrassed me at times, but it made him happy and proud.

CHAPTER FOUR

The North Side of Pittsburgh, USA

In the fall of 1972, Joan and I moved out of Grandpa Bill's house and rented our own apartment in an area called Fineview, still on the North Side. I was almost six years old. We lived on Sandusky Court, in a drab housing project that overlooked the city. I had a fine view of downtown, Three Rivers Stadium, and Mount Washington from my bedroom window. Our apartment was small, and we did not have any fancy furniture, but I did have my own bedroom. I even had plenty of closet space since I did not have many clothes. I had one dressy outfit, featuring a red jacket, dark blue pants, and a wide-collar light blue shirt. I also had a pair of Pittsburgh Steelers pajamas, which I cherished.

Joan did her best to find a nice place for us to live. At that time, many properties would not rent to families with small children. The properties that did allow small children were often in bad neighborhoods and beset with rats, roaches, or noisy tenants. We stayed at Sandusky Court for only a year. We continued to move around for the next few years to escape difficult living conditions. As we moved, we stayed on the North Side.

We rarely had money to spare. We often lived on government welfare assistance since it was a big challenge for Joan, as a single mother, to find affordable childcare on a working class salary. But what we lacked in money, Joan more than compensated for with love.

Because of Joan's love and the sacrifices she made to ensure I had at least a minimal amount of clothes and food, I see her as my real mother, just as if she had given birth to me herself. We had limited financial resources, but she always put my needs above her own. She also maintained a well-kept home. Although I later came to know my biological mother, no one can take Joan's place, as she dedicated herself to giving me a strong foundation in life.

When I was six years old, I saved all year to accumulate about thirteen dollars so I could give Joan "whatever she wanted" for a Christmas present. My mother told me that what she wanted most was an electric can opener, priced not so coincidentally at $12.99. She seldom asked for anything solely for herself. Years later, when I was a twenty-one-year-old college graduate, I needed some items to get settled in my first apartment of my own. In addition to the plates and linen and other items I "permanently borrowed" from her, one of the things she kindly gave to me was that same can opener, which I used before it finally broke after twenty years of service. She was a very giving person.

As a kid I grew uncomfortable with being poor—that is, poor by American standards. I struggled being poor partly because of needs and wants, and partly because of pride. When I was six years old, an incident that hurt my fragile pride evolved from a simple trip to the grocery store with one of my friends. My friend's family sent him to get two small jars of baby food for his younger sibling. I remember each jar costing about twenty-nine cents back then. On the way home we stopped for some reason, and he asked me to hold the bag with the baby food inside. While we were waiting, the brown paper bag slipped out of my clumsy hand. The two jars broke. My friend said, "I can't show up at home without this baby food. My momma will kill me." So, I went to my mother for the fifty-eight cents, but she didn't have it. I was embarrassed to have to tell my friend that I would have to give him and his mother the fifty-eight cents the following week. From then on, I had an acute awareness of money and the fact that my family lacked it. I knew I would have to work hard if I wanted to prosper.

My mother is warm and kind, with an excellent sense of humor. But thankfully she was strict with me since I needed the discipline. Although I never felt like an abused child, Joan definitely believed in the Biblical precept of "spare the rod, spoil the child." If I acted up, my mother whipped me right on the spot, regardless of where we were, while yelling, "God disciplines whom he loves." I received beatings, which I deserved, with toy racetracks, hairbrushes, and shoes—whatever she could quickly lay a hand on, even in public. My smart mouth usually landed me into trouble.

My most memorable beating from my mother came after I spent one evening in another part of the North Side when I was seven years old. Because we moved frequently, I had a habit of making new friends then walking back to my old neighborhoods around the North Side, which might be up to five miles away. This gave me an opportunity to play with my old friends, and I would bring my new friends with me. Of course, I was not allowed to be this far from home. On one occasion, some adult saw me in a distant neighborhood around sunset and called my mother. Joan was waiting for me when I returned to our apartment after my curfew. I walked in well after dark with a smile on my face. Although very relieved that I had made it home safely, she was angry about my poor judgment and making her worry. I had never seen her so upset.

She swung to slap me, aiming directly for my head. I ducked. Joan's hand hit the wall breaking her right thumb. She had to wear a cast, which extended from her thumb up to her elbow, for more than six weeks. I am glad she hit the wall and not the side of my hard head. Given that she is left-handed, I have always jokingly wondered why Mother chose to use the slow right hook.

One of the small tragedies of our frequent moves was that we lost almost all of my childhood photographs. During one of our transitory periods, we stored our possessions in a neighbor's attic while we lived with other family members. The storage, which was supposed to last for only a month or two, stretched for about ten months. At some point, our former neighbors began to use our possessions, which I guess had overstayed their welcome. To get our possessions back, we had to get police assistance. When we finally reacquired our things, we discovered that some items were missing. Most were replaceable items, but my childhood photo albums were not. Since then, I have been able to salvage a few memories by making copies of pictures that I have since seen at the homes of my various relatives. Still, many pictures are lost forever. This is why I am now meticulous about taking and protecting pictures of key events, and saving information and photos in scrapbooks.

In spite of the challenges at home, I excelled academically, even though I started school one year early. Joan had read to me frequently when I was a toddler, accelerating my development. When I was finishing kindergarten, the school wanted me to skip first grade and move directly to second grade. I would have been a five-year-old second grader. Joan did not allow it. She was concerned that my social skills would be behind those of the other second graders who were seven or eight years old. Of course she was right—although I did not agree at the time. Later, as a sixteen-year-old high school senior in fall 1983 who was shy around girls, I was thankful I wasn't already in college.

Although I was viewed by teachers as a precocious child, I was a troublemaker. I was frequently in the principal's office or in detention, usually for fighting or for my rebellious mouth. I used them both as defense mechanisms, as I lived in some of the poorest neighborhoods in Pittsburgh's inner city. In these neighborhoods, like other poor American neighborhoods, many of the habitants are socioeconomically disadvantaged African-American people who are unable to move out. But life in disadvantaged Black America, often called "the 'Hood," was not completely negative. As a kid with little money, you could still have big fun. We played games like hide-and-go-seek—which evolved into "hide-and-go-get-it" once puberty hit, giving teens the chance to grab the rear end of a member of the opposite sex. Other childhood games that required no money, equipment, or coaching included "Red Light, Green Light, Yellow Light—Stop" and "Freeze Tag."

If you had no money to go to the public swimming pool, you could always open the fire hydrant. If you had no swimming trunks, you could always just go out and play at the fire hydrant in your underwear. We used to catch grasshoppers or tadpoles in an old mayonnaise jar, punch holes in the lid, and keep the jar in our bedrooms in place of conventional pets. The annual school picnic at Pittsburgh's famous Kennywood Park featured the Thunderbolt classic wooden roller coaster with its sudden ninety-foot drop and top speed of fifty-five miles per hour. We could usually only afford to go once per year, but it was worth the wait.

If one person in the neighborhood had a ball, we could play football, basketball, or baseball, depending on the season, literally all day long. If someone had a toy such as a Big Wheel, we would have especially thrilling and treacherous near-death experiences riding down the steep cobblestone hills of Pittsburgh. We took excursions around the North Side to eat the "fruit of the land" such as berries, crab apples, and pears when there was no food at home.

Eventually, we took these excursions to another level when I was eight years old and living on a street called Brighton Place on the North Side. Lacking a convenient park to play in, we often used the nearby railroad junction as our playground, and we had big fun. We put pennies on the tracks to have them smashed flat, and played on top of the boxcars stopped in the rail yard. One day, my friend and I sat inside a stationary boxcar eating the train's cargo of oranges, passing the time away with idle talk.

"Man, these oranges are good," I said. "I can't stop eating them."

"Yeah, but I wish they had other fruit on this boxcar," he added.

"Shoot," I countered. "I am happy with these oranges."

"Do you hear something?" my friend asked timidly.

"Man, I hear a train coming," I replied. "I heard that if the caboose guy takes your picture, they will give it to the police, and they will find you and put you in the juvenile detention home. Let's hide."

We quickly jumped off of the stationary boxcar and hid out of sight under it. As the initial train passed us at a high speed, I said, "Don't worry, as soon as this train goes by, it'll be cool."

A minute later, another train passed us, also at high speed, on the opposite side of the our stationary boxcar. I was quite scared that the train we were under would also start, giving us no way out.

The look on my friend's face was that of disbelief and despair resulting from his decision to follow my suggestion and hide under the stationary boxcar. Luckily, just minutes before the stationary train moved, one of the other trains completed its passage through the junction and we were able to run to safety. During the walk back to our street, I caught hell from my friend.

"Tommie, I can't believe you got me to go in that boxcar," he jabbed.

"Man, you wasn't saying nothin' when you was eatin' them oranges. Shut up!"

Of course, he did have a point. We were wrong for eating the oranges and stupid for being on the railroad tracks. I never played on the railroad tracks after that.

An organization called Youth Opportunities Unlimited (Y.O.U.) on nearby Charles Street provided me with a positive outlet. Y.O.U. offered weekly sports and recreational activities on Tuesdays in the gymnasium of the then newly opened Columbus Middle School. To participate in the sports, you had to attend a mandatory weekly Bible class first to get into the gymnasium each Tuesday evening.

The Bible class instructor was White, and all the students were African-American. The other kids did not want to go to a Bible class, especially one taught by a White guy they viewed as "square." But they had no choice and attended somewhat reluctantly. At the time, however, I loved Bible classes, so it was a win-win situation for me. I sat in the front of the class and answered all the questions. Then I would run to the brand-new gym to play basketball, kickball, or even indoor tackle football during the harsh Pittsburgh winters. This experience inspired me later, as an adult, to run a similar Bible class and hold mentoring sessions at a Boys and Girls Club in inner-city Baltimore, Maryland. My efforts there subsequently earned me the Salvation Army "Man and Youth" Award in Baltimore.

In the winter of 1976, Joan and I vacated our apartment on Brighton Place because of difficult living conditions. We moved in with my Aunt Bessie in the Mount Washington section of the city's South Side. I enjoyed this time because I loved Aunt Bessie. It was also nice to live in a home with a backyard, instead of an apartment.

Tired of changing schools, I finished fourth grade by commuting across the city to the North Side using public transportation—a daily adventure for a nine-year-old. I took pride in the opportunity, which made me feel like the adult morning commuters, navigating buses across the city.

The bicentennial summer of 1976 was great on Mount Washington, as it was in many communities across the country. My cousins and I enjoyed frequent cookouts and almost daily trips to the local swimming pool. Aunt Bessie's sons, Dougie and Richie, were more than fifteen years older than me, but I was still able to spend some time around them. Dougie, having recently completed his tour of duty in the Marine Corps, took me fishing on the Monongahela River and gave me a lot of "big brother" advice.

I was also able to spend a lot of time with the Smiths, my second cousins who lived next door to Aunt Bessie. Michael, Mark, and Phillip Smith acted as my virtual "big brothers" for a while, along with another second cousin, Jamie Weathers. I could usually hang with them for a while, but they would try to get rid of me as evening approached so they could chase girls like normal teens. To compensate, they sometimes slipped me a couple of quarters to encourage me to go home but not tell any of the adults where they were and what they were doing.

The youngest Smith, Sonja, was like my little sister. Sonja and I grew especially close from playing together a lot. Since I was older than Sonja, I usually had my way. Sometimes, I would be Batman, and she would have to play the sidekick Robin. She didn't seem to mind being Wonder Woman, teaming with me as Superman. I would attach a towel to my back and jump down the steps, pretending I was Superman in flight.

I always tried to dream up something new to do as I became bored so easily. I was fond of putting my younger cousins Sonja, Christy, David, Christine, and Timmy up to new challenges. "Who can do a handstand?" I'd cry out. Or, "Who can do a handstand and then walk on their hands?"

I loved to see my younger cousins try so hard, and then get bruised up in the attempt. Ironically, my second cousin Timmy was also adopted, but I did not know this until I was an adult. He was totally accepted by the family, just like I was. Neither of us nor any of the young cousins knew we were adopted; as far as I knew at the time, it was never mentioned. It seems that for many families in the 1970s, including ours, adoption was still a taboo subject. No one seemed to know how to discuss adoption openly. No one, including my mother Joan, knew what to expect once the adopted child knew the truth.

CHAPTER FIVE

The Shocking News

As fun as it was for me, we couldn't stay on Mount Washington at Aunt Bessie's house forever. We needed our own place to live. But Joan did not want to return me to the tough neighborhoods and schools of the North Side. Influenced by the negative environment on the North Side during elementary school, my conduct in school and at home left plenty of room for improvement. This was clearly reflected in the subjective, qualitative section of my report cards where a child's behavior is judged. It was also reflected in the letters and phone calls from my teachers. In Joan's eyes, a phone call from a teacher regarding my bad behavior was far worse than if I had received an F in my course work.

Ultimately we moved about twenty-five miles north of Pittsburgh to a small town called New Brighton. It was November 1976, and I was just about to turn ten years old.

Joan was dating Don Gipson, who lived in Aliquippa, another small town near New Brighton. Don helped guide me and over time he became, in many ways, a father figure. In my teenage years, I started calling him "Don," and he called me "son."

Don was originally from rural Georgia. He did not have a formal university education; yet, he was one of the smartest men I ever met. He was a steelworker at the Jones and Laughlin steel mill in Aliquippa. He was later promoted to foreman. Don served on the Aliquippa City Council. Eventually, he was elevated to City Council Chairman.

Before moving out to New Brighton, the favorite "getaway" for the three of us was West Park on Pittsburgh's North Side. I loved going there. Don also knew how deeply I loved the hometown Pittsburgh Steelers. In December 1974, Don had taken me to my first Steelers game. It was American football at its highest level, a playoff game against the Buffalo Bills and their star running back O. J. Simpson. The Steelers won 32-14 in a frigid game at Three Rivers Stadium and went on to win their first Super Bowl later that season. I was ecstatic.

A few months later, Don punished me for the first time. I had been thrown out of school for fighting. My victim had reneged on a bet that I had won, and I really felt I needed those twenty-five cents. Joan and Don talked with me about my poor judgment when I arrived at home. Then, Don gave me a whipping. At age eight I resented physical discipline from him. I did not view him as a father figure until my teenage years.

Don challenged me mentally, especially on issues of history, politics, and education. He helped to nurture my growing desire to go to college, and he set the expectation for me to be a doctor. He said, "Thomas, I want you to be able to take care of me one day when I am old and sick." I embraced the idea of college, but not the delayed gratification associated with medical school. Given my underprivileged background, I never seriously considered going to school that long before I could start making money. I was somewhat shortsighted. I wanted to get paid immediately after just four years of college.

Don attended my first Pop Warner League football game with my mother when I was eleven. He cooked me a steak dinner afterward. He seemed really proud of my performance, in which I started for both the offense and the defense and captained our undermanned team in a losing effort.

I knew that Don was frequently looking out for my interests, even after he and my mother stopped dating when I was a thirteen-year-old ninth-grader. Don stayed in contact and involved in my life, and he continued to call me "son" even though he had biological children of his own.

I often questioned my mother and Don directly about why they dragged me out of inner-city Pittsburgh in 1976 to live in New Brighton. Being a good mother, Joan wanted me to live in a better neighborhood and attend a better school. Initially, I was not happy with the move. I was leaving my friends and cousins in the city, and I had a hard time being one of the few African-American children in the school.

New Brighton was predominately White, and lower to middle class. I remember only five African-American children, including myself, out of about 175 fifth graders. While I scored high on standardized tests, I did not get straight A's in fifth or sixth grade because of my lack of focus and general unhappiness about living in New Brighton.

Constant racial jokes and slurs confronted me in New Brighton, and I retaliated initially by developing and nurturing prejudices of my own against White people. I fought back, literally and figuratively. Feeling victimized, I inexcusably blamed anything that went wrong on racism.

I once debated with friends in New Brighton regarding the merits of two of the best players in the game of baseball at the time. Dave Parker of the Pittsburgh Pirates was my favorite. Jim Rice of the Boston Red Sox was the other subject of the debate. Both players were Black. In the midst of the friendly debate, I jokingly attacked with, "Rice has lice." One of my White friends came back with "Parker is darker." I am sure he meant no harm that day, and that he never thought about it again; however, I wonder how many Americans, including African-Americans, think that being "darker" is a negative thing.

Joan and a ten-year-old Thomas. July 1977.

By the middle of sixth grade my struggle with race in New Brighton Middle School reached its low point. One day, in despair, I briefly wondered if my life would not be better if my skin were lighter to match my wavy hair so I could pass as White. This changed just days later, after I watched a mini-series on TV on the life of Dr. Martin Luther King, Jr. This TV series, and subsequent readings about Dr. King, educated me on the civil rights movement and made me feel proud to be African-American. I was moved by the noble struggle of the civil rights movement. I was proud that leaders like Dr. King used intellect and nonviolence to win their battles. I was humbled by the sacrifices that people made so that I could live a better life. Strengthened by Dr. King's legacy, I was less vulnerable to the barbs of my White New Brighton classmates.

Now confident as an African-American, my eleven-year-old, sixth-grade psyche suffered an enormous jolt one spring evening.

"Tommie," began Don, "your mother and I want to talk with you. Have a seat."

"Why? I want to go back outside."

"Just sit down, please," said Joan. "Now, you know that I love you very much?"

"Um, yeah."

"Ever since you were a baby, you have meant everything to me."

I looked at her, wondering if I had been caught doing something wrong. But, I couldn't think of any recent misdeeds.

"I want you to know that for years and years, I tried to have a child. But I was not able. Finally, the doctors told me that I would be unable to have a child. Do you understand?"

"Well, I guess," I paused then admitted, "not really."

"I was unable to have a child, so I adopted you when you were a little baby. Ever since then, you have been a joy to my heart."

"You know, your mother and I love you as much as any man and woman have ever loved a child," added Don. "Even though she did not give birth to you, that doesn't change the fact that you are her son and that she has a profound love for you. And you know that I have always told you since you were young that I loved you as a son, just like my other son, Donnie, Jr."

"So I am adopted?"

"Yes," said Joan. "I waited and waited to get you. God allowed us to be together, so you are my special prize. You needed a home, and I so desperately wanted a son."

"Where are my real parents?"

"We don't know anything about your biological parents. That information is sealed by law."

"That's true," added Don. "The idea is that once people give up their children for adoption, then the new adoptive parents take over as parents in that child's life. It can be quite difficult to adopt, and your mother had to go through more than two years of waiting to get you. She was trying to adopt a child before you were even born. You two are both so fortunate to have found each other."

"But, this doesn't make sense. I even look like you, Mom," I implored. "I look like I am a Lowry. I look just like my cousins. We have similar features and complexions. Strangers tell us all of the time that I look just like you."

"I know that you look like a Lowry, and you do fit in quite well with your cousins," my mother explained. "The fact that you are adopted will not change anything. None of your cousins, except your oldest cousin Jackie, even know you are adopted, because they were all too young to know. They are not going to treat you any differently, just as I have never treated you any differently."

"I had prayed," Joan continued, "that God would let me know the right time to tell you. God has helped me to know that now is the time for you to know. Until now, I did not feel you were old enough to understand."

After a long silence, Don asked, "Do you have any other questions about this?"

"No."

"Do you want something to eat?" Joan asked.

"No. I don't know. Maybe, I guess."

"How about if we go and get you something, maybe Long John Silver's?" Joan asked. "You like that, right?"

"Yeah."

"Okay, if you have no other questions, we will be back in about thirty minutes with your food."

With that, they left me at home, alone with my thoughts. As an eleven-year-old, it was shocking and burdensome for me to handle this revelation. I didn't ask to be an adopted child. I felt deserted, as if this kind "adoptive" family of aunts, uncles, and cousins was not my own. I had so many questions. Why the "secrecy" that surrounded my adoption? Why wasn't I raised with this knowledge from infancy, through childhood, and into my teens? Why tell me at that particular time? What made age eleven better than seven or seventeen to share the news? At the time, I felt as though I had been living a lie. I felt like there was no one I could talk to about my situation. I lived a good distance from my cousins in Pittsburgh. I didn't feel any of my new friends in New Brighton would be understanding or supportive. I was in many ways alone. The reality of suddenly finding out that I was adopted left me hurt, confused, and resentful. I couldn't even sleep.

My feelings surfaced a few days later during another conversation with my mother as we talked about going to see my favorite Aunt Bessie. "I don't feel like going. I would rather stay here and just play football with my friends," I said.

"Do you want me to tell her what you said?" questioned Joan.

"I don't care. She's not my real aunt anyway. This is not my real family."

My caring mother tried to talk to me during the subsequent days, but I kept my feelings to myself. After about three weeks of quiet reflection, I began to accept that my adopted family completely loved me and cared about me. Because of this love, I decided that they were my real family. With the exception of two brief discussions, I did not talk again to Joan about the adoption until February 1992 during my MBA studies. To me, there was nothing to discuss. She loved me. She was my real mother. The Lowry family was my real family. There was nothing more to say.

No one, not even the adults, talked about my adoption. I was treated like any other cousin. Before that important conversation at age eleven, my mother tried to protect me from the truth to spare my feelings. She was convinced that I would not understand. I was told decades later that her theory was put to the test when I was four years old when a man who was then married to one of Joan's sisters told me, "Joan is not your mother."

Today I write off his comment as the fruit of suppressed meanness. I am not sure why he said such a thing. Confused at the time, I fled in tears to Joan. She covered the truth so well that I had forgotten about the incident completely. After comforting me, she set out to confront him. Finding him alone, Joan made it clear that he had no right telling me that she was not my biological mother. I was her son, and she was responsible for making sure that no physical or emotional harm came to me.

Once I accepted the idea of being adopted, things returned to normal for me at age eleven. As the months passed, my feelings about New Brighton improved. I began to focus on school, enjoyed learning, and soon I saw all A's on my report card. Being poor, I had realized that my best opportunity to gain admission to, and financing for, college was to get all A's in middle school and then in high school. I was motivated by my poverty, and I saw college as a way to improve my financial future. New glasses probably helped improve my grades, as I was very nearsighted and had been since the second grade. Getting by with bad eyes all those years, I was forced to rely on my listening skills to decode the fuzzy lines the teachers were writing on the chalkboard. When that was not enough, I would repeatedly go up to the front of the room to sharpen my pencil. I would memorize what was on the board on the way to and from the sharpener. Joan had asked me about my eyesight during elementary school but I would always dodge the question to avoid getting glasses.

At the same time that my grades improved, I began playing on the football and basketball teams, and performed well.

By seventh grade, I began to be increasingly comfortable in New Brighton. I overcame my retaliatory prejudices against others and became more idealistically fair and open-minded. I decided that as an African-American, I could not attempt to justify prejudice against Whites by reasoning like some of my friends that, "The Whites mistreated us first. They put us in slavery and still hold an inordinate amount of economic and political power compared to Blacks." While there may be some truth in these statements, they do not justify prejudice. I was learning from my hero, Dr. Martin Luther King, Jr.

New Brighton Middle School was definitely not Nirvana, however, and I was still maturing. I once verbally threatened to choke my American History teacher after she made a tasteless joke, stating, "The slaves escaped at night because it was harder for the masters to see them in the dark." She had already made many insensitive comments to me throughout the year, especially during the discussion of the book *Uncle Tom's Cabin*. She made similar remarks to the Black students who preceded me in the previous two years. This was the last straw for me. She thought her comment was funny. The other students in the room, who were all White, did not understand why I was upset. When I made my threat, she was completely shaken and never made another racist remark to me again. After my class left her room, she spent her whole next period, according to my girlfriend who was in that class, talking about me and how shocked she was. She was actually a pretty good teacher who taught me a lot about American History. We had a love-hate relationship. I think she liked me as a student, but her repeated racist comments were insensitive and foul. It was equally wrong for me to physically threaten her, but I didn't realize it at the time.

Participating in sports was the key to my adjustment in New Brighton. Sports are extremely important in western Pennsylvania, and my success in sports as a New Brighton Lion made me an accepted member of the scholastic community. Sensing this acceptance, I was able to overcome the occasional encounters with prejudice. I learned that sports had the potential to provide a way to pay for college and definitely provided skills that carried over to other parts of my life. For example, sports taught me how to be a part of a team, to be responsible, to set goals, and to be healthy and physically fit. I also learned to be a leader, to take direction from a manager or coach, and to win graciously. Most of all, sports taught me how to learn from defeat and to bounce back stronger the next time.

CHAPTER SIX

Once a Lion, Always a Lion

At New Brighton High School, I thrived academically. I maintained a 3.8 average during my first two years. My friends would ask, "What's up, Thomas?" I typically responded, "My grades." I did not lack confidence in the classroom. I was also fortunate to be relatively popular. I did, however, lack confidence in the dating arena. But I faced bigger challenges than dating.

During part of my middle school years, my mother Joan had worked as a home healthcare nurse, which provided a measure of working class financial consistency for about two years. When I entered high school, however, my mother suffered a back injury and could no longer work. This ultimately put us back on welfare for the rest of the time I lived with her.

The summer of 1981, before the welfare checks started coming, was especially tough. While enduring "two-a-day" summer practices for the New Brighton Lion football team, there was almost nothing to eat in our apartment. I faced true hunger every day. The aggregate effect of these circumstances left me mentally and physically drained. Joan had to have been even more hungry during this time as I ate most of the little we had. She always put my needs above her own.

By February 1982, welfare checks were coming in and things were relatively stable. Although there were financial challenges, somehow there was always a good time waiting to happen. In my case, it sometimes came when Don stopped by the apartment.

In 1982, although he was no longer dating my mother, Don took me to a basketball game at West Virginia University. His son Donnie, Jr., played for the Mountaineers, a Top 20 basketball team that year. Don bought me a game program. Out of all of the game programs sold, there were ten that had a special number on a specific page inside. Just before halftime, they called, by number, the holders of these special programs down to the floor. I held one of the lucky programs. The ten of us were each given a basketball and allowed to take a single shot from half court. Those who made it were promised a trip to Jamaica with all expenses paid for two people by a local West Virginia travel agency.

It is said that those with a sun sign of Sagittarius are lucky. I took my shot. BANK-SWISH! It went in.

The West Virginia cheerleaders picked me up and carried me around the floor in a victory lap. Dazed, I would not have known what happened if I had not been given a picture later. It was great to win the vacation trip, but it was the beginning of a dilemma. I asked myself who I should take with me to Jamaica. Don, after all, had taken me to the game and given me the game ticket and the program. Or, I pondered, should I take my mother? I also knew that Joan and I needed the cash more than the vacation. What would we do for spending money in Jamaica? People on welfare don't have discretionary cash for vacations abroad, even if the trip itself is free.

Since we did not have phone service in our apartment, I used a neighbor's phone a few weeks after my big shot and called the travel agency down in West Virginia. After a few days of deliberation, they told me that commercial value of the trip was fifteen hundred dollars and agreed to give me one thousand dollars in cash. I took the money. We didn't get it until July 1982, four months later. I gave much of it to Joan to pay the rent and some other bills, as well as to buy food. Joan spent nothing on herself. I was, however, able to buy a ninety-nine-dollar "boom box" radio, a few clothing items, and a forty-dollar pair of running shoes to be used for my eleventh grade track season. It was my first pair of proper running shoes. During my ninth and tenth grade track seasons, I had trained for running in my high-tops from the basketball team, definitely not a good strategy for injury prevention for distance runners.

Meanwhile, I continued to juggle sports and academics for the rest of my sophomore year. New Brighton High School required that sophomores take a history class called World Cultures. The class was really European history, sprinkled with Asian history and some world geography. We learned virtually nothing about African history in this class. In fact, I finished high school without learning about African history or anything significant about the accomplishments of African-Americans. I knew nothing of Lewis Latimer, who patented the process that greatly improved the quality of carbon filaments and helped make Thomas Edison's electric light a production reality. Nor did I learn of my eventual Alpha Phi Alpha Fraternity brother Garrett Morgan who invented the traffic light and the gas mask. Dr. Charles Drew developed techniques for separating and preserving blood that have saved countless lives since the days of World War II. Dr. Daniel Hale Williams performed the first successful open-heart surgery. With knowledge of these, and the many other accomplished African-Americans, Black youths like me would have had greater aspirations and self-esteem.

Racism and misinformation cut many different ways at New Brighton, with devastating effects. Sometimes my Black "brothers" in high school referred to me as "acting White" when I did something positive like making straight A's, or speaking proper English. Sadly, this is not a rare experience for many educated minorities in America. In the wise words of Dr. Franklyn G. Jenifer, former president of Howard University: "Some people tend to worry that when Black people start talking about excellence that somehow that means that we are not talking about where we came from. I say it's just the opposite. If you look far enough back, you will see that we have never been a people who have been afraid of change or challenge."

My background in Pittsburgh and New Brighton is why I have spent countless hours mentoring to our youth in inner-city neighborhoods, through programs like the National Black MBA Association's Leaders of Tomorrow Program. African-Americans like me, who have reached some level of success, must do our part to counter the negative messages that bombard inner-city youth.

To this day, I enjoy a friendship with a White high school classmate from New Brighton named Tim McConaughy. Tim really went out of his way to show me true friendship, especially in eleventh and twelfth grades. He always made sure I had a ride to various school and social functions. He often loaned me money when we were at a hot dog shop or pizza parlor. It was cash that I had no chance of paying back at the time. We discussed our options for the future, as high school students are prone to do, and we had similar views on many subjects. We did, however, have differing opinions on interracial dating. He "just didn't think it was right" back in those days, in spite of our close friendship. I struggled to understand this.

I had other uneasy interactions in New Brighton. A high school friend signed my yearbook "to one of the smartest Blacks I know." I am sure she meant it as a compliment. While singing at the lunch table in ninth grade another classmate told me not to sing "that jigaboo music around here." I kicked his butt right after the lunch period. In retrospect I know that was not the correct response; I should have just walked away. During high school I was also called nigger, spook, and other slurs both to my face and behind my back. Ultimately, I learned to extract my revenge, like many African-Americans, by excelling in both academics and athletics. In addition, because I became more religious during high school, I was less prone to fighting than when I was in middle school.

As a sophomore, I earned a varsity letter as part of the Lion track team. During my junior year, I dropped football and continued to focus on basketball and track. I earned another varsity letter in my junior year during a track season capped off by my 4:29.2 performance in the mile (1600 meters) in the spring of 1983.

During the summer of 1983, I earned $3.35 per hour, minimum wage at that time, painting, cleaning toilets, and running errands for the local YMCA. Needing a few new clothes and other items, I was spending a bit of my salary at a local department store when I bumped into Wendy Dunham, a high school classmate. I learned from her that our academic class rankings had been updated as of the end of our eleventh grade year. She told me that she was ranked number two and I was ranked number one. I was surprised, so I went to the school to verify what I thought was just a flattering rumor. It was more than a rumor. It was true. I was ranked number one in my eleventh grade class academically, but only by a few thousandths of a grade point over Wendy. Glowing with satisfaction and pride, I decided that I was going to be valedictorian. All I had to do was get an A in every class, like I had already done in eleventh grade. I was confident that with such grades it would be impossible for me to lose my lead.

My neighbors were not as confident. My Black friends told me, "Those White folks ain't gonna let you be valedictorian, regardless of your grades." I heard them, but I didn't listen. I knew that I was in control. I was determined to be the first Black valedictorian at New Brighton High School. That same summer I gained additional determination to keep my class ranking after meeting Muhammad Ali. I was an age group winner at a five-mile race in Pittsburgh. I was thrilled to meet Ali. We only spoke for fifteen seconds, but meeting him reminded me

Thomas receiving a trophy from Muhammad Ali for a five-mile race in Pittsburgh. July 1983.

of his determination to overcome racism, politics, religious persecution, and other obstacles to regain the heavyweight title back in the 1970s.

Even though sports were paramount for many in western Pennsylvania, I had grown to understand that there was life beyond sports. In those years, I noticed many college football and basketball superstars who subsequently were not stars in the National Football League and the National Basketball Association. They suffered injuries, succumbed to drug or alcohol abuse, or they just ran up against competition that was better, faster, bigger, or stronger. Others who became rich superstars sometimes lost all of their money through bad investments or had failed marriages and family life. I learned that education was the key and sports was second. As important as it was for me to be a Lion athlete, I was able to keep things in balance.

I struggled in basketball during my senior season of 1983–1984. I had only average basketball talent at the varsity level and I lacked poise during the games. In the final two minutes of a game against rival Riverside, I committed two turnovers and missed three free throws. These mistakes caused us to lose the game. I subsequently lost my starting position at shooting guard.

Over Christmas break that season, I realized there was no reason to play so nervously. I concluded that even if I had a "great" season and played at the peak of my limited abilities and averaged ten or fifteen points per game, I would still not go to college on a Division I basketball scholarship. I did not have the physical talent for basketball at the Division I level. I knew I would attend college based on academic achievement. So I relaxed during my high school games, and to my surprise, I played better the rest of the season.

Meanwhile, I earned an A in every class in the first nine-week grading period. However, I stumbled in the second grading period and received one B—in typing class of all things. It was frustrating. After all, I had only enrolled in typing so that I would be more efficient at writing papers for "real classes" during college. Physics, computer science, and calculus were no problem, but I received a B in typing.

Fortunately for me, Wendy received a B in a couple of classes during her senior year, too, and I was able to extend my lead. Wendy handled the competition gracefully at every step. I won the award as Valedictorian of the New Brighton High School Class of 1984.

Some people close to me, including Joan's former boyfriend Don, immediately began talk on graduation night that I should be able to do the same thing at the college level. This was new pressure. I did not want to hear it. I was just happy to prove my doubting friends in the neighborhood wrong. A Black person could finish at the top academically.

I was the only Black male in the New Brighton Class of 1984, and I had won the valedictorian title. When I discussed the demographic realities with a White friend and classmate named Julie at our ten-year class reunion, she was surprised I was the only Black male in the class. "I never even thought about it," she confessed. "I had no idea you were so alone."

As a good friend, Julie felt disappointed that she hadn't noticed. But, she shouldn't have felt bad. As we rehashed the details of our teen years gone by, she was sensitive enough to understand that back in high school, I had been affected by racism. I responded by commenting that I had been trying to prove that a Black kid from a low-income neighborhood could be valedictorian. I had used my environment as motivation.

Unfortunately, my academic successes, track victories, and scholarship awards inflated my already blossoming ego. During graduation week, I participated with other area

Thomas during senior year at New Brighton (PA) High School. 1983–1984.
[Courtesy of Graule Studios]

valedictorians in an interview with a local newspaper. The result was a full-page story where each of the participating college-bound graduates had the opportunity to answer questions on the future of our generation, and provide solutions to problems facing western Pennsylvania specifically and America in general. My answers, at age seventeen, proved only that I was quite unpolished in the area of media relations. Some of my statements on religion, drug use, U.S. foreign policy, and the future of high school graduates who did not go on to college were outspoken and controversial, causing consternation, dissension, and embarrassment for many.

For people I was just getting to know, my ego was making a bad first impression. A female classmate who I was trying to date told me that I was getting too much attention, and that I wasn't handling it well. The last straw for her was when we were together at a graduation party for a fellow classmate and runner named Sherri. Unexpectedly, Sherri's parents gave me fifty dollars as a graduation gift, and it wasn't even my party. They gave it to me because they were Christians and heard from Sherri how seriously I took my religious beliefs and my academic pursuits. They had watched me run track as well, as I won the county championship, and then also finished second in the Western Pennsylvania Interscholastic Athletic League (WPIAL) in the mile (1600 meters). As a result, I only narrowly missed qualifying for the state championships. I was touched by the fifty-dollar gift, which was a lot of money to me at the time. I was also happy because I needed the money to cover transportation expenses associated with starting my new summer internship.

While telling my date about my excitement about the gift and what I saw as my great new summer internship, I realized she was tired of hearing about my good fortune. More to the point, she was tired of my ego. She was probably right about my ego. We didn't spend any time together after that.

However, the fact that I was making aggressive advances with the girls I liked marked an improvement in confidence for me. Before, I had been shy with the girls. I had exhibited what many considered to be a lack of charm in high school with women. It wasn't just charm; I had no money to take girls on dates, no access to a car, and no telephone at home to call girls in the evening. My clothes were far from stylish. I wore thick unfashionable glasses because I could not afford designer frames or contact lenses for my severely nearsighted eyes. Also, being ranked number one academically in your class is not typically associated with "being cool" or "having game" at the high school level. Some of my friends called me "Knowledge Nut," "Brainiac," and other funny names. It was time for me to find a new playing field where my skill set might be more widely appreciated. I needed to meet some college friends, or more specifically, college girls, who would value my focus on education.

CHAPTER SEVEN

Inroads for Success

I was recruited by INROADS, Inc., near the end of my senior year of high school in 1984. INROADS, Inc. is a national organization designed to groom talented Hispanic, African-American, and Native American youth for positions of leadership in corporate America and in their communities. It has affiliates in more than fifty cities across America. The organization builds bridges between corporate America and the minority community. The organization has since expanded to South Africa and Canada.

A great organization, INROADS delivers a win-win for the students and corporate America. INROADS cannot directly eliminate racism, but it does help address some of the symptoms of racism in America. More than thirty-six million African-Americans constitute roughly twelve percent of the U.S. population with a buying power of roughly five hundred billion dollars. However, we are not enjoying anything close to twelve percent of the wealth of the great country that we helped to build. Of course, this economic disparity is not good for African-Americans, nor is it good for America as a whole. Given demographic trends, improved minority economic clout and education are simply good business for our nation.

I am not sure why the INROADS recruiter stopped at New Brighton High School that day; we were down to four minority students in a senior class of about 175. The probability of finding minority talent in

New Brighton for the highly selective INROADS organization was statistically low. Nonetheless, I am glad that he stopped at my school.

After the initial interview with the recruiter, I interviewed a week later in downtown Pittsburgh with INROADS/Pittsburgh Director Carole Cohen. The meeting went well. I advanced into the INROADS "Talent Pool," which represented some of the brightest minority students in the greater Pittsburgh area. The majority of the students were high school seniors, plus some college freshmen and sophomores.

After two days of orientation and preparation during Talent Pool Weekend, we were then ready to compete with each other for internship slots at various companies in the Pittsburgh area. In addition to paying us a great summer intern salary, the companies also paid INROADS a sponsorship fee that funded the organization's activities, such as recruiting, coaching, ongoing student training workshops, and counseling.

The INROADS workshops included such topics as business etiquette, résumé writing, interviewing skills, leadership, college preparation, workplace interpersonal skills, entrepreneurship, personal money management, and even how to manage your boss. Collectively, we also performed a number of community service projects, as INROADS taught us to give back to our communities.

Carole was the only INROADS director in the nation who was neither Black nor Hispanic. Yet, almost none of the more than one hundred students of color in the Pittsburgh affiliate ever seemed to notice. We never discussed it. Obviously, we saw Carole as "white," and we knew she was Jewish. But more important, we knew that Carole genuinely cared about us.

She pushed and cajoled companies to create more sponsorship slots so the organization could serve more students. Her downtown office was always open to us. We knew that we could stop by anytime and talk to her about our studies, experiences, workplace challenges, and social lives. I could catch her on her way out the door at seven o'clock in the evening and begin to share my challenges with her on any subject, and she would sit back down and take the necessary time to mentor me.

Carole had grown up in Pittsburgh's East Liberty section, and oddly enough, realized as early as third grade that there was a disparity in the economic and social standing of African-Americans compared with other Pittsburgh residents. She once noticed a pair of her patent leather shoes that her family had donated to Goodwill on the feet of one of her African-American classmates less than a month later. As an adult, significant international travel to underdeveloped nations further amplified her social conscience.

During the sixteen years Carole invested in INROADS, hundreds of local minority students grew into positions of leadership in corporate America and in their communities. These days, I frequently bump into other INROADS alumni Carole helped at professional conferences around the country.

Ironically, one of the students in INROADS during Carole's first year as director was the daughter of Carole's African-American third grade classmate who had received the used shoes from Goodwill. Through INROADS, Carole was able to help this family again. This time, however, the positive effects would last significantly longer than a pair of shoes.

Since Carole enjoyed great rapport with the minority students, the fact that she was White was an asset, I believe, to INROADS. She had to make the initial "sell" to the corporations, and most of the corporate decision-makers were White. If the company representatives had concerns about sponsoring and hiring minority interns, I believe they were likely to talk openly with Carole, as opposed to an African-American person in the same position.

There were about eighty bright, talented minority students at the INROADS Talent Pool event that I attended as a high school senior in March 1984. We were competing for roughly thirty new corporate internship slots. At the end of Talent Pool weekend, we chose up to three companies with which to interview.

There were six engineering internship slots open, and I was one of about twenty students competing for them. Four of the internship slots were at locations that were impractical for me to reach every day, since

I did not have access to a car. Determined to win an internship, I took a day off from high school for two job interviews.

I put on the suit that Don had previously bought me for a high school Christmas dance. Fortunately, Don had the foresight to encourage me to select a dark gray professional suit. I took a bus to interview one morning with a local utility, Peoples Natural Gas, at its downtown Pittsburgh headquarters.

The bus turned what is normally a nice thirty-five-minute car ride into a two-hour, claustrophobic, pausing zigzag trek through traffic. I was tired and nauseated from the long bus trip from New Brighton, but I was determined to complete a serious, thoughtful interview. I pushed from my mind the reality that I was bus sick.

Since this was my first real job interview, I was extremely anxious. As I recovered from the long bus ride my energy level was initially low, in spite of my nervousness.

I began by interviewing with two people in the human resources department. Still dealing with a queasy stomach, I was then escorted to the engineering department.

"What do you want to study in college?" the engineering manager asked.

"Engineering."

"Right," he sighed. "Which discipline of engineering?"

"Probably electrical; it seems the most exciting."

"Well, being a natural gas utility company, we don't have a lot of electrical engineering positions. Most of our positions are for mechanical or civil engineering."

"Oh."

I clearly was a bit unprepared. The interview with the engineering manager was going nowhere.

The manager started to explain the work his team did with gas lines, illustrating his talk with photos. The interview dragged forward. I tried to concentrate, while listening to his monotone description.

"And this third picture illustrates how we take two-inch plastic pipe across a bridge. You know there are a lot of bridges in the Pittsburgh area," he commented, attempting to drag an acknowledgment out of me.

Suddenly, my energy level picked up. "Of course, we have more bridges than any other city in the world. What I want to know is how does your engineering team account for the weather-related expansion and contraction of the bridge when you design the gas pipes that span our three major rivers?" I asked the stunned manager.

In retrospect, as an adult with an engineering degree, it is a pretty simple question. However, the engineering manager seemed somewhat impressed that this question came from a seventeen-year-old. From that point on, the connection was there. After my insightful question, the interview went very well. I subsequently received a job offer with the natural gas company.

I finished my interviews with Peoples Natural Gas by 1 P.M. I then had a 3 P.M. interview with the Westinghouse Research and Development Center in the suburb of Churchill, east of the city. Since I lived northwest of the city in New Brighton, I was not sure which bus to take to Churchill. Somehow I figured it out and made it to the Westinghouse facility just minutes before the interview. Squeezing into borrowed dress shoes that were a size and a half too small, I threw the duffel bag holding my comfortable sneakers into the bushes and ran a quarter mile up the long, steep Westinghouse driveway for my interview. The site security guard was accustomed only to letting cars pass by, not sweaty African-American teenagers traveling by foot. However, I talked my way past the guard.

The interview went well. At Westinghouse, there was a real connection with the hiring manager, who also happened to be a serious runner. He was really impressed with my eleventh-grade 4:29 time in the mile run, in addition to my grades and other school activities. While he was ready to make me an offer, there were cutbacks at Westinghouse the following week and the INROADS position they had slotted was ultimately cancelled. I accepted the offer at Peoples Natural Gas, which allowed me to join the INROADS group.

My job in the Peoples Natural Gas Engineering Department involved running flow analysis reports of natural gas subsystems, and consequently, I developed a good understanding of how the business operated. Unfortunately, my first summer in INROADS was not a re-sounding success from the company's perspective.

I worked for Peoples Natural Gas for three months. At the end of August, I received my performance evaluation from my designated company mentor, rather than my official supervisor. I was told that my functional job performance was satisfactory, but my interpersonal skills were a problem. Basically, I came across to my supervisor as arrogant and difficult to work with. I was crushed and shocked by the evaluation. I thought I fit in well with my coworkers, especially those with whom I worked most closely. I actually rarely saw my supervisor all summer because of his vacation schedule and additional work-related time out of the office. Instead of waiting until my last day to get a formal evaluation, I should have requested a midsummer review that would have given me time to correct any problems. Fortunately, the company decided that since I was only seventeen, I would probably "grow up" during my freshman year in college. I was asked to come back the following summer, which was important for both me and for INROADS. Returning each summer to your sponsoring company was part of the INROADS process. It would have been very unfortunate if the company decided that they no longer wanted me, or any other INROADS student to replace me. That day, on my way home, I resolved to make the next summer a better experience with better results. Ultimately, my three subsequent internships were very successful.

In retrospect, the evaluation provided me with a needed dose of reality about how tough it is to be successful in the real world. Coming out of high school as valedictorian, track star, multiple scholarship winner, and INROADS intern made me think that I could walk on water. It was good that I did not start my freshman year of college with this arrogant attitude. Humbled by the negative evaluation at the end of August, I knew that when I walked onto my college campus in the fall I would have to prove myself all over again. My valedictorian title was yesterday's news. New challenges would always loom on the horizon at every stage of my life. I also learned that interpersonal skills and perception management matter a great deal, in addition to functional excellence.

CHAPTER EIGHT

Pitt Is It

As a child, I grew to love the University of Pittsburgh, affection-ately referred to as "Pitt," and to detest Penn State University. The two schools have a strong historical rivalry. I disliked Penn State University ever since 1975, when they beat a Pitt team, led by then-junior running back Tony Dorsett, 7-6 in football. I was ecstatic when Dorsett led Pitt to a convincing victory over Penn State in 1976, on the way to a perfect 12-0 record and the national championship.

Besides sports, another part of my bond with Pitt came from my Grandpa Bill. He told me stories of how, as a child, he and other Pitts-burgh Public School students sold commemorative bricks to help raise money to build the Cathedral of Learning. An integral part of Pitt's campus, the Cathedral of Learning is the tallest education building in the country. A beautiful building inside, it is an unmistakable landmark on the city's eastern skyline.

Pitt is also next to Schenley Park. I had opportunities to play in Schenley Park from time to time as a child, which meant driving through Pitt's campus and seeing the students. Because of these various connec-tions, even as a child, I visualized myself at Pitt.

As a tenth-grader, I had planned on a career as a history teacher or a sports writer. I wrote a letter to the journalism department of the University of Pittsburgh, and asked what it took to be a sports writer. I received a return letter and a signed copy of a book about baseball, written by one of Pitt's professors. I was poised to be a journalist.

However, near the end of tenth grade, I read an article that dis-cussed various majors and careers. I noticed that among four year degrees, the highest starting salaries were for engineering majors. The article noted that an engineer typically enjoyed and excelled in math and the sciences. Since I was then getting almost all A's in all of my school courses, I believed I could handle any academic major in college if I studied hard. I liked math and science well enough, so I decided I would go to college to study engineering to lift myself out of poverty more quickly.

During eleventh grade, I started catching the necessary buses from New Brighton to Pitt's campus to attend Saturday "career day" programs at the engineering school. These programs were great for me, giving me some exposure to the different engineering majors and to the engineering labs and classrooms. The career day program usually gave the visiting high school students a free general admission ticket to a Pitt football game. These tickets were granted usually when Pitt was playing a weak opponent and tickets were slightly less scarce. I loved watching the highly ranked Pitt Panthers, led then by future Hall of Fame quarterback Dan Marino, crush the opposition.

At the beginning of my senior year in high school, I had finally realized that it was only rational to evaluate other universities. After all, Pitt was the only school I had really considered seriously at that point. So I forced myself to look at other universities. In addition to Pitt, I applied to the University of Pennsylvania, an Ivy League school in Philadelphia. I also aimed for acceptance at Northwestern University, near Chicago, and Villanova University, located outside of Philadelphia. I was accepted to all four schools; however, I didn't think I could choose a school unless I visited it first. The only problem was that I had no money for expenses to visit Philadelphia or Chicago.

Soon after, I received a letter from Villanova. They wrote that in addition to being accepted for admission, I was a finalist for a full academic scholarship, including all tuition, fees, room, and board.

In March 1984, Villanova flew me and the other two finalists into Philadelphia for an interview. I met with the Villanova University president and members of his staff. At some point, near the end of the interview, a staff member noticed on my application that I was on my high school's track team. Villanova had one of the most accomplished and well-known track programs in the country and it was especially known for its distance runners. I told them that as a junior I had run a 4:29 for the mile, and that I was interested in "walking on" as a nonscholarship athlete to the track team at whatever university I attended. After my interview, I was sent over to talk to Coach Charlie Jenkins—the 1956 Olympic 400-meter gold medalist—at the track.

The campus tour, the interview, and the meeting with Coach Jenkins were great experiences. I believe my track prowess helped my interview for the academic scholarship; a week later I received a letter awarding me a full four-year academic scholarship to Villanova. It was quite an honor. But I was not enamored with the idea of going to Villanova University. A Black female sophomore student had taken me on my tour around campus earlier in the day. In addition to the tour, her job was to give me a perspective on African-American life at Villanova. This was a problem, as she had trouble finding Black people on campus to introduce to me. Almost all of the Black people she could find were members of the basketball team. Coincidentally, those Villanova players went on to win the 1985 NCAA championship the following spring. Nonetheless, after my experiences at New Brighton High, I wanted to attend a school that was a little more diverse.

Northwestern and Penn could have been the answer. But with no money to even visit either of their campuses, and the high private university tuition rates, matriculation at these universities was not very feasible. I chose Pitt, which had been my first choice all along.

Pitt's engineering program was ranked in the top twenty nationally at the time, and the public school tuition was about a quarter of the amount at Northwestern or Penn. As a Pennsylvania resident, my tuition was quite reasonable at this state-supported school. Pitt was relatively diverse, racially and culturally, and boasted a strong international student population.

Armed with my credentials as New Brighton's valedictorian, my mother's love, and optimism regarding my future, I entered the University of Pittsburgh in September 1984. I received a number of partial academic scholarships, specifically from Westinghouse, Kodak, and Pitt.

I also received need-based financial aid. Thus, I was able to attend Pitt without personal expense. My only cost was emotional, since I had no frame of reference as to what to expect. No friend or family member had ever come back from college over Christmas break or for the summer to tell this disadvantaged kid about his or her college experiences.

During my first few days at Pitt, I went to my classes and received the required syllabuses. Each syllabus, of course, noted the required textbooks and supplemental readings for the course. Every day, I just sat there, waiting for the professors to hand out the books so I could start doing the reading assignments that were the subject of their lectures. During the first few days of classes, I saw this big line outside of the university book center. In the window displays of the Book Center were best-selling fictional novels and Pitt paraphernalia, not the course textbooks, which filled the inside of the store. Thus, I had no idea that I was supposed to queue with the other students and purchase textbooks. I figured the lines were full of new students waiting to buy Pitt paraphernalia before Saturday's big football season opener. It never occurred to me that the lines were full of students buying textbooks for their classes.

Three days after I first noticed the lines, I asked a student coming from the bookstore why the lines were so long. I listened in disbelief. I had to *buy* my books? Embarrassed, I returned to my room for my syllabuses, took my place in line, entered the sweating crowd, and ultimately bought my textbooks. Luckily, I had just received my last check from that summer's internship, so I was able to afford the books.

I had trained all summer, planning to be a walk-on on the track and cross-country teams. I was in contact with the athletic department, and I had worked out based on the schedule they gave me. The summer workout schedule was not too demanding. I expected the same treatment upon my arrival on campus.

I was surprised on the first day of cross-country practice. My teammates were in great shape and extremely talented. I was sure they did much more than the summer workout schedule demanded. Pitt was already strong in the middle distances, and had one of the best 4x800 meter relay teams in the country. I knew it would be a struggle to make this team. Plus, the press of the other freshmen—mostly high school All-Americans—preceded them.

When I started at Pitt my schedule was regimented. I awoke at 5:40 A.M., weighed-in at 6 A.M., ran five or six miles through nearby Schenley Park, and went back to the dorm for a shower. Breakfast was in the cafeteria. My first class was at 8 A.M., followed by three more classes. At noon I ate lunch, read the campus paper and my mail, then briefly unwound. From 1 P.M. until 2:30 P.M., I was in my room stretching, getting mentally ready for afternoon track practice. Being a borderline walk-on, I had to give 110 percent in the afternoon practice every day just to keep up with the scholarship athletes. Every practice for me carried the pressure of an Olympic final.

The schedule of every serious runner has easy days and hard days. However, at Pitt, I even found the so-called easy afternoon practices to be challenging. My hamstrings and calves were always tight. Typically, at 2:30 P.M. I would walk to Schenley Park to join the team for the 3 P.M. practice. Practices were intense and lasted until 6 P.M. Then, it was back to the dorm for "training table," where the student-athletes were served a better dinner than the normal cafeteria fare. After a quick shower in the dorm, I went to study in the library. Usually, I immediately fell asleep with my head resting on the table. After my thirty-minute nap, I studied as diligently as possible and was in bed by midnight. Unlike many of the student athletes, I not only carried a full load of classes, but my major in engineering was demanding.

After two weeks of tough training, I survived and made the cut. I was an official member of Pitt's Varsity Track Team. Later that same week, I pulled a hamstring muscle, which temporarily stopped me from running. I began to go to team trainers for ice, massage, and whirlpool therapy. It gave me time to think. Although I was ecstatic to be a part of the track team, I was concerned about my ability to carry my engineering course load and keep my grades above the 3.0 average that was necessary to maintain my academic scholarships. Clearly, I did not have

Olympic gold medal talent. I was at Pitt primarily to become an engineer, not an athlete.

Since I was not a scholarship athlete, the athletic department did not cover my tuition. If I did not maintain a 3.0 average, I would not only be off of the track team, but I would be out of the university because of lack of money. Being a freshman, and having no record of academic success at the university level, I felt that I had to choose between track and academics. I decided to quit the track team to focus fully on academics.

When I told the coach, he was cordial and did not seem fazed. I understood completely; I was not one of his stars. I told him that I needed to establish myself during my first semester from an academic perspective. If I did well, perhaps I might return to the team in January for indoor track season. I thanked him and we shook hands. I never spoke to him again.

Once I left the track team, I began to find my comfort zone in terms of my college experience. Maybe that pulled hamstring was a blessing in disguise. I was happy to be at college and at Pitt in particular. I loved the freedom. I loved the responsibility. I loved the academic challenge. I loved interacting with people from different cities and different countries. And, I loved the fact that I had some money. It was just pocket change, but I was able to enjoy things like getting fast food anytime I wanted it. I actually did better financially than most of my classmates on campus when it came to having spending money. This was because my financial aid, plus numerous scholarships, effectively allowed me to go to school for free. Tuition, room and board, and other school fees were all covered, so I had a bit of money to spare.

With adequate time to study and sleep after leaving the track team, I entered my first round of tests. I received all A's, except for the C grade I received on my first physics test. Physics class was tough for me initially. But tutoring, paid for by INROADS, helped a lot. I ended up receiving a B+ for the semester in physics.

As the semester progressed, I continued to earn high marks, and my academic confidence grew. I studied almost every night, while most of my friends on my freshman dorm floor went to parties. I took a lot of teasing over my dedication to my books, but I didn't care.

During my first semester, I only dated a little bit and went to a few parties. I attended the home football games and participated in a couple of on-campus organizations. I was having the time of my life just by being on campus.

On a daily basis, I took a lot of mostly friendly teasing from my roommate, a White freshman from eastern Pennsylvania. He always had a good time socializing and drinking. He did everything, except study. He was an amiable person but not a good roommate from an academic perspective. This was not a big problem for me. I went to the library every night to study. When I was done and felt like goofing off, I returned to my room. There was always something going on with the crew on the twelfth floor of Tower B. Co-ed dorms were great. The guys were on floors one through twelve; the girls on floors thirteen and higher. Life was good.

A number of the White students on my floor had not consistently been around an African-American person before. Their impression of the African-American race was based largely on mostly negative media images, or their mostly negative inferences drawn from the few African-Americans from their high schools whom they did not know well. They asked me about my major and how I did in high school. I told them I was valedictorian at my high school.

When they found out my Scholastic Aptitude Test (SAT) score was 1290 out of a possible 1600—the ninety-fifth percentile on verbal and the ninety-ninth percentile on math, they were surprised. They admired my study habits, and began to find out that I was a pretty nice guy. They began to make the classic annoying comments like "I don't know any other Black people like you" or "You're different from the rest of them." I began to feel again that in everything I did, I was representing my race. As college students, these uninformed White freshmen would be among the future leaders in our region. I felt like I had to change their perspective on African-Americans. I had to be almost perfect.

I thought to myself that when these White students became engineering managers at a major company, I wanted them to be open to hiring African-American engineers. One day, when they would become bank loan officers, I wanted them to willingly give an African-American family a mortgage loan.

African-Americans should be proud of their ability to enter alone into predominately White environments like corporate America workplaces, White neighborhoods, White high schools and colleges, and perform well. Historically, these environments have often been unfriendly, even hostile. Most college-educated African-Americans can identify with hearing the phrase, "You are the first Black to (fill in the blank) in our (town or school or company or organization)." Those in the majority rarely take the opportunity to meet the same challenges and step into predominately minority environments.

These White students likely meant no harm. They were just ignorant. They had never really been around African-Americans before. College is about overcoming ignorance, both academically and socially. By senior year, I shared a good friendship with many of them. After a while, instead of questioning my credentials, they began asking me for help with their academic assignments.

As final exams approached, I knew I was ready. Although I resented having to study through my birthday, I aced the exams, one by one. After my last final, I celebrated. I was happy knowing that I had done well for the semester.

After the last freshman engineering final, a number of engineering students were chatting about the test in the lobby that connected the main dormitory towers. One of the students mentioned a problem that had been particularly tough. I jumped in and agreed that the problem was tough, but by using certain specific approaches, one could "easily solve the problem." After I elaborated with detailed information, I stayed a few more minutes before leaving the conversation with a smile on my face. I was quite insensitive. I heard later that most of the guys in the conversation resented my attitude. Unfortunately, I came across as cocky and boasting about a problem I had solved that they had not. I didn't consciously mean to be insensitive. I was just extremely happy to be done with exams, and I had assumed that they had engineered the solution as well.

I stayed around campus for the next few days and partied hard. I was hungover on the morning that Don, Joan's former boyfriend, kindly came to pick me up at the end of the semester.

My best friend Arty, then a high school senior, was with me back in New Brighton when I received my grades in the mail on Christmas Eve. I finished my first semester with a 3.8 grade point average on a 4.0 scale. This allowed me to not only keep but to increase my scholarships. I felt good, as well as relieved. I was glad Arty was there to share that moment with me.

When I returned to school in January 1985, my friends on the twelfth Floor of Tower B wished that they had studied as hard as I did. Everyone wanted to know my grades. There was also a bit of friendly competition between the freshmen engineering students. I waited a few days before telling them I earned a 3.8. They expressed disbelief. They wanted to see my report card. After they saw my grade record, it seemed as though they viewed me as some type of a "credit to my race." Similar to my high school valedictorian quest, I had again proved to my White friends that this African-American student was their equal academically.

In January 1985, I began the second semester of freshman year. I was confident I could handle the academic demands of Pitt's electrical engineering program. Leaving the track team had afforded me the chance to develop and grow in other areas besides academics and running. I wanted to enhance my growing skills with respect to leadership, confidence, and social and professional networking. I began to consider joining a Greek-letter fraternity.

Historically Black fraternities and sororities have been a central part of African-American advancement. Members of these groups, energized by the backing and mentoring from their brothers and sisters, have been the drivers for civil rights, improved education, and minority economic development. All of these groups have a stated commitment to community service.

Brotherhood was the main reason for my interest in pledging a fraternity in 1985. In part it was because I had grown up with no brothers. I wanted to experience a tight brotherhood bond, and I also wanted to be able to leverage the professional connections that a fraternity often facilitates in the United States.

I also knew that a fraternity would be a good organization through which I could demonstrate my commitment to community service. Although I had a good idea by then that I was multiracial, my socialization and my self view were that of an African-American. Therefore, it seemed natural for me to pursue membership in a historically Black fraternity. There were four Black fraternities on campus. I perceived that each could provide the desired lifetime brotherhood bond. I chose Alpha Phi Alpha Fraternity, deciding that the brothers in the fraternity were the type of men with whom I wanted to be associated. Alpha is the largest and first Black fraternity, founded in 1906. Although Alpha is a "historically Black" fraternity, we have a diverse worldwide membership. This is, to me, similar to the fact that White students attend "historically Black" colleges such as Howard University and Prairie View A&M University. The first White member was initiated into our fraternity in the 1940s.

The list of great and famous Alphamen is long and impressive. The list includes the Nobel Prize–winning civil rights leader, Dr. Martin Luther King, Jr., and Thurgood Marshall, a civil rights attorney and first Black on the U.S. Supreme Court. Former Atlanta mayor and U.S. Ambassador to the United Nations Andrew Young and W. E. B. DuBois, a historian and the key civil rights leader at the beginning of the twentieth century, are Alphamen. Paul Robeson, a scholar, athlete, singer, actor, and civil rights leader, was initiated into the ranks. Congressman

Adam Clayton Powell, Jr., influential in passing affirmative action and welfare reform bills, is a member. Publisher John H. Johnson, former three-term Atlanta mayor Maynard Jackson, and the first African-American mayors of New York, Houston, New Orleans, Cincinnati, and San Francisco were all Alphamen. In sports, Alpha is represented by the renowned Olympic athlete Jesse Owens and football Coach Eddie Robinson, Sr., among others. It is not just the famous Alphamen that attracted me to the fraternity, but the abundance of positive-minded men that may only be known in their respective local communities for their professional achievements and community service.

Some people pledge Greek-letter fraternities or sororities during their college years partially because they want to be popular. Some pledge to participate in the Greek party scene. But neither of these reasons influenced my decision. In my freshman year, the Alphas at Pitt were in a transition phase and definitely were not the largest Black fraternity on Pitt's campus. I studied so hard during my first semester that I really did not know which group was most socially influential. I eventually took full advantage of the social benefits associated with being in a Black fraternity in the 1980s, but the benefits were not my motivation for pledging.

Along with a friend who also lived on the twelfth floor of my dorm, I began to regularly visit Alpha Phi Alpha member Todd Jackson to talk about fraternity life. Todd was an upperclassman transfer student who had pledged in Cleveland. He had an experienced and well-rounded perspective on Black Greek organizations that was not limited to my campus. He helped me understand that the fraternity was not just for your college years, but for life. He taught me that the brotherhood is not limited to your school but extends to Alpha brothers around the world. My main concern was having time to study while pledging. I discussed this openly. Todd assured me that his organization had a legacy of academic success and would help me maintain my high GPA.

Following my interview with the Alphas, I borrowed a copy of the Alpha history book from one of the brothers. All Black Greek organizations had an image, or stereotypical reputation. Everyone I talked to on campus expected Alpha Phi Alpha members to be serious about academics. After reading the beginning of the Alpha history book, I knew that historically, the fraternity has played a prominent role in the area of education dating back to the beginning of the twentieth century with its Go-to-High School, Go-to-College program. Since I was academically focused, I knew I would fit in. I was convinced Alpha was right for me.

Three people, including me, were given the opportunity to pledge. The pledge program was challenging. I studied for my classes while also learning fraternity history, doing miscellaneous assignments, and spending time with the brothers. The other two guys quit by the third week. I was left all alone to complete my pledge program.

I maintained my GPA while pledging. Although I was growing to love the fraternity, academic achievement and graduation were still my priorities.

Near the end of my pledge period there was a "turnaround day," where I was able to playfully give orders to the fraternity members. This was fun. Then I entered my final week. By this time, I had incredible visibility on Pitt's campus. I was the only Alpha pledge left, and no other historically Black fraternity was pledging prospective new members during that semester.

There were some young women pledging one of the Black sororities at the same time I was pledging Alpha. During my last week, the Sphinxmen, as Alpha pledges were known, and the lady pledges had their respective probate Step Shows on the same night. Step Shows are performances traditionally performed by Black Greeks to convey their pride in and the history of their respective organizations. Sometimes, the Greeks also took playful jabs at rival organizations. It is a combination of singing, dancing, stomping, chanting, and theatrical presence. A large auditorium was packed for our performances. Although I am not talented at stepping or singing, I definitely had the sympathy and popularity points from the large crowd for doing it all by myself.

I was initiated into Alpha Phi Alpha as an eighteen-year-old freshman on March 22, 1985. When I returned to the lobby connecting the main dormitory towers, there was a giant banner made from a painted bed sheet celebrating my achievement. It was an incredible feeling, one of exhaustion, elation, and relief, all mixed with alcohol from the short party we had in my honor. Later that night, my new fraternity brothers drove me to Indiana University of Pennsylvania (IUP) for an Alpha party there. They had Sphinxmen who were still pledging. I was glad to see my "sands," those with whom you enter the fraternity, since I did not have anyone pledging beside me at Pitt. These IUP Sphinxmen were initiated the next day. It was a great weekend, with excitement on both campuses for the new initiates.

Thomas (top, second from right) and some of the brothers of Alpha Phi Alpha Fraternity, Inc.—Omicron Chapter at University of Pittsburgh. June 1985.

One of my friends was quite clear about what I should expect next: "Once you become a fraternity brother, all of these girls will not only want to date you, they will want to be your girlfriend." Immediately after my initiation, I had a lot of visibility and popularity, and a lot of opportunities to party and date women. I, however, was determined not to be perceived as some type of social elitist after becoming an Alpha. During the summer before my sophomore year, I had no interest in dating sorority girls, or the girls who were longing for the opportunity to pledge sororities.

Instead of dating women who were suddenly interested in "Thomas the Alpha," as I was known for the rest of my college days, I dated a freshman girl who was indifferent to the Black Greek scene. She was also eighteen years old. I met her during one of our INROADS activities at the start of the summer and we hit it off right away. We had a deep involvement through the summer. This was my first serious dating relationship. However, at the start of my sophomore year in September 1985, she went off to start at Penn State and our involvement trailed off. I then slowly began to enjoy my social status and date a number of women at Pitt.

I had made quite a transformation from my high school days in terms of dating. Since I had plenty of scholarship money and great summer internships, I had more money than the average college student did. Contact lenses replaced the thick glasses. I had nicer clothes; I could afford to pay my phone bill and take girls on dates. I even had money for road trips. I finally got braces for my teeth, something I achieved cost-effectively by allowing myself to be an orthodontic patient, a guinea pig for the aspiring dental students at the Pitt Dental School. Not owning a car was no big deal at Pitt, since little parking space was available and most students walked. The Oakland section of the city, where Pitt was located, offered plenty to do within walking distance, including night life. In addition, Duquesne University and Carnegie Mellon University, and two all-female colleges, Carlow and Chatham, were easily accessible. The best thing was my academic achievement was no longer a negative as it had been in high school. Women respected the difficulty of my major and the fact that I excelled in it.

It surprises some when I relate that it is difficult to separate my college experience from being an Alpha. They are almost completely intertwined. This is not because I defined myself solely as the President of Alpha Phi Alpha's Omicron Chapter at Pitt. To the contrary, I was a

Dean's List student in engineering, chapter secretary of the National Society of Black Engineers, and worked with Pitt's administration as the student representative on the university's affirmative action committee. I was an active member of an academic honor society and briefly involved in student government for financial allocations. I was, however, viewed by other Black students first and foremost as "Thomas the Alpha." This did not bother me. I accepted and embraced it. I have used it to my benefit academically, socially, and professionally ever since. Many of my lifelong friends are fraternity brothers I met while at Pitt. That is why I paid the dues necessary to become a financial life member and I plan to stay active in Alpha Phi Alpha graduate chapters wherever I live. The fraternity's motto of "manly deeds, scholarship, and love for all mankind" is something to which I will remain committed.

My personal commitment to community service was reinforced by my fraternity and manifested through my work in the community with INROADS, the Boys Clubs of America, and other organizations. I have participated in Project Alpha, my fraternity's effort to educate young men about the dangers of teen sex, including teen pregnancy and sexually transmitted diseases. In general, I loved to try to find new ways to motivate the students in these various programs and to challenge them to let go of any low expectations of themselves.

I felt so privileged to be receiving a university education. Thus, I found that it was rewarding and of paramount importance psychologically to give back to urban youth. I felt that these inner city teens had a lot in common with Thomas Brooks, circa 1981, so I wanted to help them. It was not only good for the teenagers. I learned from these young people too. This kept me mentally young and open-minded, which has had long-term benefits for me in terms of strategic thinking, relationships, and friendships. I also had the opportunity to stay in touch with the evolving teenage culture, which I expected to help me one day when I have my own teenagers. I believe that I have done some good work. As Deepak Chopra brilliantly suggested in his book *The Seven Spiritual Laws of Success,* I found a relatively unique talent. I enjoyed practicing my talent, and I was using that talent to serve humanity. Of course, it was my fraternity brother Dr. Martin Luther King, Jr., who had wisely recommended, "Everyone can be great, because everyone can serve."

In my fraternity, I learned that the need for service did not die with Dr. King. African-Americans, in particular, faced a number of serious disparities. Technology has driven much of our nation's economic growth, but according to the National Action Council for Minorities in Engineering, less than five percent of all engineering degrees in 2002 were earned by African-Americans. African-Americans, especially young men my age, were being disproportionately incarcerated. Whites were more than three times more likely to be self-employed as entrepreneurs. To top it off, African-American life expectancy was about six years shorter. This really hit home as I began to meet older Alphamen who had pledged in the 1930s and 1940s. While organizations like INROADS were helping to improve the situation in corporate America by providing opportunities for bright young minorities, more work by all races, by government, and by the private sector was needed. Seeing the community service efforts by Alpha chapters and individual Alphamen was very inspiring for me.

When I began working as a mentor with African-American high school students, a major problem I saw was that their self-esteem was often low. This was, I believe, typically because of the amount of misinformation and stereotyping still rampant in our society.

Stereotypes related to issues like crime, drug use, welfare, and education affected many aspects of my daily life. As a result, I felt that I had to, in my interactions with Whites, personally dispel the negative stereotypes. I felt the need to be significantly better than my counterparts in corporate America in proving my qualifications when competing for the same career opportunities. I had to prove to some individual classmates and professors that I belonged in the Engineering Department at Pitt. When one has no exposure to something or to a group of people, this ignorance creates fear and negative stereotypes. Even some of America's educational dictionaries have definitions of the word "black" as "soiled; evil; wicked; cheerless; depressing." "White" has been described as "decent; pure; fair; generous." Given this perception, I was grateful that it was a White person who taught me that one could see the farthest, including the stars in other galaxies, when it is the darkest. I tried to help the high school kids I mentored rise above the negative stereotypes held by others.

Meanwhile, during my sophomore and junior years, I grew socially, dated frequently, and made a lot of friends. I was having a full college experience. I even took frequent road trips to the rival university I previously detested, Penn State. There were football games, fraternity parties, new women, and new friendships with the Alphamen at Penn State. In the end, I must admit that I almost started liking Penn State, the university. I now only dislike their football team. Visiting my high school friend Arty at Penn State was great fun. He eventually became an Alpha as well.

On one trip, I actually arrived at Penn State on Arty's last weekend of pledging to see his initiation. I will never forget the "deer in headlights" look on his face when he saw me about twelve hours before his initiation. He was shocked to see me and probably assumed that I was there to add some last minute challenges to his pledge program. Of course, I had no such intention. I was only there to celebrate his achievement. I was proud of him.

At Pitt, I was having the time of my life during my junior year. My grades were good. I was president of my Alpha chapter. It was the university's bicentennial year, and I was elected homecoming king. This gave me additional visibility on campus and in the city as a whole. By now, I also had a happy relationship with a great girlfriend.

"Everybody thinks they're 'The Big Man on Campus,'" my fraternity brother and future physician Vaughn Clagette told me one day in January 1987. "We think, we as individuals are 'The Man' because we are doing well academically and have bright futures. We are Alphas and we are well known and popular socially. We are leaders in many on-campus organizations. We are having more fun here than we ever could dream of while we were in high school. However, we are only big in our own little world. For example, whoever is president, as an arbitrary example, of the Korean Student Association probably thinks he is 'The

Man' also. Same with the back-up walk-on punter on the football team in his small clique. In a few years, we will all be in totally different worlds, bigger worlds. However, while we are here in this little world, we all think we are 'The Man.' Let's make the most of our time here. Let's have fun, but also live by the fraternity motto of 'manly deeds, scholarship, and love for all mankind. You don't want to look back thirty years from now and have any regrets about your college days."

Vaughn was right. We were completely convinced that we were "Big Men on Campus." Of course, the bigger they are, the harder they fall.

It was a tough Valentine's Day weekend in 1987. I had three major exams to study for the following week, and thus no time to spend with my girlfriend. My fraternity chapter had taken on a pledge group, and I had to go along with Vaughn and some other brothers to a meeting on Friday night with the graduate advisor for our chapter.

At the time, Vaughn was dating a girl who sometimes hung out with my girlfriend. On the way home, we met up with some other brothers and decided to stop at the home of one of my girlfriend's female comrades. We needed to unwind and wanted to see some friendly faces. What we found was Vaughn's girl there with another guy. It was a very bad scene. I immediately looked on the street for my girlfriend's car. It was not there, but I was becoming worried. I had remembered hearing a rumor from a month before about my girlfriend "hanging out" with some guy. I knew nothing specific, but the rumor was making me very uneasy that night.

The next day, I confronted my girlfriend about my concerns. She assured me that the guy was "just a friend" and that they were not together that weekend. To make a long story short, by Sunday, I had clear evidence that she was lying. My heart was wounded and my ego crushed.

During all of this drama, I was not studying. I did poorly on my exams. My mother, Joan, was in the hospital with food poisoning. I had some conflicts with one of my roommates. Buckling under all of the distractions, I inexcusably received an "F" in one of my classes that semester. Some say that everyone has at least one bad semester, but I was really disappointed with my results.

When my nightmare semester finally ended, I moved out of the dorm and into a house on Walnut Street in Pittsburgh's upscale Shady Side neighborhood in May 1987. I was able to live there because I shared a house with seven other people and paid only $210 per month. This was a great deal at the time. The other members of the household happened to be White, including one roommate who was Jewish, and three were women. Six were graduate students or established professionals and two of us were senior electrical engineering students. Living with this group was a good experience in communal, multiracial living. It was like the MTV reality TV show *The Real World,* just a few years too early and without the TV cameras. I stayed there until I graduated in May 1988, learning a lot about valuing diversity and how to resolve differences.

Meanwhile, Don had moved to Cleveland, where he was diagnosed with leukemia. His condition was discovered during my sophomore year of college. I had gone to visit him in Cleveland fairly regularly in 1986 and 1987. In general, he seemed to be making good medical progress through chemotherapy by the middle of 1987. Our friendship was great at that point. He saw me as an adult son, and he was the closest thing to a father that I had ever had.

On the Fourth of July weekend 1987, I went to visit Don in Cleveland. I joined Don and his girlfriend at a restaurant and discussed with them my love life and outlook on women. In the middle of the conversation I saw a tall, cute girl walk into the restaurant with her mother. She was thin, yet shapely. Although dressed casually, she appeared elegant to me. I stopped what I was saying and commented, "What I really need is a girl like her."

Don smiled and then ordered, "Go over and introduce yourself to her."

I explained that I felt uncomfortable approaching the girl with her mother there. I wasn't completely honest, as I also didn't have a high opinion of Cleveland women at the time based, unfairly, on my experiences with another girl I was already casually dating. I also unfairly assumed that the cute girl in the restaurant probably wouldn't be too bright. Don, being a native Georgian and southern gentleman at heart, went over and introduced himself to the mother and said that his son would like to meet her daughter. After watching Don, I went over and met the daughter. Her name was Julie.

Julie had a brilliant mind, and we shared common goals and interests. I made a date for the Fourth of July, and spent the entire day with her. She completely erased my silly stereotypical views of Cleveland girls. She was a bright engineering student who was well informed on national and global issues.

Don ran subtle interference when the other girl I was already casually dating in Cleveland inexplicably came by his apartment unannounced. I was around the corner at the apartment complex pool with Julie, and it could have been an embarrassing scene. Don liked Julie, and watched out for my interests and hers. Although our dates didn't lead to marriage, Julie and I have remained friends.

I saw Don again on December 30, 1987. I had just completed a job interview in Boston. I decided not to return directly to Pittsburgh, but to take a detour flight to Cleveland to see him. After disembarking from the plane, I called Don at his apartment. His girlfriend answered. She said that he was not feeling well and might be asleep when I arrived there.

Don awakened when I entered his apartment, but he did not get out of bed. We spoke briefly, then I quickly went to sleep, being exhausted from the trip and interview.

When I awoke on the morning of New Year's Eve 1987, Don was up and sitting in the living room in the wheelchair that he used frequently. We talked for a while. It was a good conversation, but what I remember most of all were his last words to me: "Make sure you spend time with your mother," he stated, with fondness for Joan.

I then went into the kitchen to fix breakfast. Don went back to his bedroom. The next thing I heard was his girlfriend screaming.

I ran back to the bedroom. Don was on his back and unconscious. I attempted CPR but was unable to pry his jaw open for what seemed like minutes. Don's teeth were clenched down on his tongue. Finally, I pried his mouth open and I administered CPR. I hadn't practiced CPR since health class in eleventh grade. His eyes had rolled back in his head. He was dead even before the ambulance arrived. At the time, I blamed myself for not being able to do a better job at CPR.

It hurt to lose him. It was the first time that I lost someone I loved. Since that experience, my New Year's Eve festivities always include thoughts of Don, and I always offer a toast in his honor. I wished that he would have been able to see me graduate from college only a few months later. I know that it would have meant a lot to him.

However, when I graduated from Pitt in May 1988, my mother, Grandpa Bill, Aunt Bessie, and my cousin Kim were there. Grandpa Bill was bragging all the way. He was proud of my bachelor's degree in electrical engineering, and proud that I would subsequently spend four years working for Westinghouse, his former employer.

On the way out of the Civic Arena graduation ceremony, Grandpa Bill stumbled and nearly fell. That scared me. I suddenly realized that

Thomas' graduation from the University of Pittsburgh, joined by Grandpa Bill. 1988.

he was getting old. It would soon be up to my generation to carry on for him. By earning my degree, I had overcome a huge challenge. But the race was far from over, and there were more hurdles to scale.

CHAPTER NINE

Survive and Advance

After graduating from Pitt, I accepted a job offer to join Westinghouse Electric Corporation and their Engineering/Management Professional Development Program. The job entailed four rotational assignments before I would settle into a permanent job function.

My first two assignments were at College Station, Texas. As a native of the East Coast, I was not excited about being assigned to a small rural town in Texas. When I arrived in College Station, I felt quite alone. I did not know a single person west of the Mississippi River. It was scary and exciting at the same time. Texas A&M University was there, and the historically Black college Prairie View A&M University was right down the road, halfway to the city of Houston. Fortunately, my Alpha brothers at both of these universities really took good care of me socially, and made me realize that I was not alone in Texas after all. I was even more pleased with my previous decision to become an Alpha. I often quoted to myself from the poem *House of Alpha* I learned while pledging: "Goodwill is the monarch of this house. Men, unacquainted, enter, shake hands, exchange greetings and depart friends." I lived its thesis.

At age twenty-one, with a new job, a new car, and an outgoing personality, I had no trouble meeting women on these campuses. Given that I knew my stay in College Station was temporary, I began to enjoy myself and definitely made the best of being there. I also spent many of my weekends ninety miles away in Houston.

I had been a devout Christian since my teenage years, but lost my religious focus in college. Once I settled into life in College Station, I began to refocus on religion. After a few months in Texas, I only wanted to date women who shared my religious beliefs. I felt this would help me in my spiritual journey; I had a yearning to be compatible religiously with a woman before falling in love and eventually getting married.

That prospect came about soon enough, for while I was in College Station, I met a great girl who was a native of Texas. By 1989, I had moved to Maryland to complete the final two rotations of the Westinghouse program. Coincidentally, at the same time, my new love was accepted to a master's program at the University of Maryland. I decided that it was fate or God's handiwork, so we were soon married, despite the fact that we had difficulties during our engagement. I believed, fervently, that God would help us through it and make our marriage strong.

I worked full-time for Westinghouse during the day and matriculated at the University of Maryland MBA Program as a part-time evening student. It was the most miserable, difficult period of my life. In a typical week, I spent no less than fifty hours at work, plus I had MBA classes and MBA case groups. I also taught and attended Bible classes, enduring long commutes through the traffic of the Baltimore and Washington, D.C., suburbs. I had no free time to have fun for myself. On top of the schedule strain, I was not the greatest husband in the world, and I felt as though my difficult marriage was strangling me. There was no joy in my life, whatsoever. I was trying to survive the challenges and advance through them, somehow. I did not see any light at the end of the tunnel, not even an oncoming train to put me out of my misery. To make matters worse, in March of 1991, Grandpa Bill died at the age of eighty-two. I was not surprised as his health was steadily fading, but it still hurt. I am glad I spent time talking with him each week that final year before he left us. I dedicated that semester to him, and earned A's in all three of my MBA classes in spite of my full-time work schedule and challenging overall life situation.

As America won the so-called Cold War and defense programs were cut, I was lucky to survive two massive layoffs of more than a thousand people each at Westinghouse during 1991. I believe that one reason I survived the layoffs was because I was a junior engineer, and I made significantly less money than some of the more experienced ones who lost their jobs.

Although layoffs will always be a reality in corporate America, I decided that I would try to never let myself be as vulnerable as I was then. While in corporate America, I intended to make sure that I was in a strong, growing industry; defense was not a growth industry in 1991. I wanted to make certain that I was with a strong company. Westinghouse had a number of challenges at this time, difficulties that the stock market reflected. I wanted to make sure that in the future, I was in a growing department; Westinghouse had redundant test engineering groups at the time, so there was no opportunity for growth. Finally, I wanted to be certain that I was working on a product that had exciting growth and revenue opportunities.

Having completed my MBA, I wanted to get out of the declining defense business and accepted an offer to work with a large, high-tech firm in Houston, Texas, in July 1992. This job was a great opportunity to work in strategic marketing in a growing business unit. A fraternity brother, and now a good friend, Ron Wages, interviewed me at the University of Maryland. He helped to get me in the door for an interview. I appreciated this, and I was able to take it from there with the hiring manager. I soon received a job offer.

My new job allowed me to travel all over North America, and occasionally internationally, giving me a broader perspective of the world. Things were starting to turn around for me by 1993. I was in a new city with an exciting new career. However, at the end of an all-night discussion with my wife, I knew that my marriage would never be happy. We had been in counseling since 1992, but it just wasn't helping. In spite of my previous religious beliefs against divorce, I knew that night it was time to end the marriage. She was a great person and a beautiful woman, but we were a bad match as a couple. I should have realized this during our engagement. When I thought about my life as a whole that night in 1993, I broke down and cried in front of her because I felt that I had little to show for the previous four years. Most of my friendships were weaker because of the time spent on working toward my MBA, working on my chaotic marriage, and working on my religious faith. These factors denied me the necessary time to cultivate and nurture true friendships. My religious faith was eroding; I was convinced that I had wasted a small chunk of my life, and I felt like a failure because of the impending divorce.

As I struggled with the demise of my marriage, I started hanging out at an exotic dance club in Houston in 1993. One Saturday night, I went to the club to unwind. Houston was my wife's hometown, so I did not park my car in front of the club, still trying to keep my attraction to these clubs a secret.

I parked around the block in front of a veterinarian's office. I regularly purchased lap dances from a number of girls for ten dollars each, and dropped the most money on a girl whose stage name was Chocolate*. Still legally married, I viewed this as less tempting than going out to a conventional nightclub where women might be interested in dating me. For me, the exotic club was a safer alternative since I had no interest in a relationship with any dancer.

After a number of lap dances by Chocolate, I left the club. It was about one o'clock in the morning. When I returned to the veterinarian's parking lot, my car was gone.

My soon-to-be-ex-wife was living out of state, and I was temporarily living with her sweet and accommodating parents. They were quite religious and probably would not have looked favorably on anyone coming into the house well after midnight. I knew I couldn't call them and say, "Please come and get me. I have been hanging out at an exotic dancer club, and I can't find my car."

Seeing a dim light inside the vet's office, I pounded on the glass door. I banged over and over again on the glass. Finally, a cleaning person emerged.

I asked, "Have you seen my car?"

"No speak English," was the reply.

"Where is my car?" I repeated.

The same answer was given by the cleaning person: "No speak English."

"Uh, *donde la*. . . uh…auto?" I knew then that I should have chosen Spanish over French in high school.

After a series of elaborate hand gestures, she pointed out a small sign on the window. There was an address and a phone number for a towing service. I tried to stay calm.

I went back around the corner to the loud crowded club to use the pay phone. I called six times, but no one answered at the towing service. I was desperate now.

Spotting Chocolate in the middle of a table dance, I didn't hesitate to interrupt the proceedings. "Chocolate," I pleaded, "I need your help. My car was towed, and I need a ride to the lot."

"I can't do it. I caught a ride with Greg*, the bouncer, tonight."

"What am I going to do?"

"All right, let me finish with this customer and I will holler back at you after I see if Greg will drop you off."

"Thanks. I really need this."

Finally, she came back with an answer. "He can do it," she reported, "but we don't close for another hour. Then I have to change, and Greg will have to stick around until all of the people have cleared out of the parking lot."

Ah, the club's parking lot, I thought. If only I had parked there. It was getting late.

It was 2:30 A.M. when Greg barked, "Chocolate! Dude! Let's break out of here!"

I let Greg know that I appreciated the ride to the lot. I was beginning to feel optimistic that I would have my car in a few minutes. However, upon arrival at the towing graveyard, my hopes were dashed. "There's no one here," I lamented. I began to yell, "Hello! Is anybody here? Hello! Is anybody in there?"

"What are you going to do?" Chocolate tried to be supportive.

"I don't know. The lot is dark and it is so big, I don't even know if the car is in there."

It was 3 A.M.

"Maybe I can squeeze through this gate," I reasoned. "There is a lock on it, but there is slack in the chain." It never occurred to me that I was trespassing until after I had successfully located my car. While inside the gate, I went up to the small office building.

"Hello! Is anybody in there? I just want to get my car out of here. Hello! I have the towing fee!"

No one answered. Back outside the gate, I wondered out loud how I was going to get my car out. I sat on the curb with my head down.

"What do you wanna do?" yawned Chocolate. "It is getting late."

"Let me think for a min—," I started to say.

"Maybe I can shoot this lock off and we can open the gate," Greg offered.

"Huh?" I didn't even know he had a gun. Before I could verbalize how bad of an idea this was, the first bullet hit the lock. Then, I actually became hopeful. However, after three shells had hit the lock and then the ground, the lock still held strong. It was just like the old TV commercial from the 1970s that demonstrated the strength of the lock.

Chocolate, still in the car, voiced concern about the loud shots, "The police are going to come," she warned.

Soon the gun was empty and six shells were on the ground, but the lock remained intact.

It was 3:30 A.M.

Seconds later, while pondering my situation, I heard sirens. The police were on the scene, three cars and six officers strong. We were placed separately in the back of the three cars. Two men, owners of the lot, emerged from the small office building. They had chosen to ignore my pleas previously, and called the police once they heard gunshots. Now I was worried that they would tell the police that I had trespassed.

After talking with the owners, one of the officers climbed into the car where I was being held. "Give me your driver's license," he commanded. "Now, what went on here?"

"Uh, I just came to get my car out of this lot," I stammered. "It had been towed."

He typed my info into an onboard computer in the police car. They ran a background check on me.

"Who fired the gun?"

"I don't know anything about any gun. I don't have a gun. I just came to get my car back."

"Where did you park it?"

"I parked it in front of a veterinarian's office."

"Why did you park it there on a Saturday night?"

"It was next to a club that I went into. I didn't think it was a problem on a Saturday night to park there. I had parked there on previous occasions."

Basically, my story was that I was just here for my car, and I was determined to stick to it.

"Were you the one that broke in through the gate?"

"I didn't break in. I was just looking for my car. I came here with money to pay for the towing costs. This guy was nice enough to give me a ride. I had called this lot six times on the phone and these people did not answer, though they were obviously here. When I arrived here, I yelled for someone to come out to allow me to pay for my car. They ignored me. I just slipped through the fence for only a second to verify that my car was even in this lot. I didn't touch anything inside the lot."

I knew then that I was in deep trouble. I also realized that we were lucky the police decided to ask questions upon their arrival as opposed to just shooting.

After running a check on Chocolate, they found that she had written a number of bad checks and there was a warrant on her. She was arrested. Greg was arrested for possessing and discharging an unregistered gun. My background check came back clean, of course. Fortunately for me, the owners decided not to press trespassing charges. The police seemed disappointed that I could not be arrested.

Although I was released, Greg and Chocolate were arrested as a result of trying to help me. I felt bad for them. It was 4:30 A.M.

After the officers left, I sat, stunned. I still did not have my car. I was left only with the owners of the lot.

"You need to pay us $150 to get your car back."

"What? This is crazy. It normally costs about forty-five dollars to tow a car. I will give you fifty."

"We will give it to you for eighty dollars. It is your fault that we have been out here all night."

Since I had about eighty dollars on me, I agreed and gave them the money.

"Now, just show us your ID," one of the owners said, "and we will give you your car."

I looked in my wallet for my driver's license, and I quickly realized that the police had never given me back my license. And I thought things could not get any worse.

"We cannot give you the car without the driver's license."

"Look. You all heard me calling for you. If you would have answered, I could have had my car more than two hours ago. Here is my social security card. I also have credit cards with my name on them. I can tell you everything that is inside the car. The insurance papers have my name on them. Give me the keys to my car!" I shouted.

Relenting, they let me drive my car off of the lot. A minute later, I pulled over to regain my composure. I was free, and I had my car back. However, two people who tried to help me were in jail. I wanted to help them, but I wasn't sure how to do so. Also, I really did not know Greg, the bouncer. He carried a gun, so I was vaguely concerned that he would want to extract some "revenge" against me because of the circumstances. I felt it was important to try to help both of them.

I didn't know where the jail was, but drove in the general direction of downtown. When I saw a police car, I did a U-turn and aggressively sped after the police car like a madman with the intention of asking directions. When I finally caught up the with the police car, we were in the dark, behind a strip mall. The cop wasn't at all happy, and he gave me a severe tongue-lashing. "What in the hell are you doing? Are you trying to kill yourself?"

"I was trying to follow you because some of my friends were arrested. I need directions to the jail."

"I am back here on police business. Get the hell out of here now before you get hurt!"

Soon thereafter, I caught up with another police car and obtained the information I sought. Men in custody were kept in a downtown jail. The women were detailed in a west side facility. I went downtown first. It was 5:30 A.M.

Walking into the station, I went up to the desk and said to an officer, "I am looking for a guy named Greg who was arrested a couple of hours ago. I want to see if I can help bail him out."

"What is his last name?"

"I don't know. He was arrested in front of a towing company lot on the south side."

"Well, even if you knew his full name, it wouldn't matter. Anyone arrested tonight will be in the holding area downstairs for a few hours. They won't show up on our computer up here for a while. You might want to come back in a few hours."

Discouraged, I left, and went to the west side to look for Chocolate. Because I talked to her a lot between table dances, I did actually remember her real last name. I was able to verify that she was at the jail, but I would not be able to see her for a couple of hours. It was 8:30 A.M., a bright and sunny Sunday morning.

I finally returned to the home of my wife's parents after grabbing some fast-food breakfast. I bumped into my father-in-law.

"Um, Thomas. Are you all right?"

"Yeah. Um...it has been a beautiful morning."

I was not about to share any more information and quickly went upstairs. I was hoping that he would assume I was just returning home from the 6 A.M. church service. I knew this was unlikely, but I decided not to worry about what I could not control.

After a shower and change of clothes, I went back out to the west side jail and talked to Chocolate. She told me that she expected to have to pay a fine, but would be out later that day. I promised to stop by the club later, but only to give her money to help make up for the fine she was going to pay. I had no intention of hanging around the exotic dancer club. She also told me Greg's last name, but when I arrived at the downtown facility, I was denied access because I was not a member of Greg's family. Later, when I met Chocolate at the club, I gave her some money to help reimburse her fine and Greg's bail. She promised to give it to Greg whenever he returned to the club. I had no choice but to trust her. After all, I was going out of town on that following Wednesday.

For my subsequent trip, I was scheduled to rent a car, which would be impossible without a driver's license. Desperate to find my license, I went to the police station on Sunday night but missed the start of the shift, and all of the officers were out. To make matters worse, I did not remember the name of the officer who took my license. I returned at the start of the shift on Monday night and talked to a few of the officers who were on the scene. None had my license. In the process, I was forced to again explain what happened to the sergeant in charge of the shift. I was afraid that I would be arrested as I detailed what happened. Instead, he agreed to try to help me and told me to return on Tuesday. When I showed up for the start of the shift on Tuesday night, my license was there.

After returning to Houston from my trip, I stopped back at the club to see Greg. He was outside with some of his friends. "Greg, what's up?" I said, trying to sound cool, calm, and collected. "It's me, Thomas. Um...did you get the money from Chocolate?"

"Yo, I got it. Thanks, dawg. I appreciate it. That cash was right on time."

"Well, I appreciate that you tried to help me. I felt bad you were arrested for trying to help me."

One of his friends chimed in, "Don't feel bad; you didn't tell him to start bustin' caps to open the lock. That was on him." Everyone cracked up laughing, except me. I had made a big mistake. I was just relieved that it was over and Greg had no hard feelings.

M y wife and I had tried to save our marriage, and the aforementioned counseling in 1992 did not help. In the end nothing worked, and I made my decision to file for divorce in August 1993. The divorce was not finalized until early 1994.

The disappointment I felt over the divorce filing decision hit home while traveling one Wednesday night in late August 1993. I was in the northern part of North Carolina. Looking for something to do, I went to a small party in an Elks Lodge in Chapel Hill. The University of North Carolina was on summer break, so those attending the party were local people, not university students. It was still early when I arrived at the lodge. I sat at the bar slowly nursing a beer. Hip-hop music blasted across an empty dance floor as I stared blankly at the muted TV, watching a show called *Love Connection*. On this game show, contestants select one out of three members of the opposite sex for a date. The couple dates, then they come back on TV and tell the audience about their respective experiences. When the selection process started on this particular show, they showed the three potential bachelors. Under their faces came a display with their name, age, occupation, and "status." Status referred to single, widowed, or divorced. When I saw the display of someone with "STATUS: DIVORCED," I felt terrible. At that time, I naively felt that this same label would follow me forever and would make it difficult for me to find anyone to date.

Later that week, I traveled north to the Baltimore/Washington, D.C., area. I called my friend and Pitt fraternity brother Jon Gee. We made plans to go out that Friday night. I had not seen Jon since I finished graduate school the previous year, and in the rush to meet up with him I forgot to eat.

As Jon drove us to the club, I told him about my problems and my impending divorce. He was very insightful and supportive, but somehow his words did not help much. We arrived at the club early. We sat at the bar and started drinking, reminiscing about college, and telling fraternity stories. Knocking back the drinks pretty quickly, I became intoxicated. As the designated driver, Jon had stopped drinking early. Although I was expecting to be rusty in terms of my interactions with women, I still had a couple of women all over me on the dance floor. During a break, I joined some of the women at their table. Jon saw me later, surrounded by women and having a great time. Soon thereafter my head was on the table. My last memory was of the bouncer dragging me to the door, about to throw me out of the bar because I had passed out. Jon spotted the chaos, ran over, negotiated my release from the bouncer, and helped me to the car. After laughing at me, Jon dropped me off safely at my hotel room.

The next day, I met up with an old friend in Maryland named Veronica. I found Veronica attractive both physically and intellectually. Once again, I discussed my troubles and impending divorce. She said all of the same things that Jon had told me the night before. She was supportive and was convinced that many good women would still want to date me once my divorce was finalized. Her supportive words resonated with me more clearly than Jon's, probably because she was a woman.

I went to Atlanta a few weeks after my D.C. trip. It gave me an opportunity to spend time with my old friend Vaughn from Pitt. Vaughn took a break from his work at the hospital to hang out with me. I talked with him also about the challenges I was facing. Like Jon and Veronica, he tried to be helpful and supportive. I talked with him about how my religious faith had affected my lifestyle after I left college. I had been married and I had focused my time on sharing my faith, not on partying. This lifestyle change affected some, though not all, of my friendships.

I shared that some of my friendships had changed during the previous three years because I then had less in common with the lifestyle of my friends. After a few days hanging out in Atlanta, my relationship with Vaughn was firmly reestablished. Together, we both learned a lot from each other about friendships and the two-way effort required to maintain them.

Vaughn told me of a friend he had met in Pittsburgh named James Harrison. They had met while James was working on his master's degree in Architecture from Carnegie Mellon University and Vaughn was in medical school. James was also an Alpha and a Houston native who had just returned to his hometown. Vaughn suggested that we meet each other in Houston. He asked James to introduce me to a few folks and show me around.

In November 1993 I met James, who was hanging out with two other Alphas, Brett and Louis Fontenot, at a Houston jazz spot. Along with Al Henson, the four men were all friends since grade school. They grew up together, went to separate colleges, yet joined the same fraternity, Alpha. I became friends with them from the start. In just a few weeks, I felt like I had great friends in Houston.

My friendship with James developed quickly. Despite earning a master's degree from one of the best universities in the country, James initially had been having some trouble finding a job. He was also just getting used to a long-distance relationship with his girlfriend. Since James wasn't working and I had few other friends in Houston, we frequently had time to hang out together. We helped each other through a difficult period as I worked through the divorce, and he looked for a job.

Roughly a month after we met, James received a job offer with an architecture firm in Dallas. I was happy for him. But when he left, I missed hanging out with him on a regular basis. However, I stepped right into his spot among our group of friends and on the larger Houston African-American social scene. For this, I can thank Houston natives Brett, Al, and Louis. They took me along to numerous parties and events. Any woman I wanted to meet, they introduced to me. Their respective female "significant others" gave me the same red carpet treatment. Because of these guys, I quickly went from being overlooked to being well connected on the Houston social scene. The guys taught me to never go second-class when doing things for your boys, and also that you have to put work into growing friendships. We formed a strong road trip crew for events like Mardi Gras, the World Cup, and the Super Bowl.

James knew how to cheer me up when I was down. In early 1994, after my divorce was finalized, James was back in Houston for the weekend. On a Friday night, we went from party to party. I was having a good time with James, but I was a little down about problems with a new girl I was dating. Near the end of the evening, James and I stopped at a nightspot with live music. After a full night of barhopping, I had to go to the bathroom immediately. I asked James to go to the bar and get me a beer. When I came back out of the bathroom, I saw James across the room talking to a group of White girls at the bar. I relaxed where I was, just enjoying the band.

The group of women around James kept growing, but I didn't go over. A few minutes later, I noticed the women motioning to me to join them. As their requests became emphatic, I finally walked over to the bar toward James. Before I could get to him, the women approached me and hugged on me with their hands on my back and butt. I looked directly at James trying to get some clue about what was going on. The women were still all over me, and they began to ask me to dance for them. Finally, I uncovered what was up. James had jokingly told them that I was a male exotic dancer, a stripper. He told them this because one of them was getting married the next day, and they were out for the night for a bachelorette party. It was crazy, but I briefly played along with the gag. I told them that I couldn't dance here because it was a public place. The women went and got the owner and secured his permission. So I said I couldn't do it in public because I had a day job in corporate America and someone might see me. Of course, nothing ever came of it, but we had a good time. "Nothing but foolishness" became our motto.

Near the end of 1994, James, knowing I was then open to the idea of finding a girl in Houston for a serious relationship, tried to set me up with a beautiful graduate student he knew. To do this, he created a diversion so that I could meet her. He invited about fifteen people, including her, to gather at a patio bar and restaurant. James was already living in Dallas, so the "official" reason was to have a get-together for James since he was back in Houston for the weekend. After a few hours of eating and socializing, James hadn't shown up. Everyone wondered out loud, "Where's James?" I didn't sweat his absence. I had identified the girl he had told me about and began to flirt with her. When everyone was ready to leave, James showed up with his classic fashionably late entrance. He eventually pulled me aside and said, "This is all for you. None of these people know why they are here. This is all for you!" The girl never came around to show any tangible interest in me, but I really appreciated James' effort. Besides, I did meet another cool girl at that gathering who I soon started dating.

James, Vaughn, and I, along with some other Alphamen, starting taking regular vacation trips in the 1990s that we referred to as the ABT, or "All Boyz Trip." Since all of us grew up in urban environments, we make certain these trips allow us to get in touch with nature. We have visited the Grand Canyon, California Wine Country, and Yosemite National Park. White water rafting in Montana's Glacier National Park was outstanding, but brutally cold. We then used our brains to plan the subsequent trip and went sailing in the warm British Virgin Islands. The ABT has frequented Cancun and the nearby Mayan ruins. We have skied in Breckenridge. While surrounded by nature, we discuss how we can be better people, better husbands to our wives, and better men in general. We have taught each other a lot about friendship. We share problems we are having with our extended families. We do not let each other down when it really matters and continually encourage each other to dream about many different dimensions of success. We always share our goals with each other and provide constructive criticism when our fellow brother is screwing up. Thanks to my friends, as well as my own character and determination, I had survived a tough period and found a way to advance through it. Anyone could benefit from a group of friends like this, especially as one undertakes a major endeavor like building relationships with one's biological parents.

CHAPTER TEN

Two Bouquets for Mother's Day

In July 1992, when I finally knew the general story of my birth and my biological families, I was proud of the heritage and background of both of my birth parents. I was happy to know specifically which country in Africa my paternal family was from. I began to dream of eastern Africa, specifically Kenya. Additionally, the idea of having some ancestors who were Lithuanian Jews was compelling. I was pleased that both of my biological parents were intelligent and accomplished, and lucky enough to have attended college. I was not surprised to see my biological family members described in the July 1, 1992, letter from Judy Scott as having "easygoing" personalities. It was a propitious sign to see many broad interests, from philosophy to art, and even baseball.

I also realized that the adoption agency's written account of the circumstances was twenty-five years old. I knew the account had been filtered, interpreted, and paraphrased by at least two different people, Judy Scott and some other agency employee back in 1966. I wondered if I would ever get to talk with both biological parents to hear their perspectives on the decision to relinquish me for adoption. Of course, their perspectives would also be a quarter-century old and subject to fading as well.

While I contemplated these thoughts, I received a second letter from Judy. It was dated July 21, 1992. Amazingly, the post office quickly routed the letter to my forwarding address. I had left Maryland and had relocated to Houston that same week.

Judy wrote that she had called my biological maternal grandmother. Luckily, the grandmother had lived in the same house in Dorseyville outside of Pittsburgh and had kept the same phone number since my adoption. This grandmother put Judy in touch with my birth mother.

I was surprised. I had not expected Judy to pursue this. The fact that my biological mother had written to the adoption agency years before, asking them to put a notice on file stating that if I ever sought information or contact that she would be open to contact from her child, no doubt facilitated this. I didn't know then, of course, but my biological mother had also researched groups like the ALMA and had previously registered in their database. She guessed that if I ever contacted ALMA, I would likely get the advice to contact the adoption agency and if she put a letter on file, she could save the annual fee for being in the ALMA database. This was important to her, as my biological mother was supporting her other four children, and every penny counted.

In the second letter, Judy wrote that my biological mother was "living in England." The maternal grandmother had told Judy that she was certain that my birth mother would want to be in touch. Judy wanted my consent to distribute my identifying information. I called Judy immediately and confirmed my willingness to make contact with my biological family. Although I was *previously* satisfied with only the written report, I was now thrilled about the possibility of real contact with my two birth parents. Judy subsequently forwarded my name and address to my birth mother.

My biological mother, Dorothy Blazier-Wallstein, typed a one-page letter and photocopied her picture onto the upper-right corner. She faxed the letter with picture to Judy at the adoption agency in Pittsburgh. The agency sent it to me in Houston immediately, using a next day delivery service. I received the letter in early August 1992. At last, I had a letter from my biological mother and a picture of her. It was great.

For months, I had been slowly gearing up emotionally and gathering a lot of information to get ready for a protracted search. Then, it all happened so fast. I had a positive feeling about the pace of the developments, but I felt somehow unprepared.

The fax had come through pretty well. Although I knew Dorothy was still relatively young, I was surprised by how young my biological mother looked in the picture. I felt that I looked like her. I was pleased to see that she had a London address, and thought that it would be great to visit Dorothy and tour London for the first time on the same trip.

I don't know how much time Dorothy spent working on the initial one-page letter, but when I initially read it, I thought, "This is very good for the moment." She wrote:

Dorothy Wallstein
London NW3 3HU
England

Dear Thomas,

I cannot describe my feelings of overwhelming love, joy and relief to hear news of you through the agency. I have worried so much about you and would have given anything simply to know that you are alive and to know something of how you are doing in this difficult world. I still have so little information about you, simply that you now live in Maryland and have worked for Westinghouse. I have also learned a little about your adoptive parents and your progress during the time when you were fostered. Although I understand that your life will have been challenging and difficult, this simple information has brought such comfort and joy to me. I feel so proud of you making this courageous search for yourself! I have always felt or hoped that you would rise to the challenge of your existence, and saw you as a strong and special human being.

I do not know what you need from me at this point in your life. You may not even be sure yet yourself. I am anxious that you should get what you need as and when you need it and that I should not impose my wishes in any way. But I do hope you will give me news of yourself, as much as you can! I am trying not to get too hopeful about the possibility of seeing you, in case you simply want information. But I do not want you to think, for even a moment, that I would resist the suggestion of a reunion!

I have had a further five children since you were born, your first half-sister, born in Switzerland in 1970, sadly died when she was only four hours old. A year later, your second sister, Lotus was born. She has known about you since she was thirteen and is now nearly twenty-one studying to be an actress. She and I were together last night when I got the first news of your interest. She, too, is so excited to have news of you; she has always had a strong sense of her own relatedness to you and also understands how much you mean to me. She is a wonderful young woman.

You also have three half-brothers. Atom, who is eighteen, lives with me and recently finished the British equivalent of high school and works at Domino's pizza with ambitions of being a disc jockey, being crazy about house music at the moment. Jade who is sixteen and Derwent who will be fifteen in December have lived with their father for the last two and a half years in the northern part of England, though they are about to arrive for a three-week vacation.

I have lived in Britain since 1970, apart from eighteen months that I spent in Florida when your sister was a baby, and now live in a small, but comfortable apartment in London. I work as an organization development consultant, though for many years I had a career in holistic medicine and I still do a bit of teaching and clinical work.

There is so much that I want to say and ask, but it is difficult to know what more to say here. Perhaps you would like to know what I look like. I am forty-five years old, 5'5", dark brown (and gray!) hair, weight 126 pounds. I am healthy, as are all of your siblings.

I will stop now in order that I can fax this to Judy Scott who has kindly agreed to send this to you by overnight courier. I would be so happy to hear from you! You may call collect if you would like. If you get my answering machine, please leave your number and the times when you will be in. I have not yet told the boys about all of this so would appreciate it if for now you simply ask for me and leave your number.

I do hope to hear from you soon. I don't know how you would like to address me, so for the moment…

Sincerely,

Your natural mother

I responded to Dorothy's fax by typing a five-page letter. I summarized my life up to that time, and included details about my years with Joan and experiences at Pitt. I also enclosed a picture. She told me later that after she read my letter, she put it back in the envelope and sighed, "I can die now. My son is alive and well." A few days later she happily realized that she didn't have to die then, that she could enjoy getting to know me. She responded with a long letter in mid-August, filling in many gaps in my knowledge.

Soon, we were talking on the phone for the first time. Insensitive to international time zones, I suggested that we talk after my workday was over. That was 6 P.M. for me. Of course, since I lived in Houston, it meant a midnight call for Dorothy.

Our phone discussion began uncomfortably. After all of these years apart, and all of the letter writing, we didn't quite know where to start.

"Dorothy," I began, "I know from the information provided by the adoption agency that you went to Europe to pursue a possible abortion. I really want to thank you for not having an abortion." Although it was quite blunt so early in a conversation and so early in our relationship, it was direly important for me at the time to convey this right away. Dorothy offered no immediate comment on the subject.

After a pause, Dorothy started telling her story: "Well, there is some background that set the stage for your arrival. I went to Penn State University after working in the summer of 1965 as a camp counselor in upstate New York. I was interested in psychology, philosophy, and comparative religions and thought I might use my Penn State education as a social worker or psychologist. I joined a club for international students."

"You know, I grew up with a dislike for Penn State. I was always a Pitt fan, and I attended Pitt. It is sort of painfully ironic that I was conceived at Penn State." I paused. "You were from Pennsylvania, right? What could have made you want to join a group of international students?"

"I had considered joining the Peace Corps. I guess I was idealistic, almost naively so, about the concepts of brotherhood and the global human family," replied Dorothy. "It was at a meeting of this club that I met your biological father, Mboga Mageka Omwenga. Mboga was a graduate student and he had a lovely smile. We only dated briefly. He seemed like the type of man who would fight selflessly for higher principles. You were conceived on March 6, 1966; I was eighteen years old at the time. We had gone on a date, and we had gone back to his apartment.

"During the sexual embrace with your biological father, I remember sensing your presence distinctly, a beautiful energy hovering, waiting near my right shoulder. I perceived this energy to be the beginning of a baby who would overcome cultural and racial division. I did not want to get pregnant per se, but there was a moment when I specifically remember surrendering to *you*. Thomas, I knew instantly I was pregnant. And in that moment of direct perception, I had a great sense of calm, clarity, and love for you."

Dorothy continued. "From that moment of conception, I knew that you, Thomas, would be special, that you would build bridges across the races. Specifically, I perceived that you were to change things, to build a better world, and to do so in the face of great adversity. I was

convinced you would bring people of different races and cultures together. I never forgot or denied this perception in the years after you
were born or as you grew into manhood separated from me."

A few weeks later, after official confirmation, Dorothy told Mboga
of the pregnancy. Not long thereafter, she left Penn State. Eventually,
she got back in touch with him, and they continued to write to each
other until I was legally adopted.

"How did you decide what to do about your pregnancy?" I calmly
asked.

Dorothy's voice quivered a bit. "Thomas," she began, "it was an
extremely difficult period for me. Before making the decision to give
you up for adoption, I did fly to Sweden to seek an abortion. Abortions
were legal and easier to obtain in that country in the 1960s. I traveled
with the money from my own part-time job in the university cafeteria,
and the money given to me by a friend in the dormitory. I also hitch-
hiked part of the way. My parents were not yet aware of the pregnancy,
so I was unable to ask them for money."

"How do you think your parents would have felt about you being
pregnant, especially with me being an African-American baby?"

"Well, let me come back to that question, if that's okay. On the
ferry from Copenhagen, Denmark, to Malmo, Sweden, I met a young
woman named Lena Lundahl. On the boat ride, I told Lena the story of
my predicament. Lena took me to her family's home in Sweden on a
lake near Vaxjo."

I could hear Dorothy softly crying over the phone. I was glad to be
hearing the story of my origins, but I wondered if I was pushing for too
much information, too fast.

"Are you okay? Do you want to take a break from answering my
questions?" I asked.

"No, I'm fine," she replied through the audible sniffles.

"Okay. So, did Lena want to help you get an abortion?"

"Lena was just trying to be nice to me, in general. Lena's parents
spoke no English, but they went out of their way to be kind to me. The
parents arranged for a doctor to come to the house to examine me the

next day. The doctor said that the pregnancy was too advanced for an abortion, and asked if I didn't feel the baby's kicks."

"Why wasn't I kicking?"

She didn't answer the question directly. "The next day, Thomas, I did feel the kicks for the first time. I am now sure that I had been blocking them out. I wasn't yet facing the reality of your impending arrival."

"Okay, so it was too late for you to have an abortion. What were your options?" I asked.

"The Lundahls took care of me for three weeks. They encouraged me to stay in Sweden to raise my baby there. The government paid people to have babies because of Sweden's low population."

"I could have been a Swede? Are there any Black people in Sweden?"

"There are. Unlike America, single parentage and racism were nonissues in Sweden according to the Lundahls. I, however, was concerned about the potential cultural and linguistic challenges. So, I chose to leave Sweden. I still wanted to go back to Penn State and back to the life I had known before getting pregnant. I was not yet able to put you first."

"I can understand that. You were still a teenager."

"Yes."

I was happy to be talking to Dorothy. But she was crying again, although she indicated she was able to continue.

"So, how did I come to be born in America?" I asked, as the crying subsided.

"The Lundahls paid my passage across the North Sea to England where I knew my mother, Maryan, was visiting relatives. I met her in London and told her the story of my pregnancy. Previously, I had told my parents that I was just taking a summer trip to Europe to see the world."

"How did your parents feel about you being pregnant, especially with me being a Black baby?"

"Well, I am still getting to that part. I don't want to miss any details for you along the way."

"That's fine. Please take your time."

"Well, I spent the rest of the summer of 1966 in London. I had a cheap charter flight ticket that did not allow a return to the United States until September. While I was in London, I read several books on pregnancy and natural childbirth and I began my prenatal visits. The whole process of being pregnant fascinated me, and I was determined to be wide awake and to avoid drugs during labor if possible. Um. Well, I lost my train of thought."

"That's fine. Dorothy, are you okay?"

"Yes. Well, let me answer your questions about my parents. My father, George Allen Blazier, Jr., wanted me to have an abortion. He did not want me in the house while I was pregnant. He did not want the neighbors to see his daughter in this condition and felt this was a disgrace to the Blazier family. He told me this directly. My parents also were decidedly not thrilled about the fact that the baby was to be multiracial. I was interested in keeping you and raising you by myself at one point, but my father was definitely against it."

"Did you feel like raising me was not an option because of his views?"

"That's a fair question. Thomas, you have to understand that it was a different era in terms of race, and in terms of empowerment for women. As for raising you myself, I felt somewhat powerless to address some basic life issues. Where would I stay? I could not raise you in my father's house. Where would I work, and who would take care of my new baby while I worked? I wanted you to have a good home, but I was not able to give it to you then."

I could hear pain in her voice. I heard the sniffles and knew she was trying to hold back her tears.

"Dorothy, I think I understand the situation you were in. I am not judging any of your actions from 1966. I am just asking questions to gain a general understanding about my background. Don't sweat it, okay?"

"Okay." After a few deep breaths, Dorothy continued, "My father agreed that I could live in a trailer in some park in Pittsburgh until I could enter the Zoar Home for Girls. This was a place where unwed expecting mothers could live and get medical attention until their babies were delivered. The child would then be given up for adoption, and the mother would work at Zoar for about six weeks afterward to help the incoming pregnant mothers. I spent the final weeks of my pregnancy at Zoar."

"It sounds sad, like you were all alone," I commented.

"I did feel alone." Dorothy acknowledged. "Being an unwed mother was not accepted by American society during the mid-1960s. That is why I was hidden away. My mother came periodically to visit and to bring me food. My father did not come to visit me at Zoar. Overall, I would summarize the behavior of the specific staff members who cared for me at Zoar as dreadfully punitive. In a few of the staff members, I perceived an unstated desire on their part to mentally and emotionally punish the unwed mothers-to-be for getting pregnant. It was an awful place but full of nice pregnant women."

"Ever since I found out, at age eleven,that I was adopted," I stated, "I wondered if I knew my correct birth date."

"Your birth date is completely accurate. I was wide awake and was not aided by pain-killing drugs for the birth, which took place in Pittsburgh. This approach was met with disapproval by the obstetrician who thought he should play a bigger role in the performance. I was dismayed that you were unnecessarily held upside down and slapped, even though you had already given a healthy cry. The obstetrician and nurses also seemed annoyed when I insisted on seeing and holding you right after the delivery. They tried to whisk you away, likely afraid that maternal bonds would take over. Thomas, I felt bad that both my mother and I were only able to hold you briefly back in December 1966."

As soon as I was carried to the nursery, Dorothy asked to see the placenta. The obstetrician obviously viewed this as strange, but Dorothy was fascinated by childbirth. Also, she thought this was possibly her way of "having control" of what was a pretty powerless situation and vicariously claiming something for all of the effort. They were even more annoyed when she asked, from her self-taught knowledge of obstetrics, "Is it a Duncan placenta or a Schultze placenta?" The doctor working between her legs ignored her. She insisted. Finally, he mumbled, "A Schultze." Later she said, "I didn't think there was any particular health virtue. But I took some pleasure in that; I just knew my baby would have the more attractive shiny and smooth Schultze placenta instead of the ragged and lumpy Duncan."

Feeling that the Lundahls had helped her to give me life, Dorothy gave me the name Erik. This is a Nordic name that conveys great manly strength. She was told the name would probably only be temporarily used by the foster family, not kept for the long term. She was inexplicably pressured to consent to my being circumcised. Again, she felt powerless. She had real misgivings about it, but the pressure of medical conventions at that time strongly favored having the procedure, and she agreed.

In those days, Dorothy related, all babies were put in a nursery behind a big window, away from their mothers except for specific planned feeding times. I was put in the back of the nursery, and the nurses fed me, not Dorothy. This kept the unwed mother separated from her child. "Thomas, after you were born, I was not allowed to see you again until the day we left the hospital. Then, as an adoption formality, I was required to accompany you on the ride back to the Zoar Home for Girls where I symbolically handed you over to their care."

"Was that the last time you saw me?"

"Fortunately, there had been another girl at Zoar, who was expecting twins at the same time you were born. We had befriended each other before your birth. Sadly for her, the twins were born early and died. Being a trained nurse, my new friend took a job at the home and was therefore one of the nurses charged with your care. She would secretly let me see you regularly, Thomas. And she would not just prop your bottles, as was the usual routine for the babies there, but sat with you and fed you personally. This was a great comfort to me.

"For years, I carried a memory of the last time I saw you as a baby. I remember that you were looking straight into my eyes, knowingly and calmly. I touched your birthmark on your right cheek. Given that you would not be my baby to raise, I was becoming dangerously moved by motherly instincts toward you. As you moved your lips, obviously wanting to suck, as all babies do, I felt totally unprepared for my instinctive maternal responses to be awakened. I had denied that I would raise you for all of those months. For a moment, I instinctively desired to nurse you. Terrified, I hurriedly put you back in the crib and rushed away. Over the years, I punished myself for not saying a more proper and less rushed goodbye."

"Well, maybe we can fix this," I said. "Maybe we can have a reunion and meet each other and say proper hellos."

"That would be fabulous," Dorothy breathed with great relief.

After my birth and subsequent adoption, Dorothy was depressed over losing me, and afraid of her future. She went through a brief but ugly period of heavy drinking, having received no counseling about the pregnancy, birth, or loss. She had confided in a young man, who she had met in New York in 1966, telling him she was en route to Sweden to pursue an abortion. He had tried to help talk her out of the abortion and showed her kind affection and wrote to her throughout the pregnancy. But by 1967, his interest had waned, which added to her depression and isolation.

At my birth, Dorothy was told that there was "something wrong with the baby's blood," which delayed my adoption. She received no further explanation. I found out later that I was slightly anemic at birth. My blood test was fully normal at the age of three months. Dorothy had no knowledge of this later test; over the years, she was left only with the fear that I had leukemia or some other life-threatening ailment. In spite of her requests, they gave her no further information. "The medical people seemed to regard me as having no rights of information about you at all," she said. "They clearly judged me as a real slut and a heartless bitch for giving you up for adoption."

After the pregnancy, while working for the airline, she was in Detroit when the urban riots of the late 1960s were breaking out across America. When I was officially given up for adoption in May 1967, Dorothy went back to Pittsburgh to sign various papers at a hearing. As she flew out of Detroit, she could see the fires from the riots burning.

She landed in Pittsburgh, which had experienced disturbances at the same time. The riots scared her, making her feel inadequate and lost, fearing that she was turning her mixed-race baby loose to face an uncertain future in a tough world and a nation divided over race, war, and vast social and political turmoil. She remarked later, "It seemed as if I were walking in a dream, the memory of the hearing is one of me just looking on rather than taking part. Again, I had a feeling of helplessness and fear for your future and little more than numbness about my own."

After this, Dorothy was told that I was placed with a "mixed race professional family." Like most Blacks in America, my adoptive family is far from having one hundred percent African blood. Dorothy was still given no comfort on the issue of my well being. Later, while researching the topic of X-ray use during pregnancy, she found that X-rays could cause leukemia and the prognosis for childhood leukemia at that time was poor; she even feared I might have died without ever knowing she cared about me.

The education and life that Dorothy had started as a freshman at Penn State University was interrupted forever by her pregnancy. Her mother, Maryan, hoped Dorothy would return to Penn State. But psychologically, Dorothy was unable to return to university, being too depressed and confused. She was stigmatized by leaving school and, like many others in the "Baby Boomer" generation, was quite disillusioned with life, politics, and the war in Vietnam. Relates Dorothy, "I had no mental model for how someone could leave and go back to college. I think I was not empowered enough to even find out if it were possible.

"But now," continued Dorothy, "twenty-five years later, my son felt empowered enough to inquire about me. This road to a possible reunion all started for me when I received a message on my answering machine from someone at the agency, saying that they wanted to speak to me about some business I had with them in 1966 and asking me to call them back. I was so excited. I knew you must be alive! And I hoped that I might hear what I most wanted to hear, that you would like to make contact with me, and maybe meet me. I called them back and learned that you were asking for information about your biological par-

ents and your adoption. They asked if I would be willing to be contacted by my son, now called Thomas Brooks. Of course, I said 'yes.' I
asked if she would give me your address so that I could write to you.
She would not do that but agreed to forward a letter and photo that I
faxed to her. She gave me only basic information; I learned only that
you were alive, and that you had been working in Maryland.

"I felt phenomenal joy and apprehension," added Dorothy. "I was
lucky that Lotus just happened to be staying overnight with me that
day, before she took a flight out of the country the next day. Lotus had
known of your existence since she was thirteen years old. This meant I
could share the news with the person who best understood what the
news meant to me and who also had her own deep longings to know
you."

Now that we had made contact again on the phone, Dorothy was
not only excited about meeting me, but anxious to meet my adoptive
mother, Joan. Dorothy wanted to thank Joan for her courage and for
her commitment to me at a time when Dorothy was unable to provide
such care. I wasn't convinced that it was a good idea for Dorothy and
Joan to meet right away, but I was glad that Dorothy said during our
very first phone conversation, "Joan was and always will be your mother."
Having raised four children, Dorothy understood the sacrifices Joan
must have made for me. Dorothy stated that my relationship with her
must never undermine my relationship with Joan, or cause any resentment. I agreed, and as a result, I was determined to take things slowly in
terms of arranging any meeting between the two of them. I was, however, anxious to meet Dorothy myself.

Dorothy and I were reunited in Houston Intercontinental Airport
about 10 P.M. on Tuesday, September 29, 1992, and we spent a week
together. The time together was surprisingly comfortable and natural.
Maybe I should not have been surprised, since I was carrying her genes.
She observed that I had the "Rittenburg nose, posture, and hand gestures" like her grandfather David Rittenburg.

The first night, we stayed up until 4 A.M. in an all-night diner, drinking tea and talking, even though she suffered from jet lag and I had to go to work the next day. As I expected, the reunion meant a great deal to me in terms of my journey to discover more about my identity and heritage. But I am convinced the reunion meant even more to Dorothy. For her, the process was exciting, healing, and at times painful and disturbing. She had to relive all of the memories of family and societal pressures associated with giving birth to a Black baby in the 1960s. She had to deal with the memories of letting me go. The week together in Houston stirred in her a lot of memories, doubts, and feelings, many of which were not altogether comfortable for her. The reunion greatly accelerated her healing process.

Thomas reunited with his biological mother Dorothy in Houston. September 1992.

"Thomas, I worried that you might not like me," Dorothy confessed, "or that you might even have a lot of anger or hate toward me. I didn't actually believe that, but I worried about it, and accepted that it was a realistic possibility. If that had been the case I was determined to show you that I loved you and always had, whatever patience or effort it would take."

I asked, "How did your family and friends react to the news of my reappearance?"

"My mother's first reaction to the news was one of protection of me," said Dorothy. "She didn't want me to be hurt. I told her that I didn't care if Thomas was a U.S. Senator or a serial murderer, he was my son and I was not going to turn away from him again.

"Some of my friends and acquaintances warned me about feeling overly optimistic about my son's 'real motives,'" Dorothy added. "I was conscious that some of this was rooted in prejudicial images people had of 'young Black men,' which offended me deeply, and my reply was always the same: 'Thomas is my son and I will not turn away from him again.'

"Thomas, can I ask you a question?" she interrupted herself.

"Of course. Actually, you just did," I said with a smile.

"How was it for you, growing up as a multiracial child?"

"To most Americans, I am not perceived as 'mixed' by people who don't know my heritage. As a young child, I once referred to another child as a 'half-breed' as he was multiracial. Joan immediately scolded me. Although Joan was told during the adoption process that I was multiracial, I did not know I was multiracial as a youngster. Joan did hint at my multiracial heritage a few times while I was in high school. I assumed I was multiracial by the time I started college. However, race was irrelevant for me by then, so I never pursued this issue through a detailed discussion. My knowledge of my multiracial background was not completely confirmed until I first talked to Joan earlier this year about looking for my biological parents. The socialization of my adoptive extended family was clearly Black, or African-American. In fact, during my elementary school years, virtually my only interaction with

White people came about at school thanks to school bussing and integration measures, as there were no non-Black people in my lower income neighborhoods on the North Side in the 1970s."

I continued, "I can even remember when I was about four years old, another kid in the Manchester section of the North Side was teased for being a 'half-breed.' I was not because my family was viewed as Black, and I was not seen as having so-called 'half-breed' features. During the early 1970s era of "Black Power," it was not at all popular to be multiracial where I lived. Both Blacks and Whites ostracized those who looked multiracial. The other kid looked multiracial; he had a light brown Afro, his skin was sort of light brown or beige, yet pale and freckled at the same time. I was perceived as Black, so I was accepted by at least one group. Sadly, both Whites and Blacks generally rejected the other kid during that period."

By the end of our week together in Houston, Dorothy and I knew we were beginning an unusual but exciting friendship. We were both opening up, both sharing. She was trying to remain calm, attempting to allow me to set the tone for our interaction. However, I could tell that it was hard for her to hold back. As soon as I took any step forward, she immediately matched the step in kind. She wanted so much for me to like her. As we talked, I agreed with her that our newly developing connection was a relationship built on the need to overcome adversity, to challenge mediocre cultural norms and divisions; it was becoming a relationship of great significance. We have shared, since my conception, a nonverbal understanding of a kind, and now, we had done what we needed to do to come together again. By the end of that week, we had laid a foundation to pursue our mutual goal of becoming good friends.

CHAPTER ELEVEN

From Europe to Haight-Ashbury and Back

On a spring day in 1889, two-and-one-half-year-old David Rittenburg's two oldest brothers took him into the nearby town. There was nothing unusual about the trip. Harry and Israel, David's two brothers in their twenties, were sent by their parents to get supplies. David, born on November 16, 1886, to Jewish parents George and Mariana Rittenburg, was the youngest of thirteen children. They hailed from near a town called Qwalk on European soil that has been controlled by both Lithuania and Russia over the decades. Little David was just tagging along with his big brothers.

While the three brothers were gone on the supply run, their parents and the trio's ten other siblings who stayed behind were murdered by Orthodox Russians. It was a religiously motivated pogrom, an organized and officially encouraged massacre and violent persecution, against Jews. For much of the century, young Orthodox Russians were taught to hate the Jews because they viewed Jews to be Jesus Christ's killers. The Orthodox Russians were inflamed against the Jews living in the area, feeling that these Jews had no true loving ties with Mother Russia.

When the three brothers returned home to the scene of the carnage that engulfed their home, they knew they were now alone. Not only had their home been burned to the ground, but the Russian terrorists had also leveled almost all of the Jewish homes in that area. The only things that the trio had left were the supplies they had just purchased and the scant change left over from the transaction.

Harry and Israel managed to escape on a boat to Boston by way of Germany and Italy, riding in steerage class. After passing through the trauma of Ellis Island and arriving in the United States, they hawked clothing from a pushcart in Boston.

Eventually, the two older brothers opened their own clothing shop. Saving their earnings, they managed to send for David many years later. David was to become my great-grandfather.

A neighboring Gentile family had protected David after the murders and the sudden separation from his older brothers. The Gentile family hid the Jewish youngster from the prying eyes of the army and the Orthodox Russian church. There was a network, a sort of "Underground Railroad" of Gentile families who did not agree with their priests and prelates with respect to the Jews, and they passed David from family to family. This network enabled David to safely cross Europe. As a result of his odyssey, David eventually learned to speak in thirteen different languages.

David arrived in America when he was thirteen years old. He polished his command of the English language in night school, and worked in a warehouse during the day for three dollars per week. Out of the three dollars, he used two dollars for room and board and saved the remaining dollar each week. David later pursued an engineering degree and graduated from the Massachusetts Institute of Technology (MIT).

In 1917, at the age of thirty, David attempted to enlist in the United States Army. Initially refused because of his age, the grateful immigrant American begged, leveraging the fact that he was an engineer to sway the outcome. The army needed engineers in World War I. Thus, he was eventually accepted in the United States Army 101st Engineers—American Expeditionary Forces. The United States had given him safety and the religious freedom to practice Judaism. Thus, my patriotic great-grandfather wanted to serve his adopted country.

As a soldier, David made a distinguished mark with his courage and excellent character. His military leader, Captain Swan, said that David was the "cleanest man in the army." David was also the only Jew in the troop.

The U.S. Army was accommodating to David's religion. In the spring, the army sent loads of matzo, the brittle flat bread eaten at Passover, for David to eat. Sometimes, because of logistic issues, matzo was the only food available for the entire group, leading the other troops to jokingly ask my great-grandfather, "How long does this holiday last?"

David fought in three major World War I battles in France, including Chemin des Davies in February 1918, Toul Sector from March to June 1918, and Chateau Thierry in July 1918. At Chateau Thierry, David was shot in the left ankle and taken prisoner by the Germans. Because he had a name that sounded German and spoke German, the enemy soldiers in charge of the POW camp called him a traitor and refused to feed him or give him medical attention. A humanitarian organization gave him limited care, but his leg was severely damaged.

It was not until June 12, 1919, about eight months after the war was over, that David was released from the POW camp. Because his leg did not receive timely and appropriate medical attention, he had a permanent limp.

David's wife, my great-grandmother Betty Kahn, was born in what is today known as Kaunas, Lithuania, which was then known as Kovno, in July 1898. At the age of two, she was taken by her parents from Kaunas to Leeds, England, to escape the religious pogroms and also secular persecutions inaugurated by the Russian state against the Jews.

Betty's father, Myer Kahn, was a Rabbi. Betty was one of nine children, five girls and four boys. Myer died in his early forties when Betty was finishing the 3rd grade. His family was left with no means of support.

With the death of her father, my great-grandmother Betty was pulled out of school to do the housework, while her brothers found odd jobs to help support the family. To earn money to keep the family going, Betty's mother Leah did laundry for the neighbors.

Betty had a lovely voice, and for years she aspired to be a famous singer. A theater company recruited her, but her mother would not let Betty pursue a musical career. This spawned continuous friction between the two women.

While the animosities intensified between Betty and her mother, an older brother of Betty's moved to America in pursuit of a job during World War I. He settled in Boston. In 1921 Betty decided to escape her mother and moved to Boston, where her brother was.

Betty later moved in with a female cousin, Fannie, who also lived in Boston. Fannie was married to Harry Rittenburg, my great-grandfather David's older brother.

When David returned from the war, he took a civil service exam. The exam revealed to the government his proficiency in languages. They then sent him to work on Ellis Island in the Immigration and Naturalization Service as an interpreter. David was later promoted and sent to work in Derbyline, Vermont, at the Canadian border.

In 1922 David decided to take a two-week vacation and headed back to Boston to visit Harry and Fannie. It proved to be more than an ordinary visit. It was on this vacation that David met Betty, the woman who would become his wife.

Fannie encouraged David to take Betty around town. Every day for two weeks, David and Betty shared time together. The couple took in all the activities around Boston and discovered that they enjoyed each other's company. Betty was romanced in a most classical way. When David left Boston to return to his job in Derbyline, she began to write him, filling the pages with the day's happenings and subtle messages of endearment.

They traded letters for months. In due course, David proposed in a letter. Betty accepted via letter.

David mailed Betty five hundred dollars to buy an engagement ring. Betty spent the entire amount on a beautiful one-carat diamond, and then wrote a letter to David saying she needed another $150 for the setting. David complied and sent the money.

David and Betty were married in New York City in February 1923, while traveling to David's new assignment in Key West, Florida. Betty was not fond of Florida. Tired of the heat and the mosquitoes, Betty soon demanded that they transfer. They moved to Detroit, where David worked on an immigration ruling board with the Immigration and Naturalization Service on the Windsor/Detroit border between Canada and the United States.

A middle-class Jewish immigrant family from Lithuania living in Detroit, Michigan, of all places, David and Betty personified the "American dream." They had two children, my grandmother Maryan, who was born in December 1923, and her younger brother Milton.

Maryan excelled in school, skipped a couple of grades, and graduated high school at sixteen. She had dreams of being a doctor. Although David was intelligent, honest, and fair, he was also old-fashioned and conservative. He discouraged his daughter's dreams of a medical career because of the cost, as well as the fact that he did not want his daughter to see naked men.

At age sixteen, Maryan began her post-secondary education at Wayne State University in Detroit. There, she fell madly in love with a great-looking psychology student named Julius. Julius was a native of Romania. He had a thick accent, one that time never dulled after years in America.

After World War II erupted in 1939, the United States began to consider placing Japanese-Americans in detention camps. Since Romania was aligned with Axis powers Germany, Italy, and Japan, Julius was concerned that he might be put in a detention camp.

On December 7, 1941 Julius and Maryan were on a date, driving about sixty miles to Toledo to swim in the warm pool of a salt mine. It was then that the news of Japan's attack on Pearl Harbor exploded over the car's radio.

Julius sharply turned the car around, dropped Maryan off at her home, and went to enlist in the U.S. Army. He did not want to be seen as an Axis sympathizer. Maryan was devastated by Julius's actions and his impending departure. When Julius told her he was not in love with her, it hurt her even more.

Still somewhat upset because of Julius, Maryan met a soldier named Milton at a military dance ten months later. He was about to ship out for battle, but wanted to marry before going to war. Maryan agreed, wanting to prove that someone could love her and would want to marry her. Maryan's parents approved of her betrothal, as the young soldier Milton was "a good Jewish man."

The wedding date was set for January 1943, but Milton lost his nerve and failed to return in late December 1942 to finalize the wedding preparations. When Maryan located Milton, he told her that he "loved her like a sister." That was exactly what Julius had told her. As the new year of 1943 rang in, Maryan was without a fiancé and very depressed.

Maryan's eventual husband-to-be came from the Blazier family of western Pennsylvania. Based on extensive research, the first Blaziers were believed to have come to America around 1750 from the Alsace-Lorraine area, a historically disputed border region of Germany and France. Sometimes the family even used the more German moniker "Blazer," depending on which country was in control of the region.

My great-grandfather George Allen Blazier, Sr., known as Allen, had been born in May 1890 in Esplin, in the Pittsburgh area near the Ohio River. A popular community activity in Esplin was ice skating on Chartiers Creek. It was here that Allen first met the beautiful Margaret Emelia Hankey, who equally enjoyed the popular winter sport. Their courtship ended in marriage in 1916, when Margaret, a first generation American of German extraction, was just seventeen years old. Margaret's parents, born in Europe, were named Friedrich William Huhnke (Hankey) and Josephina Theresa Marks. Friedrich had been born in Drausnitz, West Prussia. Josephina had entered the world in Bohemia, Austria.

During World War I, Allen worked in a defense plant in Oakdale, Pennsylvania, that manufactured munitions for the government. One day an accidental explosion killed several people. Fortunately, it was his day off. Like my other great-grandfather, David Rittenburg, Allen had a near miss with death before fathering my grandparents. In later years he took his children to see the remains of the factory. It had never re-opened after the explosion.

Allen and Margaret's young family began to grow in 1918 with the birth of my maternal grandfather, George Allen Blazier, Jr., known as George. Siblings Bill, Peg, and Bob followed over the next six years.

Before the Christmas season in 1925, Margaret wrote letters to Santa Claus for all of her children detailing how good they were and how they all deserved the presents they hoped to receive from him.

Then pregnant, my great-grandmother Margaret carefully placed each child's letters securely into the crevice of the fireplace behind the gas jets, where Santa was sure to see them. As the family anxiously awaited the coming of the invented seasonal character, Santa Claus, they also anticipated the March arrival of the fictional stork. They were a closely bonded family. The kids were anxious to find out if they would have a new brother or a new sister. In March 1926 they were told that they had a new sister. The baby's name was Betty Jean Blazier. George, Bill, Peg, and Bob all lined up alongside their mother's bed. Margaret turned the covers back to show the kids their new sister. When their father came in, they all celebrated, but it was short-lived. Their beautiful, giving mother passed away three weeks later. The cause of death was believed to be "child bed fever," caused by the doctor's poorly sanitized baby delivery instruments.

The family then moved in with Allen's parents. Grandma Blazier was extremely strict with the five children, and Allen was feeling the inhibitions of living in his parents' home again.

At age eight, George felt the loss of his mother more than the other children did because of the nurturing closeness he had experienced with her. In addition to the difficult loss of his mother, George suffered throughout his life with mastoiditis, an inflammation of the mastoid bone on the side of the head behind the ear. Mastoiditis is usually caused by a routine bacterial infection that spreads from the middle ear. His medical condition was later complicated by epilepsy and abscesses in the brain, which eventually led to his total loss of hearing in one ear. As a youth, he also coped with scarlet fever, mumps, diphtheria, chicken pox, and measles.

When he was thirteen, George and a friend built a boat out of some boards. When completed, they hauled the boat down to Chartiers Creek on the bed of his Sherwood Spring Coaster wagon. The boys had grand visions of floating down the Ohio River to the Mississippi River, and all the way to New Orleans. They never went very far. Those privileged to ride in the boat had to bail water out as fast as they could, or suffer the dire consequences of a swim to save their own lives.

Grandmother and Grandfather Blazier began to feel the pressures of responsibility related to the five children, and hired a succession of young women to help at home, but none of them lasted long. During this period, Grandmother Blazier became terminally ill with cancer and died in December 1931. George was thirteen, and the other children were ages eleven, ten, seven, and five.

When the children did not meet Allen's expectations, he consistently put them down, which made some of them feel inadequate and inferior. Allen conducted long lectures, and allowed his frustrations to spill over to the children. Allen and Grandpa Blazier, with their wives both deceased, often disagreed openly on how the household should be managed. These displays of domestic discord were quite disconcerting and had a negative effect on the children in their care.

Almost four years after Grandma Blazier's death, Grandpa Blazier died in September 1935. Shortly afterward, Allen told his five children that he and their Aunt Ida, their mother Margaret's younger sister, would marry. All five of Allen's children thought it was a great idea. Their father and Aunt Ida were married in November 1935. Aunt Ida and her sons, previously cousins but now stepbrothers to George, moved into the Blazier home.

Allen's five children were suddenly living by a new and confusing set of domestic rules that Aunt Ida seemed to make up for her convenience. It soon became obvious that she favored her own biological sons. George, who was then seventeen, voiced his objections to what he felt was unfair treatment, articulating the considerable discord in the household. Allen was forced to make some hard decisions.

Aunt Ida would win out. She persuaded Allen that his son was destroying the harmony of their family and subsequently George left home at a tender age. Eventually, under similar pressure, Margaret's other children did the same.

O ne of George's first jobs was driving a truck loaded with oysters from Virginia to Chicago. He liked the freedom of the open road and continued driving for many years.

While attending Wayne State in Detroit, Maryan worked in the payroll department for Long Transportation Company, a long-haul trucking company. George drove a truck for the same company. His typical route at that time was between Chicago and Pittsburgh. One day, this itinerary changed abruptly. The company scheduled George to make a run from Pittsburgh to Detroit so he could visit the company headquarters to adjust a payroll discrepancy. It was there that George met Maryan. It was January 1943, mere days after Maryan's fiancé Milton had ended their relationship. George was twenty-four and Maryan was just nineeen.

After Maryan had adjusted the paperwork to his satisfaction, George was happily on his way with his paycheck. By chance they bumped into each other again later that day at a nearby diner. George approached her, saying, "You're the only familiar face I see in here. Do you mind if I join you?"

They enjoyed a nice chat, and Maryan told George about a number of things to do in Detroit. George got on the same streetcar she took. She commented that she would be getting off at Wayne State to attend her class. Surprisingly, George jumped off the streetcar when Maryan did. Instead of carousing around Detroit, he went with her to her evening class. He politely asked the professor for permission to enter. Afterward, they went to an arcade and a novelty shop, and then to a restaurant. They were having a great time.

George was planning to enlist in the army for World War II on January 12, 1943. At the noisy restaurant, he told Maryan that he was depressed because he had no one to write him. There was no one to care if he lived or died. Maryan mentioned that she was depressed because she had been left by her Romanian lover Julius, and then subsequently by her short-term fiancé Milton. Her comments about her love life were startling to George. But it was not as abrupt and unexpected as her next query.

Maryan said, "Ask me to marry you."

"What? I have only just met you!"

"I promise I'll say 'no,'" she pouted, "but it will make me feel better."

After looking around at the other patrons, George obliged.

True to her word, Maryan refused.

Hours elapsed and the crowd at the restaurant thinned. During this time, George thought deep and hard. Finally, he leaned forward and queried, "Will you marry me?"

Maryan was surprised. "I already told you I wouldn't have you," she reminded her new friend.

George looked her in the eyes and whispered, "Listen, I've got a serious plan."

"What are you talking about?" Maryan laughed.

"I just came to Detroit to get my final paycheck," George continued. "I am going to enlist for the war as soon as I get back to Pittsburgh, and I have no one to write to me. You are unhappy at home anyway, so we can get married and I will send you my army pay of fifty dollars per month. You can use that for your living expenses in Pittsburgh. All you have to do is write me once a week. If I get killed, you would get the ten-thousand-dollar insurance policy proceeds. If I survive the war, we can just get the marriage annulled."

George's argument seemed reasonable to Maryan. His proposal allowed Maryan to prove to friends and family, and to herself, that she could get a husband. George would benefit by having someone to write to him.

The next morning the young couple met at 7 A.M. and took the legally mandated blood tests. George then left Detroit and drove the company's truck back to Pittsburgh. Maryan headed down to the Marriage License Bureau.

"What is the name of the groom-to-be?" the official asked.

"George Blazier, Jr."

"What is his middle name?"

"I don't know."

"How old is he?"

"I don't know."

"When is his birthday?"

"I don't know."

"Was he ever married before?"

"I don't know."

"You don't know very much about this man, do you?"

"No."

"Well, he will need to come in here and provide the answers to these questions."

Maryan was stupefied. She hurriedly contacted the man she knew so little about, urging him to return to Detroit at once.

On Friday night, January 8, two days before George was due in Detroit, Maryan's mother Betty Rittenburg received a phone call. A friend had noticed in the newspaper that Maryan and George were listed under "Marriage Licenses Applied For." Betty had never heard of George. At dinner that night, David Rittenburg asked his daughter in a low, stern voice, "Who is George Blazier, Jr.?"

"How did you find out about him?" startled, Maryan asked nervously.

Raising his voice now, David repeated, "Who is George Blazier, Jr.?"

"I have known him a long time from work," she lied. "I didn't tell you we planned to get married because I knew you wouldn't approve because of our religious differences. But I have been dating him ever since I started working."

Both David and Betty were incredulous, and Betty was especially upset about learning of her daughter's impending wedding from a friend.

On Sunday night, January 10, Maryan received a phone call from George. "I need help," he blurted.

"What's the matter?" Maryan asked. "Where are you?"

"I'm in jail."

"What do you mean you're in jail?"

George explained, "There was an automobile accident. I was a witness to the accident. Since I'm from out of town, I'm being detained in case I'm needed to be a witness at the hearing the next day. The only way for me to get out would be for someone locally to vouch for me."

There was a moment of silence. Then he asked, "Can your father come downtown to the jail and sign for me?"

"If my father agrees to help you, let me do all of the talking when he starts asking you questions about our relationship. I need to cover up my lies. You just back me up."

George agreed.

David went down to the jail with Maryan. After George's release, the trio drove back to the Rittenburg home. When they arrived, they were confronted by a host of family members who had assembled specifically to talk Maryan out of her decision.

Maryan's extended Jewish family was horrified that she would marry someone they had not had a chance to get to know. Even worse in their minds, he was an uneducated working class Gentile. Family members even tried to bribe Maryan with promises of an elaborate wedding and honeymoon if she would delay the wedding six months. It would take

George this long to finish his initial military training. The real agenda of the family was to change her mind during this six month period and get her to cancel the wedding.

Maryan continued lying to validate her story. David still didn't buy her story about the relationship. He pulled Maryan aside, interrogating her, "Are you in trouble?"

"No, Father, I am not pregnant."

"Then I don't understand this," exclaimed David as he walked away.

In spite of these obstacles, George and Maryan obtained their marriage license and were married the next morning in a church. It was a little over a year since the December 7 Pearl Harbor bombing that prompted Julius's decision to enlist in the army. Although Maryan's Orthodox Jewish parents would not attend the wedding ceremony, they did host a small brunch after the wedding. After the brunch, the couple rushed to catch a train for Pittsburgh.

After the couple departed Detroit, Maryan's family then sat *Shiva*, from the Hebrew for "seven," a week-long period of intense mourning observed by immediate family members following the death and burial of a loved one. Essentially, Maryan was ousted because she married a Gentile. It took many years to fully repair the separation. Although she eventually reunited with her family, the time apart was difficult.

W ith their trip to Pittsburgh complete, George promptly attempted to enlist in the army on Tuesday, January 12. The Army refused to enlist him because of his chronic ear infection and partial hearing loss.

He was supposed to return to Maryan later that day, but he stayed away for three days as he struggled with the bad news. On Friday, January 15, he finally returned to his Pittsburgh apartment where Maryan was staying and told her the news.

"We might as well go back to Detroit and have this marriage annulled," George said.

"Why?"

"The army turned me down. I am 4-F; no army for me."

"I'm not going anywhere. I can't go back home and admit I lied. I'm dead in the eyes of my family."

"What do you want to do?"

"I can't go home," Maryan repeated.

Being proud, stubborn, and determined, Maryan said after a long pause, "We are two intelligent people. Everybody else thinks they are madly in love going into marriage and that they will live happily ever after. We don't even know each other, but if we work at it, we can make a marriage. We can make it work!"

George had to think about it. It was not what he intended—he had hoped for a pen pal, not a full-time wife. By tradition, they weren't truly married since the marriage had not been consummated. After much thought and discussion, the couple decided to consummate the marriage a few days later.

Maryan had stillborn twin boys eleven months after they married. Although disappointed, George and Maryan decided to try again. In 1944 she gave birth to my uncle, Robert Thomas Blazier. The family usually called their new addition Bobby.

My great-grandfather David Rittenburg with the toddler who grew into my Uncle Bobby. Photo from the 1940s.

George's mastoiditis led to brain abscesses and he was often hospitalized, enduring eight brain surgeries over the years. Maryan worked in a real estate office, trying to keep up with all the bills. Maryan stood bravely by his side while George endured comas and brushes with death as a result of the abscesses. Bobby was placed in a children's home for six of his first eighteen months while Maryan worked to pay off George's large hospital bills.

The family lived on the South Side of Pittsburgh in Beechview, and then moved across town to East Liberty. They subsequently rented three different dwellings before buying a home in 1953 in Dorseyville, just outside of the city. Maryan still lives in that same house, more than fifty years later. She recently described the marriage as good in many ways, but also tough because of her husband's ill health and medical bills. George passed away on March 14, 1989.

George's brother, Bill Blazier, remembers him as an intelligent and ambitious person. George's trucking business involved hiring drivers for his trucks, managing repairs, and organizing other facets of the business. He spent many lonely days away from home. George was a deep thinker with philosophical interests. He was a lifelong seeker. When he became interested in a subject he explored it thoroughly. He had a different mindset than Maryan, who concentrated on a career, running the home, and being more "socially sophisticated." Their interests did not always converge. George delved into books such as Napoleon Hill's *Think and Grow Rich,* Dale Carnegie's *How to Win Friends and Influence People,* and the works of several philosophers. He even pondered the metaphysical writing of Edgar Cayce. George adhered to no dogma. His search never ended, and it had a formative effect on his daughter, Dorothy.

My biological mother, Dorothy Jean Blazier, was the final child born to Maryan and George. She was born in May 1947, part of the baby boom generation.

Dorothy told me that while the family was living in East Liberty in the early 1950s, she befriended a girl named Michelle*. They were best friends, and their mothers were friends. The girls spent their days roller-skating and skipping rope. Michelle's father had committed suicide when she was very young. Michelle's mother, Kate*, struggled to cope with the situation.

When George was not sick he drove tankers of asphalt and petrochemicals from coast to coast. Unfortunately, this meant being away from his family for weeks at a time. Maryan, alone most of the time, decided to let Kate and Michelle move into her home. Dorothy was seven at the time. This decision enabled Maryan to work full-time while Kate tended to the children and kept the house.

Dorothy had a close friendship with Michelle but found Michelle and Kate to be disruptive borders. The household dynamics changed again when Dorothy was sixteen, and Kate remarried and moved away with her new husband. He apparently wanted Kate, but perhaps not the responsibility of raising her daughter. When Kate moved out, she left Michelle behind in Maryan's care. Kate had notarized papers drawn designating Maryan as Michelle's legal guardian.

Maryan, generous to a fault, treated both girls as her daughters. She even dressed them similarly in their preteen years. As a teenager, Dorothy sometimes felt her mother preferred Michelle. Dorothy also felt the community's disapproval of their unconventional family situation. Dorothy dealt with it all by being an honor roll student, but also by getting into trouble at school. Her behavior frequently resulted in her being sent to the Principal's Office or to Detention Hall.

Dorothy lived in working class Dorseyville, but she attended the predominately upper-class Fox Chapel High School since Dorseyville was designated to be part of the Fox Chapel School District. Although Dorothy was a hard worker, a majorette, a debating team member, and a yearbook editor, she was unruly and political, and she felt like a misfit at Fox Chapel High School. Because of this, many students and teachers viewed her as being "from the wrong side of the tracks."

It didn't help that her older brother, Bobby, had made himself notorious at Fox Chapel High because of his somewhat abrasive personality and constant quest for attention using all the wrong techniques. The teachers expected the same behavior from her. At times she didn't disappoint them, speaking her mind more than most students. She was very vocal about the civil rights abuses of the 1960s and the growing conflict in Vietnam. While hardly anyone spoke out about either issue in overwhelmingly conservative and upper-class Fox Chapel, Dorothy spoke of their inherent wrongs and how the country was poorer because of them.

Dorothy felt socially inept at high school but did better with older students enrolled in the local universities. Many expected her to excel at the university level. They thought she would follow her older brother's lead and enroll at the University of Pittsburgh, where he had gone. To defy expectations, she refused to go to Pitt. She wanted recognition for her own ability and not because she was Bobby's sister. After serious deliberation, Dorothy decided to matriculate at Pennsylvania State University in the fall of 1965. In early 1966, in the second semester of her freshman year, she met my biological father, a Kenyan named Mboga Mageka Omwenga. Dorothy and Mboga conceived me in March 1966.

My birth in December 1966 was as natural as possible, given the circumstances. Dorothy shocked many by advocating natural childbirth. Natural childbirth was distinctly uncommon in the United States in the 1960s. After reading a book on the Lamaze method, my birth mother was determined that I be born as nature intended. She was so convinced of the correctness of the French physician's conclusions, that when it came time to give birth, she refused all painkillers. Dorothy focused on Lamaze's natural breathing technique, much to the consternation of her physician and the group of medical students invited to watch the procedure. She was strapped down, her legs held in stirrups, before they cut her perineum. Despite this discomfiture, I had little problem entering the world and cried lustily.

The milk of human kindness did not flow at the time of my birth for Dorothy or for me. There were no Florence Nightingales. Instead the nurses attending the birth were callous and hard-hearted. They whisked me away within moments after my natal cry. There was no fanfare.

Rather than being welcomed into the warm bosom of a loving family, Dorothy surrendered me to foster care almost immediately after I was delivered on that cold December morning in 1966.

Maryan suggested to Dorothy that she should not mention the birth of the multiracial child, which also occurred out of wedlock, to anyone. Dorothy was even told not to mention it to her older brother or "her future husband." Maryan advised her daughter to "forget the whole ordeal."

Dorothy's father was even less receptive. Dorothy later reflected that she had no memory of George ever talking about my birth before his death in 1989. My conception and birth definitely strained Dorothy's relationship with her parents.

Unknown to her parents, the pregnancy that Dorothy was instructed to keep secret was the first thing nearly every lover would discover in an intimate moment. Dorothy was left with severe stretch marks on her abdomen, breasts, and buttocks—deep and wide grooves that looked as if they had been carved with a knife. The pattern of torn skin and lines, which remained bright red for many years, meant that she could not have followed her mother's advice to tell no one about the pregnancy. They were painfully obvious and spoke volumes about what she had endured.

To escape the emotional pain related to her strained family relationships and the child that she let go, Dorothy moved to Detroit. She felt that for her own sanity, she had to distance herself from her immediate family in Dorseyville.

She got a job with the company then known as Northwest Orient Airlines. Dorothy lived in a downtown apartment building where many working singles lived. She shared a one-bedroom apartment with another airline employee.

As she met new friends in Detroit, no one suggested that she return to Penn State or attend another college. She was also afraid to ask her parents to help with tuition following the trauma of her pregnancy. With low self-esteem and little self-confidence, she became a regular drinker. As the alcohol intake continued, her courage diminished further until all self-confidence disappeared. Dorothy believed she had nothing left in life, leading her to continue drinking heavily. She felt lost and alone.

"I began to fantasize a lot about suicide and finally decided to do so by jumping off the Golden Gate Bridge," Dorothy later confessed to me. "I am embarrassed to say it, but I had romantic images of leaving 'my heart in San Francisco' like the Tony Bennett song. I had never been there and knew nothing about the place, except that a 'cool' friend of my brother's was now living there. I decided to get a 'drive away car' with a friend and travel out there with the vague but serious plan that I would try to get a new job as a stewardess, or throw myself off the bridge."

When Dorothy arrived in San Francisco, she went to see her brother's friend. He let her stay in his apartment in the now famous "hippie mecca" of Haight-Ashbury, a neighborhood she knew nothing about. He suggested that she meet him that night at the Fillmore Auditorium where there was going to be a concert by "some guy named Jimi Hendrix." Dorothy explained, "I did not know who the artist was, but hearing the words 'concert' and 'auditorium,' I assumed it must be classical music. So I put on a dress and some fashionable white boots and found my way there."

While standing on the steps waiting for her brother's friend, Dorothy observed the other concert goers as they entered the building. They were dressed in psychedelic clothes, hats, and beads, making her stylish black and white dress and daring white boots look out of place. Her brother's friend arrived and simply handed her a little pill.

"Eat this," he directed.

"What is it?" she asked.

He told her that the pill would make her enjoy the concert more. Trusting him completely, she swallowed it. She learned later that the pill was LSD. That unforgettable Hendrix concert and the acceptance she found with his friends later that night while listening for the first time to the Beatles' "Sergeant Pepper's Lonely Hearts Club Band" saved her from thinking further about suicide. "It was just like the Beatles' famous lyrics," related Dorothy. "I got by with a little help from my friends."

Suddenly, the world seemed to have a place for her. Dorothy found meaning in the world of "flower power" and "consciousness raising." She was still bereft about the child she gave up, but the young people in Haight-Ashbury did not judge her. Instead, they encouraged her to talk about it, meditate, and take care of herself.

Dorothy remembers thinking that if she had found Haight-Ashbury sooner, she may have been able to keep her baby boy and start a "New World Order" where White girls could raise Black babies in a supportive and peaceful climate. That was the magic of the 1960s in San Francisco. Haight-Ashbury in the 1960s was a unique place and time. She still thinks that period, and the love and insight she found there, saved her life and made her eventual reunion with her son possible. She confided in me after our reunion, "I was then able to explore different world views and different lifestyles. I started to understand the meaning of freedom, love, and learning, beyond the acquisition of knowledge. I started to discover my own potential to think outside of my conditioning, and I started to develop a relationship to nature and to understand my place in the world."

A lover, in that time of face painting and so-called love-ins, comforted her about her severe stretch marks by saying they looked like a lovely "sunburst." She knew there was nothing attractive about them, but the gesture was appreciated.

Gradually, Dorothy came to terms with the separation from her child and the end of her stint as a Penn State University coed. She began to enjoy the freedom and excitement of the 1960s and 1970s. She became involved with an underground newspaper that questioned the Vietnam War and supported Civil Rights. She witnessed Black Panther rallies and took part in various protests. She attended numerous performances by the Grateful Dead, Jefferson Airplane, the Doors, Janis Joplin, Sly and the Family Stone, Bob Dylan, Joan Baez, Santana, the Rolling Stones, Credence Clearwater Revival, and countless others who spoke through their songs to her generation. She even saw Jimi Hendrix a second time.

It is also significant to note that she was introduced to so-called "alternative" medicine, which later became her career. Plus, she learned about organic farming and yoga, which greatly influenced her life. She stopped eating meat as well.

I mentioned to Dorothy that drug use, beyond alcohol, was completely foreign to me to this day. I certainly discouraged drug use in the students I mentored.

Dorothy explained that after her first "trip" on LSD, she continued to use psychedelic drugs, "We used primarily LSD and marijuana. I never used injected drugs. I avoided heroin, cocaine, and the people who used them. Our intention was to use psychedelic drugs as 'mind-expanding agents,' not simply for kicks or as an escape. For us, this was a religious and idealistic quest."

Dorothy admitted that she was "deluded and naive" about the risks associated with LSD and marijuana. She deliberately avoided the other drugs because she knew they were dangerous. She felt an almost religious "duty" to use LSD regularly, to keep her head "clear" and free of illusion. She later realized that drugs were dangerous and unnecessary for a truly religious life.

This period in Dorothy's life provided an expensive but valuable education. "I found drugs opened my consciousness to greater learning and inquiry," Dorothy detailed in measured sentences. "I felt that I learned a tremendous amount of information while on drugs. I did not use drugs to escape or to party, but to learn and to heal. I later saw that this was sometimes an illusion, but even that fact was something that I learned while taking them. I was a person who intended to use drugs to 'tune in' and to make the world a better place. I never used them to 'tune out' as life was still to be experienced. Some may laugh, but I viewed taking drugs almost as a sacrament. I would take LSD in the forest or with friends who also sought answers and to change the world. I also used LSD or marijuana at concerts and love-ins, but mainly with intimate friends."

Dorothy became pregnant again in San Francisco as the Vietnam War dragged on in the late 1960s. The conception was a deliberate choice she made with her lover. As it was with my conception, she knew immediately she had conceived. She "saw" something she was sure was the baby and was thrilled. Dorothy and the baby's father planned to move to Switzerland to have the baby in a politically neutral country. They believed that if the child were a Swiss citizen, he or she would never have to face a war-related draft. Incorrectly convinced of the safety and benefits of LSD, she naively took the drug once during the pregnancy, about three weeks after conception. She then "felt" something happen to the baby she knew she was carrying. She felt the baby had been damaged. From that time on, she rejected LSD and other drugs because of her pregnancy. She also wanted to be more connected with the people who did not use drugs. She wanted to "drop in" again.

Throughout the pregnancy, which went full term, doctors assured her that the baby was normal. The tests and scans indicated that all was well, but Dorothy remained convinced otherwise as she prepared to have the baby. She could not ignore her perception that there was something wrong, and found herself unable to prepare for the baby with any enthusiasm. However, she hoped the doctors were right. She bought a crib and diapers, and she crocheted booties and sweaters. When her labor started, Dorothy intuitively knew that she would not have a healthy baby. A few hours later, to the complete shock of the obstetrician, she gave birth to an anencephalic child. Anencephalic babies are born without most of their brain and typically die shortly after birth. The baby could survive in the womb, but its lungs couldn't work without a developed forebrain. The Swiss medical team kept the little baby girl, whom Dorothy named Discovery, alive for only four hours.

Dorothy was devastated. Determined to find out why the baby girl died, the doctor did a number of tests. He discovered that Dorothy had a disease called toxoplasmosis, which is spread by cats. Dorothy had often been around and was scratched by cats while living in California. The doctor was sure that this viral disease caused Discovery's condition.

He instructed Dorothy to have her blood tested again and he predicted that the virus would be out of her system in six weeks. It was.

In spite of the doctor's diagnosis of Discovery's cause of death, Dorothy blamed the LSD and her "own stupidity." She felt enormous guilt and shame. She wished she had avoided drugs before conception and during pregnancy.

The loss of this second child, after previously giving me up for adoption, wounded Dorothy deeply. Dorothy and the baby's father moved to England, where they began an intensive study of acupuncture. Their grief and self-accusations over the death of their child proved too much for them to handle together. They later separated, but remain friends to this day.

"Losing Discovery," related Dorothy, "was another devastating blow. I thought she would make up for my loss of you, Thomas. Apart from that one acid trip, I had been so careful about diet and exercise. I really wanted to care for the baby. But when I lost my second child I really didn't know how to handle it. Discovery's body was never returned to me for burial and I was never able to even hold her. Mentally, I felt her loss. Physically, my full, hard breasts were the size of melons and I had no child to relieve the pain, reminding me of my loss. The sense of failure, helplessness, and overwhelming grief were the same as when I lost you. The hormonal ravages of post-natal depression, which can happen to any new mother, especially hit those who lose their babies. I was also in a hospital in a country where I could not speak the language. I had no counseling, no family nearby. I had a dreamlike feeling of watching helplessly as my life went by. I thought I handled it well, but I really didn't allow myself to grieve Discovery's death until fifteen years later, through psychotherapy.

"I had also thought that I had done something wrong while I was carrying you, Thomas," Dorothy continued. "I feared I had not eaten enough vegetables or something during pregnancy. I was particularly concerned years later when I learned that X-rays during pregnancy could cause childhood leukemia. Thomas, I had been carrying you in a breech position. Before your delivery, an X-ray was done to determine the type of breech. Later, as a homeopathic medical practitioner, I treated a six-year-old child who actually died of leukemia in a case where X-rays during pregnancy were the likely cause. I feared that you, my first child, might not even be alive. I never received any word to let me know you were okay. I had carried you for nine months, and had given birth to you. After Discovery died, I had to cope again with all of the painful memories associated with letting you go."

While in England, Dorothy later met and married Francis Hannon, the man who would father her other four children. They were married for about ten years before drifting apart and eventually divorcing.

Dorothy had met Francis at Brockwood Park School in England while she was there for public talks given by educator and philosopher J. Krishnamurti. Francis wanted a family, and Dorothy was desperate to be a mother. They were married about two months after they met.

She told Francis of the son she had given up for adoption and also of the short life of Discovery. Francis was very supportive. Less than a year after the wedding, a baby girl they named Lotus was born to the couple in Wales in October 1971. At last, Dorothy had a baby to hold and nurture for the long term. Dorothy exclaimed with maternal passion, "With each of these pregnancies, I tried harder and had more knowledge. I improved my diet, my knowledge of pregnancy, obstetrics, and medicine. I initially thought that having Lotus would make up for losing Discovery. But even though Lotus was the greatest gift, I realized fully that neither of my first two children could ever be replaced."

Lotus was followed by three sons, Atom, Jade, and Derwent. In her efforts to give her children the best possible care, she breast-fed them for a long time, seven years in total for the four children. In her enthusiasm to return to a more natural, traditional form of health care and child raising, Dorothy began a career in holistic and homeopathic medicine. Memories of her father's illnesses also influenced her decision to pursue a career in homeopathic medicine. Dorothy devoted as much time as she could to her new career. She made certain that it evolved around the school hours of her children. Dorothy was so concerned with caring for her children that she built her clinic in the ground floor of their home so that she could be available to them.

In 1974, Dorothy qualified as a homeopathic medical practitioner. She later became the Founder and Principal of the Northern College of Homeopathic Medicine in the United Kingdom, a college that offers four-year training programs to healthcare professionals. She served on national committees concerned with the development of medical and ethical standards and national curriculum, addressed international medical conferences, collaborated on numerous publications, and appeared on radio and television. As the first nondoctor homeopathic medical practitioner to work in the National Health Service, Dorothy directed a three-year research project sponsored by Saint Mary's Hospital Medical School. This work attracted the patronage of the Prince of Wales, the attention of the Minister of Health and the national media, and led the way for the development of a new postgraduate program at the University of Westminster. Her team's work was published in the *Journal of the Royal Society of Medicine*.

The loss of her first two children clearly affected how my biological mother raised Lotus, Atom, Jade, and Derwent. Even with all of her career accomplishments and the prestigious Sloan master's degree she earned in 1991 from the London Business School, she was able to put her children first. While she deeply enjoyed raising four children, she still spoke of her first born, the boy she gave up for adoption. "I thought a lot about the son I gave up. I wanted to find him, but I did not want to intrude on his life or that of his new family. I thought the timing was critical and had to be determined by him. I decided to just make sure he could find me if *he* wanted to and to just 'call to him' through the cosmos. I always looked for him on the streets of Pittsburgh when I went back for visits. I fantasized endlessly when he was different ages, about how I could find him and watch him from afar, going into school or playing with his friends. My heart was always open to a reunion. By the time of our reunion in 1992, I was more than ready."

CHAPTER TWELVE

Roots and Reunion

"Why stop now?" I asked my supportive Houston friends in the fall of 1994, although I knew it was a rhetorical question. "My relationship with Dorothy is now well established. I would like to discover my African heritage. I want to find my Kenyan biological father Mboga Mageka Omwenga."

According to the documents I had obtained from the adoption agency in July 1992, my Kenyan father's exact age was unknown, which I found peculiar and authentic at the same time. He was said to be about twenty-six years old, five-feet nine-inches tall, 150 pounds, with thick kinky black hair, brown eyes, and medium-dark skin coloring. I jokingly decided that he must have had some strong genes to cause me to be as dark as I am since my biological mother is White. His description as outgoing and friendly matched how I perceive myself to be.

Given conditions in many parts of Africa, I was not completely surprised that the document stated that three of his five brothers had passed away. I was surprised, however, that the document stated that he "had sisters but the girls don't get counted." From this I perceived that my father had not really, for whatever reason, been given the opportunity to open up to my biological mother. Maybe she didn't know the answer. That specific statement in the document didn't seem credible to me at the time. I reminded myself that the agency's account from 1966 had been filtered, interpreted, and paraphrased by at least two different people.

I was pleased to read that my father was a graduate student in political science. His level of academic achievement, especially given the lack of educational opportunities for Africans during the 1960s, was impressive to me. I assumed that he must have been intelligent to have made it out of Kenya to study in the United States in the 1960s.

Not much was mentioned about my paternal grandmother. According to the documents, my paternal grandfather was said to be the son of a "chief." I felt good about this; maybe it boded well for the development of my leadership skills.

Although I only knew my father's name, thanks to Dorothy, and not much about Kenyan culture, I began to think of myself as half Kenyan by 1994. For example, I began to feel passionate about an issue from the sports pages that showed that, sometimes, even the excellence of Kenya's star runners may not allow an escape from racism. In the mid-1990s, some road race directors in the United States were accused of discriminating against Kenyan runners. Yet, Kenya was the dominant nation in the 1990s in terms of producing world-class distance runners. Some American race directors had been excluding some Kenyans from competing by placing a limit on the number of foreigners that could enter a race. Another tactic was to offer prize money to American runners only. This made it more likely for an American to end up on the victory stand, since elite Kenyan runners often did not make the long trip for zero prize money. These tactics were used even if the winning times of the American runners were not competitive with other winning race times of athletes from around the world.

I understood that the stated purpose was to encourage excellence and fan interest in American distance running. But, most of the American distance runners were White, which led to the accusations of discrimination. What may have been true, though not directly stated, was that for American corporate sponsors, White American winners were believed to be more "marketable." Kenyan athletes looked different, and although they usually spoke English well, it was often not their first language. As a patriotic American who happened to have one-half Kenyan blood and a bit of knowledge of marketing, I had a unique perspective. I felt that honoring the sustained excellence of the Kenyans would drive the American distance runners to be more competitive over time. I believed that the American public could eventually find foreign athletes marketable if their exploits were promoted properly. Some of my running friends thought that I was biased; my allegiance to Kenya was growing stronger.

Reading Alex Haley's *Autobiography of Malcolm X* and watching Spike Lee's epic film about Malcolm X had significantly influenced me. One of many points that was not lost on me was that Malcolm's later views were profoundly influenced by his trip from the United States to Mecca. Instead of just hearing about the culture and practices of fellow Muslims in the Middle East, he went to Mecca and experienced them firsthand. I decided that even if I could not find my biological father in Kenya, I would still benefit greatly in terms of identity and heritage by traveling to my father's homeland.

Understanding and learning about my Kenyan heritage was important to me. Growing up in the United States, I understood the cultural plight of many African-Americans. Because of slavery, most African-Americans have no ties to the history of their African ancestors. They have been robbed of their heritage, history, and culture. Without this knowledge, it can be easier for some African-Americans to be negatively influenced into thinking that African-Americans are somehow inferior to other groups. Of course, this is not the case, but it has taken some Americans a long time to realize this after nearly four hundred years of miseducation, discrimination, and oppression in North America, Europe, and the Caribbean.

In November 1994, I met a helpful woman who lived in Kenya named Fatma who was visiting friends in Houston. She was an acquaintance of a woman I had dated in Houston. Based on my biological father's name, Fatma was pretty sure that my father was a member of the Kisii ethnic group. As a travel agent, Fatma agreed to help me arrange a safari game drive in the Maasai Mara/Serengeti area once I landed in Kenya, and to provide any help she could to find my father.

A coworker named Paul gave me great advice on logistics in Kenya after he visited there a few months before my trip. His input on lodging, transportation, safety, and the Kenyan authorities was especially valuable given the limited time I would have in Kenya to find Mboga. Paul had taken a sabbatical from his job and spent one year traveling around the world to finish setting foot on all seven continents including Antarctica before the age of thirty. At that point in my life, I was just beginning to embrace the idea that the world did not begin and end with the United States. After talking to Paul about his world tour, I began to feel that my trip to Kenya would not only allow me to find my father, but would allow me to accelerate my overall growth as a world citizen.

My departure to Kenya was set for late December 1994, and was to provide me with my first exposure to Africa. Although she previously traveled most of the world, Dorothy had never been to East Africa. She agreed to go with me to help me find Mboga. She wanted to aid me and she also wanted to share the experience of a few days on animal photo safari. Without assistance from Dorothy before and during the trip, I would have had little chance of finding Mboga. I wouldn't even have known his name.

When my grandmother Maryan Blazier heard about my plan to go to Kenya, she gave me a thousand dollars to help with the costs of the trip to find my father. This gesture was quite touching, as I was now accepted by Maryan, the matriarch of my recently acquired family. I was glad she supported my quest to find Mboga.

The preparations for Kenya were tiresome. I obtained a prescription for antimalarial medicine. I took shots to prevent yellow fever, cholera, tetanus, and hepatitis A. I also contacted the Kenyan embassy for an entry visa.

After flying out of Houston, I stopped in London to meet up with Dorothy. While in England, I met Mosomi Moindi through my sister Lotus. Mr. Moindi, a Kenyan, was the deputy director of the Kenyan National Tourist Office in London. He was smart, enthusiastic, and full of creative ideas on how to find Mboga. Specifically, he knew of one person with the last name Omwenga, who worked in the Treasury Building in Nairobi. He could not recall the man's first name. Mr. Moindi added that the national Minister of Science and Technology may be of help since this Kisii cabinet member was said to have been recently reunited with his American child, presumably conceived while the minister studied in the West. Mr. Moindi assured us that Kenyan culture would nearly guarantee that my father would want to be found.

Early on Saturday morning, December 31, 1994, Dorothy and I landed in Nairobi, Kenya, to begin our search for my biological father. I knew it was going to be a difficult trip for Dorothy, from an emotional perspective. She had to readdress all of the tough issues that she dealt with in 1966. She was forced to deal with memories of how she was treated by friends and family while pregnant with a Black baby in the United States during the racially charged 1960s. She was forced to reflect on her thoughts about a possible abortion and her ultimate decision to give me up for adoption. Shackled with her past decisions, Dorothy made the best of it and proved an entertaining, enlightening, and worthy traveling companion.

Since our reunion more than two years before in September 1992, Dorothy and I had become close friends. She had helped me in many ways. With her Sloan MBA background and management consultant experience, she was an excellent peer advisor as I refined my career aspirations. She set a good example for healthy living and gave me more insight into vegetarianism, yoga, and homeopathic medicine. Her extensive travels motivated me to want to see the world, which helped me develop my perspective as a world citizen, not limited by race, religion, nationality, or political ideology. I found her to be very politically aware, and I always learned something when I talked politics with her, even if we disagreed on some issues. Generally, she had a wealth of life experiences and I felt lucky to have her as a friend I could consult with about almost anything.

We landed in Africa at four o'clock in the morning at Nairobi's Jomo Kenyatta International Airport. *Jambo, Kenya!* Since my teenage years, I had yearned for an opportunity to set foot on African soil. I kissed the ground as soon as I got outside the airport. I was very tired since I had not been able to sleep on the flight, but I was drunk with excitement about the idea of actually being in Africa.

I had not previously traveled to the southern hemisphere, and on the way to the hotel I noticed that the stars in the sky were beautiful and different from those seen from the northern hemisphere. At the hotel, I was struck by the loud sounds of roosters crowing to welcome the rising sun, and the fact that the water went down the drain counter-clockwise in the Southern Hemisphere. Unfortunately, I knew no Kiswahili other than the word *jambo,* which means "hello," and a few other words and phrases. Fortunately for me, most Kenyans, especially those in Nairobi, spoke English.

Like many African nations, Kenya had been exploited for decades by European colonialism. In the case of the land that would ultimately become Kenya, the exploitation was at the hands of the British, and it lasted until 1963, when Kenya gained its independence. This is why most Kenyans speak English. English is the "official" language of the government, and Kiswahili is Kenya's "national" language. Kiswahili is a language that was formed by Bantu African and Arab traders doing business along the East African coast. In Kenya, most of the written word is in English and about ninety percent of the spoken word is in Kiswahili. Most rural people also still speak their specific ethnic group language when they are at their home village.

During our first day in Nairobi, Dorothy and I stocked up on bottled water and mosquito repellant. We then met up with Fatma, who I had met previously in Houston. Fatma went out of her way to be helpful. She arranged our safari, and then, speaking Kiswahili, helped us to call all of the Omwengas in the 1988 Kenyan Phone Directory. Surprisingly, there were no Omwengas listed in the 1994 directory. Unfortunately, we failed to reach anyone who had ties to Mboga, and some of our calls were not answered. Fatma, however, was optimistic. She expected to receive some additional assistance from a policeman and a lawyer who were both Kisii.

Since it was New Year's Eve, Dorothy and I went to a party that night at Carnivore's, a combination game restaurant, bar, and dance club. There were about four thousand people there from all over the world. Many were expatriates from India, Europe, or the Middle East; the remaining others were Kenyans. At midnight, hugging Dorothy, I held up my bottle of Kenyan beer to honor the memory of Don Gipson, who had died seven years earlier on New Year's Eve, 1987.

After the clock struck midnight, bringing in 1995, I met an American girl who recently graduated from an Ivy League school in the United States. She was in Kenya on a Fulbright Scholarship for a year of research. We talked for about thirty minutes and agreed to meet later in the week. She seemed impressed with my search for my biological father. Her support fueled my determination.

Dorothy and I stayed up in our small room after the party until 3:30 A.M., repacking for our safari trip that was only a few hours away. I was again unable to sleep. Getting out of bed at sunrise, I went for a run for about forty minutes. After a quick breakfast, Dorothy and I went to Nairobi's small Wilson Airport for our flight to Keekorok Lodge in Kenya's Maasai Mara area, bordering Tanzania's Serengeti National Park. Exhausted, yet excited about our upcoming safari adventure, we decided to take the trip on Sunday and Monday since it was New Year's Day weekend and the closed government offices would be of no help to our search for Mboga.

The Sunday morning flight on the twin-propeller plane was bumpy, but the view was beautiful. We snapped pictures from the window of the plane as we flew across the Great Rift Valley. Besides producing so many world class distance runners, I learned that the Rift Valley is the area where the African continent is rifting apart. It is believed that in millions of years, the African continent will split into two, with a narrow ocean filling the present Rift Valley. The same process is believed to have taken place along the Red Sea where the Arabian plate has separated from the African plate.

Arriving at Keekorok and deplaning, we took a walk around the camp looking at monkeys, elephants, and giraffes in the distance. Dorothy could not stop talking about the giraffe that stared right at her. After lunch, we listened to a short lecture from a Maasai warrior. According to him, "All cattle in the world were given by God to the Maasai people. Many of the young Maasai men live off of the blood, milk, and beef from the cattle. We drink the blood by tapping into the vein of the neck of the cattle while they are still living. We only take enough to drink, without killing the cow. Anyone else in the world that has cattle has wrongfully taken them from the Maasai. The Maasai will regain those cattle by any means necessary."

Cattle are a symbol of social status among the Maasai, with the emphasis placed on quantity instead of quality. Overgrazing has contributed to tremendous environmental degradation in areas where the Maasai live. Also, the Maasai warriors are still well known for being fearless lion hunters. If a vehicle carrying Maasai drives through the game park, the lions will take off as soon as they smell the Maasai or see their trademark red clothing from a distance. The Maasai, however, were having trouble maintaining their traditions as more and more Maasai were being educated and influenced by Westerners.

A day later, we made it to a Maasai village. They had small homes with ceilings roughly five feet ten inches high. At six feet one inch, I had to crouch down constantly.

A bearded Thomas (on left) in Kenya's Maasai Mara National Park. January 1995.

They let their goats and sheep sleep inside their homes at night. The cattle slept in their own shed. During the day, the cattle grazed just outside of the village. Small holes in the huts at the ceiling served as windows to let air in and smoke out as they cooked. Roughly thirty huts were arranged in a large circle to form the village, and there were huge piles of cattle dung inside the circle of huts. You had to watch every step to avoid a messy situation. There were flies everywhere, including many on the children. The flies did not seem to bother the adults.

We paid five hundred Kenyan shillings, about $12.50 at the time, to get into the village. The Maasai tried to sell us beads and cloth. The village was pretty humble, so I wondered what they did with the money from the continual stream of tourists.

The Maasai were quite friendly and accommodating to us tourists. While holding a Maasai spear, I felt like I could throw it through someone fifty feet away. The aerodynamic design, length, and weight of the spear were really impressive.

On Sunday, after the lecture and a short nap, Dorothy and I took our first photo safari, or game drive. *Safari* is the Kiswahili word for journey or expedition. A game drive consists of a driver taking tourists around the expansive national parks, looking for animals to watch and photograph. The sights were slow for the first thirty minutes, but the excitement quickly picked up. We saw a large male lion, *simba* in Kiswahili, who had just finished feeding. We also saw one of his lionesses and the cubs, with blood all over their mouths from their earlier feast. The lionesses do most of the hunting while the males protect the pride from predators. The males, however, eat first after a kill is made. The lions left little for the hyenas, vultures, storks, and cranes to pick over later. These birds were all circling or standing nearby waiting for their opportunity. As we started to drive away, we saw the freshly devoured buffalo carcass a short distance away in the high grass. Later, we saw five elephants, including two small calves, which walked across the trail right behind our parked safari vehicle. Over the next two days we saw antelope, ostrich, wildebeest, cheetah, warthog, gazelle, hyena, zebra, and rhino. The animals were amazing in their natural habitat. We even watched two cheetahs stalking a huge herd of antelope. It was a truly outstanding day.

As night fell, my mood changed. I was totally paranoid about the malaria threat since mosquitoes were abundant. I went to bed after spraying mosquito repellant all over my body. I wore my running tights and a long sleeve shirt. I slept under a mosquito net, which was standard equipment at Keekorok Lodge. The antimalaria medicine I was taking caused extremely vivid dreams. The subject of each dream was a meeting with Mboga. Each dream seemed to assure me that I would find Mboga in spite of the time constraints for this trip, and that our reunion would be positive.

We flew back to Nairobi on Monday around noon to continue looking for my father. Since it was a government holiday, the city moved at a slow pace. I was not able to reach Fatma all day to see if she had any luck with either of her Kisii contacts. Since Fatma was not with me, I did not call the remaining Omwengas we had not yet reached from the old 1988 phone directory. It was a struggle for me to communicate well on the phone, even in English, given the difference in accents. In addition to the difference between Kenyan and American accents, the phone lines were full of static.

I integrated my running workouts with my search for Mboga. I ran down to the offices of the *Daily Nation,* the leading East African newspaper. I decided to place an ad that would run on Wednesday, January 4, as I had missed the deadline for Tuesday. I tried to make the ad as discreet as possible, since I did not know if Mboga had ever told anyone in Kenya of my existence. The ad ran:

OMWENGA FAMILY

Looking to locate Mboga Mageka Omwenga of Kisii ethnic group regarding Penn State University Alumni Association. Contact Thomas Brooks, Room #168 of Sagret Hotel Equatorial by Wednesday, or call USA +1 (713) 555-1212 after Wednesday.

I wished that I had submitted the ad sooner.

Unable to locate Fatma, Dorothy and I met my American Fulbright scholar friend for dinner. I had not seen her since we met at the New Year's Eve party. At the end of dinner, Dorothy was tired, so we twentysomethings went to a night club. Some of the clubs in Nairobi seemed to be filled with quite a percentage of African prostitutes, along with Western men there to pick them up. Or, maybe it was the hookers picking up the men? Nonetheless, I was glad to be with my American companion because she provided continued encouragement for my up-coming search for Mboga, and because the aggressive hookers left me alone while I was in her company.

Although I made no value judgments on the prostitutes or their clients, I knew that the HIV rate in Africa was already growing rapidly. In fact, according to the Global Health Council, sub-Saharan Africa has the world's highest incidence of HIV. This is not to say that we don't also have a major AIDS problem in the United States, but the AIDS statistics in Kenya made me especially sad. The other thing that struck me was the beauty of some of these women, especially those from So-malia. They were tall and glamorous; I counted about five that were just as beautiful as supermodel and Somali native Iman.

Tuesday morning, the search for Mboga began in earnest. Dorothy and I went to see Dr. Zachary Onyonka, a contact I received from Mr. Moindi while we were in London. Dr. Onyonka was a Kisii who was said to have gone to school in Syracuse, New York, in the mid-1960s. We felt that he was our best lead since he was in America at the same time as Mboga. Of course, Dr. Onyonka, whose official title was Min-ister for Research, Technical Training, and Technology, was a busy member of the Kenyan Cabinet and was not in his office at the Utalii House. His secretary was gracious and told us that Dr. Onyonka would be back at four o'clock that afternoon. We asked her to help us look for the two Omwengas whom we had heard worked in the Treasury Build-ing. After forty-five minutes of calls, she could not locate them.

Things that we took for granted in the United States, such as online phone directories, email, and phone calls that go through instantly, were

scarce in Kenya in 1995. The secretary referred us to another government employee, Dr. I. A. Onyango, also a Kisii. He was very helpful
even though Dorothy and I went to see him with no appointment. He
spent so much time trying to help us that I wondered what he was
supposed to be doing in terms of his actual job duties. Before lunch, Dr.
Onyango found a lead of someone with the "Christian name" William
Omwenga who he thought could possibly be my father. Many Kenyans
have both an indigenous name and an additional "Christian name."
However, when we returned after lunch we found out from Dr. Onyango
that William was not related to me. Dr. Onyango's friendly secretary,
Winnie, agreed to help us put in inquiries to a couple of well-connected
Kisii men that she knew. The names we were given were Henderson
Magare and Nyang'au Omwenga.

During the lunch hour, we stopped by to see Fatma at her office.
We learned that she had been with her sick father the day before and
thus unavailable. She told us that her Kisii policeman and lawyer friends
were not able to produce any leads.

We then visited the U.S. Embassy in Nairobi, the eventual site of
the August 1998 terrorist bombing. The consular officer tried to help
us, but the embassy only kept visa records for one year from travel.
Thus, Mboga's travel records from the 1960s were not available. The
Consular Officer suggested that we check a Kenyan government building called Sheria House to look for birth records, or maybe the Kenya/
USA Association to network with people who might know my biological father.

At 4 P.M., we returned to the Utalii House to see Dr. Zachary
Onyonka. We were told earlier that he would be back by then. He failed
to return at 4 P.M., or at 4:30 P.M., or even by 5:30 P.M. We waited
patiently the whole time since we thought he was our best lead to help
find Mboga. His secretary encouraged us to stop back again the next
day. Oh well, cabinet members are busy people.

Dorothy and I walked down the main street of Nairobi, Kenyatta
Avenue, after we left Onyonka's office. At 5:45 P.M. it was still sunny
and the downtown street was crowded. Dorothy and I parted company,

briefly, so I could buy an extra suitcase and she could shop for some souvenirs. When I met her on the same busy corner five minutes later, I learned she had been assaulted. A man had tried to rip off her shiny, fake gold necklace. She was not hurt, but definitely shaken. The thing that disturbed her more was that she also saw an emaciated man who looked like he was literally dying in the street.

Returning to the hotel, we had to move together to a different room. The window did not close fully in room 168, and I was nervous about the mosquito and malaria threat. I called and asked the newspaper to alter the ad to include the new room number, 170, but I doubted they would get it right. In a developing country, you have to be flexible and alter your expectations and contingencies accordingly.

Dorothy, tired from the day's search, was not interested in going out. Fatma was tied up with her sick father, so I went out with my Fulbright scholar friend again. We had a great time eating and talking in a suburban area called the Westlands, nice by even Western standards. Under British colonial rule, before Kenya gained independence in 1963, there was residential segregation based on race. The Westlands used to be part of the European section of Nairobi during the colonial regime. Asians lived in estates in the Parklands area while Africans lived in areas such as the Eastlands. These patterns still seem to be maintained, but now are wholly driven by socioeconomic status rather than race. Since 1964, there has been no segregation in Kenya based on skin color. But there does seem to be an "economic apartheid" where the better schools, neighborhoods, hotels, and hospitals are outpriced for many. Well-to-do people of all races still live in the Westlands, including many expatriates.

Returning to the hotel from the Westlands, I slept fitfully. I was awake and had already taken a run when Dorothy woke up on Wednesday morning.

"Dorothy, I think we should go to Sheria House, as the consular officer had suggested. I would like to be there by 8:30 this morning."

"Well, Thomas, I am tired, so I would like to get some more rest, and then go to breakfast."

"Well, I guess that's okay," I said uneasily before pausing. "But I wanted to go to Sheria House to check out birth records early this morning, before our first appointment at 9:30 A.M. We can just grab some food from downstairs and eat it during our taxi ride."

"I want to sit down and have my breakfast. This is the first I have heard about Sheria House. You are not keeping me in the loop on the research plans. I feel like you are treating me like baggage on this trip, just going your own way at one hundred miles per hour."

"You haven't heard about Sheria House because I just came up with this idea during the night while I was unable to sleep. This is a way to maximize our time here, and will allow us to make optimum use of the early morning hours before our first appointment. It is not a change to the schedule, but an early morning addition." Tension was rising between us.

"Well, I can go with you," Dorothy replied, "but I think you need to relax. Not everyone can keep your level of intensity."

I was agitated. All I could blurt out was, "I understand. If you want to sleep in and go to breakfast, that is fine with me. I just know that this is our last full day in Kenya, and I am determined not to leave the country without making some type of contact with my father's family."

Once I calmed down a bit, I realized we were probably both frustrated with trying to do so much with so little time.

We eventually made it together to Sheria House, which happened to include the attorney general's chambers, where we obtained a mailing address to use to make written requests for birth records. While there, we talked to the registrar general, who referred me to a Kenyan named Samson Mainye Akuma. Samson directed me to a restaurant owner named Robert Ouko. When Dorothy and I arrived at the restaurant, it was not very busy. One of the workers tracked down Mr. Ouko.

"Mr. Ouko, I am Thomas Brooks, and this is my biological mother Dorothy. I am wondering if you can help me locate my biological father. He is a Kisii, who went to school in America. I understand that you went to school in America, too."

"Yes, I went to school in America, a long time ago, on a running scholarship."

"That is great. I am a recreational runner myself. What events did you run?"

"I ran in the 800 meters final in the 1972 Olympics, and I also won a gold medal for the 4x400 meter relay."

"That is amazing. I am so honored to meet you, a Kenyan Olympic gold medalist. I am a big fan of track and field. I have to get a picture with you."

"Thomas, maybe you should ask Mr. Ouko about your father," whispered Dorothy after taking our picture.

"Oh, right. My father's name is Mboga Mageka Omwenga. He is a Kisii who went to university in America in the 1960s. Mboga and Dorothy had me, and then I was given up for adoption in America. A couple of years ago, I found Dorothy in London. Now I have come to Kenya, hoping to make contact with my biological father. I was wondering if you know him, and if you might know where to find him."

"Yes, I know Mboga. He is older than I am and he left for America before I did. I am Kisii also, and your father was well known among the Kisii people. He is known for his great intelligence. He ran for political office, but I believe he was defeated."

"Do you know if he is living in Kenya?"

"I don't know. I don't know where to find him since I have not seen him in years."

Even though Mr. Ouko was not able to help directly, the fact that he knew my father gave me a strong feeling that we were close to finding Mboga.

After that there was definitely a sense of urgency. Our flight was set to leave Nairobi the next morning. The ad had run in the Daily Nation newspaper on Wednesday as planned. The room number in the ad wasn't corrected to number 170 in spite of my previous request. Later, we again went to see Dr. Zachary Onyonka. We never did get to meet him, and he never responded to the detailed note that we left for him on Tuesday. What I had believed to be our best lead bore no fruit. In a separate pursuit, I talked to a man named John from the Kenya/USA Association, who agreed to run a check on Mboga for me. In all, we pursued fourteen different people and paths to find my biological father. There were even a couple of additional leads I never had a chance to pursue.

By sunset Wednesday, our last night in Kenya, the leads from Winnie, Dr. Onyango's friendly secretary, and from the newspaper ad began to converge. When I returned to the hotel, I saw a note that said a Robert Nyamwaro Omwenga had stopped by while we were out. We then met a few distant relatives early Wednesday evening that stopped by in response to the ad in the newspaper. Specifically, there were two distant cousins, Peter Omwenga and David Obwoge, and an in-law, Rebecca Onsongo who came with her daughter, Jane Onsongo.

The conversation with these relatives was roughly the same as that with Mr. Ouko. They knew of Mboga and actually claimed to be related to me, but they did not know anything about the specific whereabouts of Mboga. Everyone was friendly to Dorothy and me. Savoring the moment, we took some pictures.

Later that evening I received a knock at the door from the hotel staff. There was a phone call for me, requiring me to walk down stairs to the cramped booth that contained the hotel's only guest phone.

"Hello. This is Thomas Brooks," I began.

"Hello! Hello!" It was a female voice.

"Hello. This is Thomas Brooks," I repeated more loudly. There was static on the line.

"I am calling from a friend's home on the coast. Can you hear me? I will only talk briefly. This is Margaret. Margaret Kwamboka Omwenga," stated the voice, rich in accent and excitement. "I saw that advertisement in the newspaper after a friend pointed it out to me. I am Mboga's daughter. Why do you need to talk to my father?"

After traveling thousands of miles, I hesitated to reply to the direct question. I had always hoped to locate Mboga, but to do so discreetly. I did not know if she knew that she had a brother from the United States. What if her mother did not know about my existence? I also knew that it was my last night in Kenya. I knew this conversation would be brief, because of the static, and the fact that she was calling long distance. So maybe it was selfishness, or desperation, or maybe the fact that my instincts felt positive, but I decided to answer the question directly and truthfully.

"I am Mboga's biological son from the United States. I came to Kenya to find and meet my father."

"Huh? You are saying that Mboga is your father?"

"Yes. I am Mboga's son. I was conceived in the United States in 1966. My biological mother, who is a White American, is here with me in Nairobi right now." I paused. Margaret was speechless, so I continued, "After I was born, I was given up for adoption, and grew up with a Black American family. A few years ago, I was able to find my biological mother, Dorothy, in London. Now I am here to find my biological father. I bring no ill intentions. I don't need money from Mboga or anything like that. If possible, I am just hoping to meet him and to continue to learn about my heritage as a half Kenyan and a member of your family."

"This is a surprise. I did not know about this, about this son from America, from my father." Margaret commented. "I was born in 1975 and always thought I was the oldest."

"I am sorry to share the news with you, this way, without getting to meet you first," I stated. "I had hoped and expected to meet my biological father first. Then he could have shared the news with you if he chose to do so."

After a long, uncomfortable pause, I added, "Margaret, I am leaving Nairobi tomorrow to return to the United States, but I would love to meet you."

"I am happy and excited about meeting you as well. I live near the coast, in a city called Kwale. It is a long trip to Nairobi, and expensive, and the roads are bad. Are you able to meet me in Mombasa, which is right on the coast?"

"I would like to, but I have to be on the flight tomorrow morning at 10 A.M. because I have to make it back to the United States for work.

It seems like there is not enough time for me to get to Mombasa tonight and then back to Nairobi for my flight tomorrow morning."

"Thomas, I am anxious to meet you."

"Is there a way you can get to Nairobi tonight? I asked. "Since you mentioned that it is expensive, I can offer to reimburse you the money for your trip when you get here."

"Let me check," my sister said. "I may be able to borrow money to take the bus. I would then travel overnight and arrive in Nairobi early tomorrow morning. I can meet you at your hotel a few hours before your flight."

"Well, I hope you can make it. We can have breakfast together if you do make it. Again, I will reimburse you the money for the bus trip when you get here. By the way, where is our father?"

"You know, I have not been able to talk to him for a while. He does not have a telephone and he has been staying in a different part of the country. I will see what I can find out."

Now, I was really encouraged. I had talked to my Kenyan sister. I was ecstatic!

Only a few minutes later, we received another knock on the door from the hotel staff. Robert Nyamwaro Omwenga, who had left the earlier message at the hotel, came back again, this time with Henderson Magare. Henderson Magare had been contacted about me by Winnie, the friendly secretary, and also by a relative with the last name of Momanyi who, at the time, worked at the American Embassy. They waited for us downstairs at the dusty, open-air hotel bar.

"Hello. You are Thomas?"

"Hi. I am Thomas Brooks, and this is my biological mother, Dorothy."

We ordered some bottles of Tusker, one of the popular beers in Kenya.

"We understand that you are looking for Mboga Omwenga."

"Yes. I am Mboga's son. Mboga, along with Dorothy, conceived me in the United States in 1966. After I was born, I was given up for adoption. A few years ago, I was able to find my biological mother, Dorothy, in London. Now I would like to find Mboga."

"I heard about you being here in Kenya. So I talked to Robert Nyamwaro earlier today," said Henderson Magare, with a giant smile on his warm face.

"Yes, I am Mboga's step-brother," said Robert Nyamwaro. "The other contact you received, Nyang'au Omwenga, is also a step-brother to Mboga. We agreed that it would be best for me, as Mboga's brother to make the initial contact with you. This is why I came by the hotel earlier, but you were not here."

"Yes, I am sorry we missed you, but I am glad to meet both of you now."

"Mboga is my brother. We have the same father, but we have different mothers. Our father had four wives. How are you sure that Mboga is your father?" asked Robert Nyamwaro skeptically.

Dorothy chimed in confidently, "Thomas was born to me back in 1966. His father was named Mboga Mageka Omwenga. I am sure about the name. I am not sure exactly how to spell the middle name, but I am sure about the name."

Initially, Robert Nyamwaro seemed cautious and skeptical about our intentions. But Henderson Magare, Mboga's cousin, effectively my uncle in the Kenyan concept of extended family, was extremely friendly and gregarious.

"I am just here to find my biological father. I hope that my arrival will not cause any problems in the family," I stated between swigs of Tusker. "I don't need money from Mboga or anything else. I have no negative intentions. There is no reason to be uneasy. If possible, I am just hoping to meet him and to continue to learn about my heritage. I am just learning about Kenya, and the Kisii people. I want to continue this process with the help of my family in Kenya. I hope to build a friendship with him, and also with my siblings here in Kenya. If possible, it would be great to eventually meet other members of my Kenyan extended family as well. By the way, I just talked to my sister Margaret on the phone. She is hoping to take a bus overnight to meet me here tomorrow. My flight leaves Nairobi at 10 A.M. tomorrow."

Still cautious, Robert Nyamwaro pulled out a picture of a handsome young African man.

"That is him!" Dorothy exclaimed, looking totally convinced. "He was about twenty-six years old when I knew him."

"This picture is from about 1970, when Mboga returned to Kenya. He was a little older than me," Robert Nyamwaro said.

"I am sure that this is him!" Dorothy affirmed, anxiously.

I was glad Dorothy had been there to make the positive identification. Otherwise, I am not sure where the discussion would have gone from there. "So, where is my father now? Is he in Kenya?"

"Mboga lives in Kenya, but he is out of the country at this time, on a matter relating to his timber business," Robert Nyamwaro stated. "There is no easy way to reach him at the moment. Maybe what you can do is to leave a note with us, and we will get it to him when he gets back to Kenya."

Hoping to put Robert Nyamwaro at ease, Dorothy and I reiterated that we wished Mboga no harm and did not want anything monetary from him. All I wanted was to meet Mboga. I wanted to gain more knowledge about my heritage as a Kenyan, as a Kisii, and as an Omwenga family member. We emphasized this in our two notes that we left with Robert. Each note included our respective contact information. I was thrilled to have made positive face-to-face contact with family members who were close to Mboga. As I went to sleep that night, I was happy, now confident that I would eventually meet my biological father. Dorothy's identification of the photo had been the turning point in the discussion. Also, I felt it was important at the time for Mboga to get not only my letter but the letter from Dorothy as well. After all, he had never met me and had never heard of anyone with the name "Thomas Brooks."

We got a 6 A.M. wake-up knock on our door from the hotel staff on Thursday. I had wanted to be up and dressed just in case Margaret made it. Amazingly, she did arrive, along with her longtime friend Salma.

They had been classmates at the Kenya High School, generally regarded as the top high school in the country at the time. Salma, a student at the Catholic University of East Africa in Nairobi, was Margaret's best friend. Salma used money intended for her school fees as a loan to Margaret to make the trip. I gladly paid Salma back.

Margaret Kwamboka, Salma, Thomas, and Fatma in Nairobi. January 1995.

I was deeply touched by the effort Margaret made to meet me in Nairobi, and spend just two hours with us. We traded basic information about each other and our families. Due largely to the Kenyan concept of extended family, Margaret immediately accepted me, and Dorothy as well. She referred to Dorothy as "mother" and was especially excited to hear that she had another "sister" named Lotus in London, who was not much older than she was. Dorothy reciprocated the goodwill right away.

I was also glad to hear that in addition to Margaret, I had two other Kenyan siblings, Christine Bahati Omwenga born in July 1986 and Machoka Rasugu Omwenga born in September 1991. I then had knowledge of a total of seven siblings, four brothers and three sisters, scattered around the world. This was amazing for someone who grew up as an only child.

"How do you think Machoka will feel to find out that he has an older brother? I hope he will not feel like I am taking his place as the first born son," I shared with Margaret.

"Thomas, you know, the first born son is usually given his father's surname. For some reason, my mother Jane Bosibori chose not to give Machoka the name of the father. So I don't think it will be a problem for Machoka. Also, he is still young, so he will be able to get used to the idea of an older brother."

I told Margaret the story of how I was conceived, adopted, and raised in the Lowry family in Pittsburgh. I also explained how I was able to find Dorothy.

"You must be determined and brave to have found Dorothy and then to come all of the way to Kenya to find Dad. I have never known anyone who would do something like this. You seem to be confident about yourself."

"I feel fortunate to have found you, Margaret."

"It was fortunate. I never read that paper. A friend saw it and saw my name, Omwenga. If she did not point it out to me, I would have never seen it. Then, I had to get another friend to let me use her phone to call you in Nairobi yesterday. You know, I was excited. I did not even go home to get a change of clothes, because I had to rush to make the 7 P.M. bus last night. On the way to Nairobi, I was just thinking about our conversation. I was not convinced that you were really my brother. I thought it might be a joke."

"A joke?"

"Yes, I couldn't believe that I had a big brother from America. But, once I saw you, I knew instantly that you were my brother. You look similar to my father when he was young."

"Do you think that Mboga will be happy to hear that I am here in Nairobi looking for him?"

"Yes, he will be excited."

"What about your mother, Jane Bosibori?"

"I don't know. I don't know if she knows about you. You know, they met long after you were born, after my father returned to Kenya."

"And Margaret, how do you feel about Thomas finding you?" Dorothy asked.

"I am happy. I had always wanted a big brother to mentor and inspire me. Thomas seems strong and confident. I think he can be a great big brother."

Robert Nyamwaro and Henderson Magare soon arrived at our hotel to drive us to the airport and see us off on our trip back to London. Fatma stopped by to say goodbye as well. Henderson Magare was still animated and friendly. Robert Nyamwaro was then also opening up and seemed comfortable being around us. He hadn't seen his niece Margaret in years. "I just enable good people to come together," I joked.

Margaret Kwamboka, Thomas, Robert Nyamwaro, and Henderson Magare in Nairobi. January 1995.

All of my newfound Kenyan family seemed confident that I was Mboga's child based on my looks and mannerisms, including Robert Nyamwaro. They seemed anxious to stay in contact with me. It was noted that some other members of the family had birthmarks similar to the one I have on my right cheek. Henderson Magare had no doubt that I was Mboga's son. They also said that they would mail me phone numbers of Omwenga family members who were living in the United States. On the flight out of Africa, I could not help thinking that my life was forever changed by this trip to Nairobi.

On the flight home, Dorothy apologized, "I am sorry I was acting bitchy on Wednesday morning."

"No problem. I could not have found Mboga's family without your help before and during the trip."

"Well, I am sorry. I was feeling a bit insecure. I was afraid that once you found Mboga that you would not want to stay involved with me."

"Dorothy, that is not going to happen. I value my relationship with you. Finding my father is not going to change that. Just like when I found you, that did not change my interaction with Joan. Don't worry about it."

This was the first time I had seen Dorothy so vulnerable in the more than two years I had known her. The funny thing is that when I first met Dorothy, I thought she was some kind of superwoman who always handled every interpersonal relationship issue so gracefully, so much better than I. I now realized she was very much human. She was still an excellent advisor and loving family member.

About a week later on January 12, 1995, Dorothy woke me up with a phone call at 3:45 A.M. Houston time.

"Mboga just called me here in London. I have just talked to him."

"What did he say?"

"I only spoke to him briefly. He is happy that we traveled to Kenya and he is willing to make contact with you. I have a number where you may be able to reach him right now."

For some reason Mboga felt more comfortable calling Dorothy first. This surprised me at the time. I now understand that this would be normal protocol for a Kenyan, to call the parent before the child, especially since he had never met me. I tried repeatedly for the rest of the night to reach Mboga, who was at Henderson Magare's office. I was unable to get through until 7 A.M., 4 P.M. Nairobi time, because of Kenya's less-than-advanced telecommunications system. Mboga had left the office, but Henderson Magare and I set up a time when I would call on the following Tuesday so that I could speak to Mboga.

Henderson Magare had told Mboga about my visit to Kenya, and Mboga then shared with him the circumstances surrounding my birth. Henderson Magare had not known of my existence before my arrival in Kenya.

Mboga had related, "Cousin Magare, I thought I would never see my son, called Erik at the time. It pained me to the extreme because of our strong African sense of family and kinship. In 1966, I felt powerless concerning the future of the baby. Dorothy was young, and therefore dependent on her parents for financial support. I was a student and a foreigner to boot. So Erik was given up for adoption, and I found out about that decision through a letter from Dorothy. At that time, I wanted Erik to be handed over to me, and then eventually to take him with me back to Kenya. But the odds were against me. They acted like I did not exist and I was not given an option. Because I thought I would never see him, I didn't inform anybody about my son, not even my own mother. But for reasons unknown to myself in November 1994, I told my cousin Peterson Nyakundi about the existence of my son. Then ironically, only two months later, I got a handwritten letter from my son who had come to Kenya to search for me after twenty-eight years."

On January 17 I called my biological father on the phone at the appointed time. As fate would have it, the quality of the phone connection was less than ideal and the static and echoes on the line were quite problematic. These problems, along with the cost of the call, kept the call relatively short. I was broke after my trip to Kenya.

"I am so glad to finally speak to you. I have looked forward to finding you," I began.

"I am glad that you came to Kenya to look for me. This is a courageous thing for you to do. I am proud of your effort. I was glad to read in your letter that you are doing well."

"It was unbelievable to meet Robert Nyamwaro, Henderson Magare, and my sister Margaret Kwamboka. I am thrilled now to have a connection to you and my Kenyan family."

"You will have to come back. You have another sister and a younger brother. You have an elderly grandmother who would like to meet with you. Maybe you can come back later this year, in December. Then you can go to Kisii, to our Omwenga homestead."

"I am happy to finally speak with you and I look forward to meeting you. I am having a lot of trouble hearing you on this phone line. I am not sure that you are able to hear me either because of the echoes and static. Is there a way for me to be able to contact you?"

We chatted some more, and then Mboga gave me his address. The search was basically complete. With Dorothy's help, I knew that we had found the right person, my Kenyan father. I now had biological parents and siblings in both Europe and Africa.

Over the next four months, Mboga and I exchanged letters that allowed us to gather basic information about each other. He was still suggesting that I return to Kenya in December 1995. After closing on my first house in March 1995, I really didn't expect to have the cash to go back sooner. At the same time, I didn't want to wait that long to meet him.

I had a one-week business trip to France in July 1995. Being in Europe, I decided to use the opportunity to make a quick two and one-half day vacation diversion south to Kenya to meet Mboga instead of returning directly home to the United States. I called Henderson Magare a few weeks in advance to see if someone would be able to meet me at the airport. On July 8, 1995, at 3:30 A.M., I landed alone in Nairobi. Walking through the dimly lit airport hallway toward the baggage claim area, I saw Henderson Magare, Robert Nyamwaro, and a person who I guessed was Mboga in the distance. After my initial feeling of great excitement, my second thought was, "How did they get through immigration without a plane ticket? Anything goes in a developing nation." It turns out we had a relative who was a senior police officer at the airport.

After walking another two hundred meters, at last I was able to give Mboga a hug. I was happy—speechless. I was at last connected to him and to Africa. I was happy that I had decided to find him. I was ecstatic that he wanted to see me. I wanted to know everything about him and his family.

While waiting at baggage claim, I chatted with my father about the long flight and noticed that more than fifty additional people were waiting outside of customs. Every time I looked in that direction, they made a huge noise. Finally, Henderson Magare told me, "They are waiting for you, Thomas!" It was touching that so many people came to meet me at 3:30 in the morning. This would be a rarity in America, but the warm welcome seemed so natural in Kenya. The Kenyans were imbued with a cheery spirit of spontaneous hospitality.

While still waiting for the luggage to appear, I walked toward the crowd to say hello. When I was about three feet away from the railing, they reached out, grabbed me, and pulled me hard into the railing. My new family was affectionately mobbing me. Hugs and kisses came from everywhere. Only six months before this, these people did not even know that I existed. Now they were giving me an unbelievable welcome. It was great, except for the slight pain in my ribs from being pinned against the railing.

My Kenyan family warmly greets me at the Nairobi airport. July 1995.

The beautiful noise they made is called *okoiririata* in the Kisii language. It means ululation and it was made by the large group of female Kisii relatives who welcomed me. They had traveled from all over Kenya.

One of these women gave me a monumental smile. It was my sweet Aunt Truphena Moraa, one of Mboga's three living sisters. She traveled from her home in Kisii, in remote southwestern Kenya, to welcome me on behalf of my aging grandmother Kemunto. Thomas Ayiera, Mboga's younger brother, accompanied her. He was from their Nyakongo home village in the Kisii district.

After almost ten minutes, my relatives let me go and I was able to go back and claim my luggage. With baggage in hand, we went to Uncle Robert Nyamwaro's house. More people were waiting for me there. There were young and old. Many relatives traveled great distances, including people from the Kisii area.

Uncle Robert Nyamwaro and his family were extremely nice and hospitable. My female first cousins, Robert's daughters, Rose, Nancy and Stella, baked two cakes for me. One cake said, "Thomas, welcome home." The other read, "We all love you." My aunts couldn't stop hugging and kissing me. The older men, including my uncles, beamed proudly.

Once everyone settled down, Mboga spoke first. For fifteen minutes he introduced me to the family. What Mboga said in English had to be translated into the Kisii language sentence by sentence for the benefit of the entire audience, as some who traveled from Kisii did not know English.

"Since 1966," Mboga began, "when Dorothy sent me a letter saying that 'Erik' had been given up for adoption, I suffered psychological pain over the loss of my son. I have felt a sense of irredeemable loss, always worrying about young Erik's well being and education. I am extremely thrilled to have contact with Erik, now known as Thomas, after more than twenty-eight years of separation.

"In Kisii culture," Mboga explained, "a father is never asked whether or not he can accept his own child. The father's acceptance of his own child is something both natural and obvious." As such, Mboga automatically accepted me as his firstborn child since I was born in 1966. Mboga later told me in a side conversation, that as an African man, he solely makes decisions with respect to his nuclear family. In this respect, he had informed his wife Jane Bosibori that he accepts me as his biological son. Mboga shared that Jane Bosibori, like my sister Margaret Kwamboka, was delighted to welcome me into the Kisii family. Margaret noted later that she had also talked with her mother Jane Bosibori about my existence. They agreed that it was not a problem for the family, since I existed well before Mboga and Jane Bosibori were married in 1974.

Mboga closed by publicly expressing his gratitude to Joan for her work in raising me single-handedly. He said he wanted to meet her face-to-face to thank her.

After his declaration of his acceptance of me as his son, I subsequently referred to Mboga as "Father." This felt comfortable for me since I had grown up without a full-time father and since Don, my strong male role model, had passed away in 1987. Even though I was just getting to know Mboga, there was no conflict, no feeling among anyone then involved in my life that some male figure was being "replaced" by my Kenyan father. This was a different situation than figuring out what to call Dorothy. Although I was very lucky to have Dorothy in my life, Joan remained the only mother I ever had in the truest sense of the word since she sacrificed her needs while raising me by herself.

I then spoke to my Kisii family for about twenty minutes, with Henderson Magare serving as interpreter. I summarized my life up to that point. I told them the details of how I found Dorothy, and about my first trip to Kenya that allowed me to make contact with Robert Nyamwaro, Henderson Magare, and Margaret. After my speech, we took what seemed like a million pictures.

My family had already kindly taken care of my hotel expense for the two days. After I got a few hours of sleep, we met at Robert Nyamwaro's house in the afternoon. I was accepted as one of the Omwenga family, especially by the older men such as my uncles Stephen Gichana Bogonko and Davidson Momanyi Omoro. The uncles, prominent real estate businessmen, gave me words of wisdom and a new Kisii name, Thomas Omwenga Mboga.

I spent much of my time in the evenings with my Uncle Henderson Magare and cousin Kefa Nyasinga. Kefa was a delight to be with. Kefa had seen the original ad that I placed in the newspaper to locate Mboga. Although he did not contact me, he checked with Uncle Henderson Magare to see what was going on. When he heard that his cousin was again coming from the United States, he made a point to be at the airport to meet me. Kefa, who managed a bus and transport business at the time, is definitely business-minded and enthusiastic about having fun. He has a good work-hard/play-hard balance, just like his American cousin. We are roughly the same age and have a lot in common. Kefa would tell you straight out, "I take many beers, many, many beers." So, he and I did some nighttime drinking together. Although I normally do not eat red meat or pork, I made one exception for an exotic dinner, feasting on zebra, gazelle, giraffe, and wildebeest at the Safari Park Hotel. Besides the meat, I also had the opportunity to try some ugali, now a favorite of mine, a Kenyan staple made with cornmeal. My old friend Fatma joined Kefa and me one night at my favorite African nightclub, Carnivore's.

"Spending two and a half days in Kenya is not enough," I was told repeatedly. "Your old grandmother Kemunto will be heartbroken to hear that you were in Kenya and did not go to see her." I felt bad, but I knew that I was due back at work in Houston. I planned, immediately, to return to Kenya during the upcoming December holiday season. Besides the "pressure" to stay longer to visit Kemunto, I felt pressure from my African family to settle in Kenya permanently, to adopt it as my homeland, and to be near my father. I was also pushed by various people to work with my family on some type of United States-Kenya business venture, to support a family member's education at a United States university, and to marry a Kisii woman. My family was definitely not shy! I took the pressure in stride, as I was experiencing cultural immersion at a dizzying speed.

During some quiet time with my father, I learned that my grandfather's name was Omwenga Ayiera. Grandfather Omwenga had four wives, sixteen sons, and by my count twelve daughters before dying on November 14, 1964, while Mboga was at school in the United States. My grandmother's full name was Miriam Kemunto Omwenga. Kemunto was my Grandfather Omwenga's first wife, and by 1995 she was roughly a hundred years old. However, nobody, including her, knew her exact age. This was because births were not registered in Kenya until roughly the mid-1950s; no national census was in place during Kemunto's childhood. I am Kemunto's first grandson that is a child of her boys. Mboga was her oldest living son. As the first grandson of the first wife, I was told that I would forever hold a special place in my family's village. I was a bit troubled with the emphasis seemingly placed on sons over daughters; however, I feel proud to be thought of as a special person in an African village.

Mboga and Thomas in Nairobi. July 1995.

On the day of my departure, I had a nice, quiet breakfast with what seemed to be some key Omwenga family leaders. The group was comprised of my father Mboga, Uncle Robert Nyamwaro, Uncle Thomas Ayiera, and Aunt Truphena Moraa. In addition to the "pressures" mentioned earlier, they added a new one. They told me that my grandmother Kemunto would not totally feel like I have "come home" until I have built a small house in the family's homestead in Kisii. "This is an important tradition," said the hardworking, wise, and articulate Aunt Truphena Moraa. "A small plot of land will be set aside for you, Thomas."

I typically believe in embracing tradition, and I wanted to leave my mark in Kisii so my future grandchildren would always be known in the village. However, after buying a house in Houston in 1995 and two expensive trips to Kenya, building a house in Kisii was the last thing I could afford. But again, I took all of these pressures in stride as part of my high-speed cultural immersion. Building a house in my family's home village was a crucial tradition. But, which of these requests was most important to my immediate family? Which was most important to Mboga, specifically? It was impossible to know this at this stage, just knowing my family for two and a half days. I would just have to worry about it later.

When I went to the airport, twenty family members arrived to send me off. I would miss them, but I had to get back to Houston and do some work. I was exhausted by the time I returned home. The search that began during MBA studies in 1992 with some casual information gathering was complete.

I have three great families on three different continents. I knew that I was fortunate. All that remained was to make it to Kisii to see my one-hundred-year-old grandmother before she passed away.

CHAPTER THIRTEEN

A Piece of Africa

Back in the States, I made first contact with my cousin in Dallas, Silas Omwenga Momanyi, in August 1995. It was great to have Kenyan cousins living in the United States. Silas told me that we had relatives in New Jersey as well. I was looking forward to meeting them all, but my short-term focus was still on East Africa.

As planned, I was working on trip logistics near the end of the year for my third trip to Kenya. The primary purpose of this trip would be to travel to my family's village in Kisii to meet my grandmother Kemunto. Once I had my flights booked, I wrote Mboga to inform him of my planned arrival in December 1995. I received a letter back from him less than one month before my trip, telling me not to travel to Kenya. He indicated that he was not able to provide financial assistance at that time.

He wanted me to delay my trip because he got the mistaken impression from my letter that I expected him and the rest of the family to support me financially for hotels and meals during my stay in Kenya. I had asked him in my letter for help with "logistics." By that, I meant only guidance on the most convenient hotels in which to stay in Kisii, and advice on how I was to travel from Nairobi to Kisii. I did not mention finances or money in my letter. I must not have been clear, and we did have two very different cultural orientations. It was simply a misunderstanding. I really wished I could have talked to him to clear this up

171

quickly. The lack of ubiquitous infrastructure in Kenya, especially telephone and email access, was frustrating for a Westerner accustomed to
cheap, real-time communications.

I immediately wrote a letter to clear up the misunderstanding. I did
not want anyone in my kind Kenyan family to spend any money on
me. The problem though, was that letters from the United States sometimes took roughly two weeks to be delivered to rural parts of Kenya.
I've been told that occasionally, the letters don't make it at all as Kenyan
postal employees sometimes open letters from the United States looking for money. So I called my Uncle Henderson Magare in Nairobi and
asked him to find a way to get a message to my father on the coast.
Having no way to ensure message delivery to Mboga left me frustrated.
I was discouraged by father's written suggestion to delay my trip, but I
was still determined to go see grandmother Kemunto in December 1995.

On December 30, I received another great welcome at Jomo
Kenyatta International Airport in Nairobi. The warmth and love of my
Kenyan family constantly amazed me. I finally met my younger siblings
Christine Bahati and Machoka Rasugu, and their mother Jane Bosibori.
Mboga, Henderson Magare, Robert Nyamwaro, and Margaret
Kwamboka were also there. After lunch, cousin Kefa picked me up in a
Mercedes Benz, and we traveled in the general direction of Kisii to a
small city called Nakuru. We sped up to 175 kilometers per hour—
roughly 110 miles per hour—on a bumpy road that was one lane in
both directions. It was a sunny day, and the mountainous countryside
was beautiful. I was amazed that the cows and goats grazing on the side
of the road never strayed onto the road, even though there were no
fences to confine them. These animals must be behaviorally well condi-
tioned. However, I was a bit nervous about vehicle safety as we raced
across Kenya.

Ever since we met, Kefa had really gone above and beyond the call
of duty to take care of me during my trips to Kenya. Henderson Magare
and others also had gone all out to facilitate my arrangements in Kenya.
After spending the night in Nakuru in lodging kindly arranged by Kefa,
we did a quick game drive in the morning at Nakuru National Park.

There were no lions there; however, Lake Nakuru is famous for rhinos and flamingos and the park did not disappoint me. Although the flamingo population had decreased as the lake shrunk, I still saw hundreds of flamingos. And, taking advantage of the fact that rhinos usually have terrible vision, I even got out of the car to pose for a picture in front of a group of rhinos that were only fifty meters behind me.

On December 31, 1995, one year after I first landed in Kenya, I rode the bumpy, dusty unpaved roads through the Kisii area to meet my grandmother Kemunto. The specific village is roughly fourteen kilometers west of the town of Kisii and is called Nyakongo. Nyakongo is in the Nyamira district, in the Kisii area. The village of Nyakongo seems to revolve around a large, beautiful tea plantation and some cattle herding. I would have assumed that agriculture and livestock would be difficult industries to sustain on the hilly terrain of western Kenya. I found out, however, that the area's cool temperatures and fertile volcanic soils have supported successful farming for the very dense population of the area. But the livestock industry faces a serious problem known as land fragmentation. The father, by tradition, has to subdivide land among his sons, who do likewise for their sons. This cycle cannot go on forever and still support the people and the cattle. Population density is a serious concern. Some Kisii people are beginning to buy land outside of the ethnic group boundaries in areas such as the Rift Valley, Narok, and the eastern coast to support cattle grazing.

The entire village seemed to be waiting for me, about five hundred people. There was singing and dancing. Everyone was touching my face, skin, beard, and hair since they viewed me as being a *mzungu,* the Kiswahili word for a European or white person. Light-skinned, wavy-haired Westerners did not come through this remote village every day. In spite of my difference in skin color, I was accepted fully by everyone in the village. Kenyan Africans seem to have almost no notion of racism, despite a history that includes British colonialism. It felt wonderful, and it was truly a grand scene.

I finally met Kemunto, my centenarian grandmother. Mboga looked just like her. It was great to see the two of them standing together. Mboga's cousin Nahashon Mumbo, then age seventy-five, gave me a handsome traditional walking stick as a gift. The villagers also presented a goat, which was subsequently slaughtered for that evening's feast. These acts of kindness demonstrated my acceptance into the Omwenga family. Kemunto then spit on my palms to give me a blessing. I was somewhat unsure of how to react, but with just a little coaching I promptly rubbed my hands together and then on my face to gladly accept the blessing. There were some short speeches and then a light meal in the mid-afternoon.

Mboga, Kemunto, and Thomas in Kenya's Kisii area. December 1995.

The men showed me the plot of land, my own piece of Africa, that I was granted to build my house in the village, just as Aunt Truphena Moraa had promised. I was told repeatedly this was a key Kisii tradition. It was also emphasized to me that I am the ranking first male grandson of Kemunto, Omwenga's first wife. The people in the village fully expected me to build a house there. Mboga and Kemunto were happy I had made it to the Kisii area and to our home village; it was a rare spectacle for a foreign child to visit the Kisii community. Kemunto was also glad to see her son, Mboga. My sister Margaret Kwamboka was also present for the celebration, back in the village for the first time in years. I was just happy to enable good people to come together.

Unfortunately, in the midst of all of this, my camera battery died as soon as I entered the village. Luckily, we found someone who was able to get a camera and take nine pictures. The whole time in the village I was thinking that I would never get any copies of the pictures. I was also afraid that the aged Kemunto would die before I could return to Kisii again to take more pictures.

"Father, now that I know you, Margaret, Uncle Robert Nyamwaro, Grandmother Kemunto and the others," I commented, "I want to know how I might be able to better fit into the family."

Mboga began, "In our Kisii culture, it is the family unit which is the synthesis of our African mind, a modern symbol of our ancient shrine and a court of law, in which we heal our souls, and where reconciliation and arbitration between and among individuals, family, and community materialize.

"It is our family unit that binds the members of immediate family together and makes them responsible for each other from the cradle to the grave. And it's through this linkage that we preserve the cohesiveness of the extended members of the family and keep the community intact. Hence our moral, emotional, and material support revolve around this unit; it is unshakable and unquestionable.

"It is through the mechanism of the family unit that we share happiness and joy and collectively endure grief and sorrow, burdens and tragedies."

"Do you think I can become part of this inner circle?" I asked.

"Thomas, you have visited our home village in Kisii. It thus became a historic occasion to our villagers as well as our clan as a whole. My blood kin received you with unprecedented warmth, rejoicing, and merriment. This occasion is reminiscent of old sub-Saharan Africa—one of the only places on earth where this still happens.

"For sure, many Western foreigners had visited our village and its environs before you. But you are the first member of our own family, born of a foreign mother abroad, to visit our home village, and henceforth your paternal ancestral home. That's why so many of my blood relatives and others journeyed from near and far to our ancestral village to meet and greet you. In the process, they displayed unalloyed Kisii culture, their ability to care, their spontaneous warmth, hospitality, and their age-old African sense of connectedness. It has been a splendid historic occasion to me in particular. It has given me special paternal pride and pleasure and hope. Above all, it made me feel proud of myself. Within our clan I have been a pioneer. I was the first to acquire secondary education; I was the first to go overseas and the first to earn bachelor's and master's degrees; I was the first to contest a parliamentary seat, though I lost the election through it being rigged by a Mafia political class.

"Only wealth has eluded me thus far. But this is for a specific reason. On my return to Kenya from the United States, had I agreed to become a sycophant, bootlicker, and a political henchman to the ruling clique I would have certainly by now become a millionaire many times over. But I chose a different path of an honest, committed, and independent-minded patriot. This is based on my personal integrity, principles, and ideals I hold dearly regardless of the consequences.

"But virtues do not count in Kenya's current political system. In fact, it is often a great liability for one to be principled or independent-minded. That is why sycophants, flatterers, bootlickers, and reckless con men, grabbers of national resources, who behave like fawning robots, have become millionaires overnight without doing any productive work. But I find this cancerous behavior to be revolting to my nature.

"However, the philosophical foundation of our culture is based on *social caring and sharing.* This seems to be diametrically in contrast with the American culture of individualism inviolate, something akin to 'each one to carry one's own cross.' Instead, in old African culture we are socialized from our childhood to 'be our brother's keepers' to the extent we are able. That is why, in fact, in our culture someone who is stingy and selfish with his or her money or property is despised and ostracized by our community as a whole."

"I think I understand." I said. "So, what should I do?"

"Whenever possible, therefore, try to assimilate some aspects of African culture. For under normal circumstances a human being yearns for self-identity and recognition, both of which are vital; so is the feeling of filial affinity."

Although he has suffered terribly because of his ethics and political views, Mboga's conscience was clear. "With the restoration of pluralism in Kenya since December 1991 and the coming election in 1997, my dream for a just, democratic society seems nigh," said Mboga optimistically. "The days of one-man rule and the creed of greed among the ruling clique are up for reckoning."

Mboga's dream still was to have Kenya's opposition groups, which advocated multiparty democracy, work together as part of a democratic government for human rights and a better quality of life for all Kenyans. I am proud of his efforts, principles, and conviction. He is an incredible example for me.

Before I left the village, I carefully observed the way the widowed wives of Omwenga, my grandfather, conducted themselves. Three of his four wives were still living, only Grandmother Bonareri was deceased at that time. More than thirty years after his death, their lives were still completely intertwined. This surprised me. The ladies lived in separate, adjacent houses and loved each other like sisters. The other living grandmothers, Kerubo and Moraa, treated me with love, just like my grandmother Kemunto, even though I was not technically part of their bloodline. To these Kisii women, I was their grandson, too. Their concept of family was overwhelming to me.

Kemunto was thought to have been a "good wife" to graciously deal with Omwenga getting the three other wives who came after her. The multiple-wife tradition is quickly dying out, since the children are now attending school instead of working at home to help the husband support the family. Today it is typically too difficult for the husbands to support more than one wife and family.

Even beyond the Kenyan concept of family, perhaps most overwhelming are the first words that Kemunto told me through an interpreter when she saw me on December 31, 1995: "You are my resurrected late eldest son Rasugu!" Rasugu, her first son born around 1925, died in his teens around 1940. Another son, Nyakundi, and two other children also died young. In fact, Rasugu and Nyakundi actually died on the same day. This forced Mboga to take the place as the eldest son in the clan. My appearance in Kisii had given Kemunto a bridge to an emotional place where the empty space left by Rasugu could be filled.

My biological father, Mboga Mageka Omwenga, is part of the Kisii ethnic group from rural southwestern Kenya. The Kisii claim a man named Mogusii as their founder and derive their ethnic group name from him.

The Kisii first entered what is now western Kenya from what is now the modern Democratic Republic of the Congo. They eventually settled on the Kano Plains during the 1600s and 1700s. Besides raising cattle, they labored as farmers and hunters. The Kisii community later morphed from individual family units to more interdependent groups with clan leadership. Common language, culture, and external enemies kept them united.

Eventually, the Kisii migrated south. There they had frequent conflicts with the Luo and Kipsigis, and later the world-famous Maasai in the 1800s. The Kisii ultimately settled in a hilly area where the weather was cooler and the soil more fertile than the Kano Plains. Today, that fertile area is known as the Kisii Highlands.

"In about the 1890s the British and their guns conquered much of what ultimately became known as the Kenya colony. When the British and other Europeans colonized parts of Africa, they imposed their culture and language and took away our self-rule," Mboga related. "In fact, in our own ethnic group language, correctly called Ekegusii, there is no word 'Kisii.' This is a word coined by the British. The correct name for our people is the Abagusii, as Gusii is the name of our land.

"The British colonial administrators, who were deployed to oversee the conquered Kisii people, reduced everything pertaining to Kisii people to a single common denominator. The people, the language, and the land were all called Kisii. Similarly, the new colonial rulers derived the word "Kenya" from the Kikuyu words "Kiri" and "Nyaga." These words mean mountain and god, respectively. Therefore, "Kiri-Nyaga" means the mountain of god, because the Kikuyu community believed that their god resided atop Mount Kenya. The British gave this name to the entire country, which now consists of roughly thirty-two million people. About two million are Kisii.

"The crafts of basketry and pottery are still practiced by our rural people, including the famous Kisii soapstone carvings. Besides the soapstone, another famous export is the 'Kisii stool' which features colored beads in decorative patterns on the seat. In terms of industry, White colonial farmers set up tea and coffee plantations where Kisii people worked. As you drive toward our village, you see miles and miles of tea farms that still exist today," Mboga explained. "At that time, land was forcefully taken away from the Africans and given to the colonists. Schools were segregated, and women were not encouraged to go to school. Finally, Nairobi University was founded around 1970 to educate anyone who met its academic requirements.

"After I left Kisii to study in America, Kenya gained its independence in 1963," Mboga added. "Now, after independence, what we have in this country is not racism based on skin color, but economic apartheid."

There are many parallels in Kenya to other places. Specifically the situation in Kenya has been similar on many levels to the treatment of African-Americans in the United States, and the treatment of the Aboriginal people in Australia with overt racial segregation being replaced by economic disparities.

"In spite of the severe impact of colonialism on Kenya," Mboga said proudly, "we retained our indigenous names, traditions, languages, and customs. Hence the culture and history remained intact. In spite of the imposed government, customs, and Christian religion, the hearts and minds of people native to Kenya were not colonized. Many people, however, had strange 'White-Christian' names prefixed before their indigenous names. But I, for one, rejected to be called by a White-Christian name. In fact, my second son, Rasugu Machoka Omwenga, has no such foreign name. But his mother insisted that her two daughters should be given so-called Christian names, Margaret and Christine."

I found out that my deceased grandfather, Omwenga Ayiera, had only one blood brother. He was called Onuong'a Ayiera, and he died in 1978. My grandfather also had four sisters. Their names were Mabera, Bosibori, Gechemba, and Nzomu.

Omwenga Ayiera also had more than a dozen stepbrothers. They shared the same father but had seven different mothers, including Nyamenia, Nyaboga, Oseko, and Magoma.

My great-grandfather's name was Ayiera Ogeto. He had a total of seven wives. One of the wives, my great-grandmother Kwamboka, was the mother of Omwenga. My younger sister Margaret proudly wears Kwamboka as her middle name.

Kwamboka was a good mother and homemaker. Her husband Ayiera Ogeto, a king and owner of livestock and farmland, was the son of Ogeto. Ogeto was the son of Isekerario and a powerful king before the advent of British rule. Ogeto ruled about half the population of Kisiiland. He was fair and sympathetic to the downtrodden. Aiyera and Ogeto were both kings, *mfalume* in Kiswahili and *eruoti* in the Kisii lanugage. During the precolonial era, each Kenyan ethnic community was ruled by its indigenous king. The title of "chief" was created by the British. Isekerario was the son of Tibichi. I am extremely fortunate to have knowledge of my African heritage, going back six generations before me.

Mboga continued. "Omwenga had a nice family life with his four wives. Kemunto, the first wife of Omwenga, was quiet and reserved during her younger years, as was Kerubo, the second wife. Bonareri was the most social of Omwenga's wives. She was efficient at running various errands. Moraa was the fourth and final wife and she bore the last of Omwenga's twenty-eight children. Thomas, can you imagine having that many brothers and sisters? Omwenga loved all of his wives and they all cooked for him.

"Omwenga was known for his good sense of humor," Mboga continued. "But my father was also strict, though he did not need physical discipline to influence his children. My father's word was enough. He had the most foresight among his kin, and also championed people who were abused or oppressed by those in power."

On another occasion, I caught up with Mboga's older cousin, John Mageka Mboga Nyaboga, now living in the United States. "Omwenga, my uncle, was a good man," John declared. "He was a leader of his area, appointed in the role of assistant 'chief' in the colonial regime. My mother and Omwenga's first wife Kemunto were 'agemates.' This means they were friends and about the same age. They were both married around 1920 at a place called Sensi when they were approximately twenty years old. My Aunt Kemunto was always involved in my life. Kemunto was sweet, polite, sympathetic, and generous.

"My Uncle Omwenga was able to keep the four wives happy. He was a good person," said John. "He knew how to manage four wives and his children. On his farm, he planted a lot of tea, coffee, maize, and sorghum, which enabled him to get money that he used to educate his children. He also had a couple of hundred cows, sheep, and goats."

John continued in slightly broken English. "Every morning after awakening, as assistant chief, Omwenga walked around the expansive area, admonishing every child, 'Go to school. Please go to school.' I remember, Omwenga came to my place around 1946, and told me and your father Mboga, 'Go to school.' Your father and I were together in first grade. We paid the equivalent of fifty cents. There were two sections, A and B. Mboga was in section B. I was in section A.

"I remember," related John. "Your father Mboga, he came to me and said, 'Please, come to the class with me, which is a better class.' So I switched sections."

"Did Omwenga remain involved in your education?" I asked.

"Yes," answered John. "At first, every evening Omwenga would come to us and say, 'Show me your work, from school, from those teachers.' But we could not, because it was on the slates that we left at the headmaster's house. It was erased every day.

"One day when we were about eleven years old, Omwenga went to the school and asked the teacher whether we were going to school. The teacher told him that Mboga and I did attend school, and that we did our work, and that we were obedient. With that, Omwenga was satisfied.

"Over the years, Omwenga continued to go around the whole area, saying, 'Go to school. Nothing good will become of you if you just stay here,'" John added.

"How did Omwenga know that education was so important?" I inquired.

"Because he was working as an assistant chief," John reasoned. "This was part of his responsibility, in general. But beyond that, Omwenga treated me like a son. I was with my first cousin Mboga almost all of the time. Mboga's father Omwenga and my father, Nyaboga, were both sons of Ayiera Ogeto. In Kisii culture, Mboga and I were considered brothers. Mboga and I would sleep in one bed, using only one blanket. We shared clothes. When we ate, we even shared the same plate. Together, we had our own special way of doing things. At 4 A.M. we would get up together to do work in the garden. We walked about five miles to school together, without shoes. We came home together and looked after the cows together. We shared everything, even as we grew older. We were best friends."

Mboga eventually went on to the Government African School, now called Kisii High School, which was the only colonial government supported public high school in the densely populated Nyanza province of southwestern Kenya. Since slots were limited, only the brightest students in the area could attend the high school. This made the Kisii High School of that era more prestigious than any local university in Kenya today. Even John, who excelled in school, was not able to go. John ended up at Kabianga Teachers Training College, where he trained as a primary school teacher.

Mboga then advised his cousin John to marry, and he helped John find his eventual wife in 1960. John quickly married, and one of his ten children is Monica Nyamwange, my cousin. Monica later earned her Ph.D. from Rutgers University, and I now visit her occasionally at her home in New Jersey.

Of the approximately four hundred students at Kisii High School in four grades, Mboga was one of the top students. After graduating from Kisii High School he worked as a teacher from February 1960 to July 1961. In early 1961, he applied for and won a scholarship sponsored by a United Nations agency to attend a university in the United States. During that time Kenya was on the verge of gaining independence from Great Britain. The United Nations wanted to make sure that some Kenyans had a western education and that the Kenyans would bring their expertise back to their native country.

Before his journey to the United States, Mboga's village helped raise money to help with his miscellaneous expenses. His cousin John also helped to support Mboga's three sisters and mother while Mboga was away from Kenya. For this, Mboga remains extremely grateful to John.

Fortified by the love of his clan, Mboga departed Kenya for the first time. Arriving in the United States in September 1961, he attended a historically Black college in Baltimore, Maryland, then known as Morgan State College, which is now Morgan State University.

Mboga's undergraduate years occurred at the height of the African-American civil rights struggle and the Cold War between the United States and the Communist bloc led by the Soviet Union. Since most of the African states had regained their independence after 1957, Mboga believed that African students were somewhat purposely shielded by the American government from open, direct racism. Mboga believed the U.S. government feared that the then patriotic home governments of these African students would be wooed to join the Communist bloc if there was evidence that their students were being discriminated against in the United States. Nonetheless, Mboga encountered raw American racism from several White men in the surrounding Baltimore community.

"After I received an admissions letter to Morgan State," Mboga recalls, "I applied for a full scholarship from the United Nations Agency for International Education. They acceded to my request, but the verbal pact was that the scholarship would only pay for my undergraduate studies that normally lasted four years. Upon graduation, I was expected to return to my country and fully participate in the so-called "nation building.""

"It took me approximately four years to graduate with a bachelor's degree in economics from Morgan State. I also wanted to enter graduate school to pursue a master's degree in political science. After a protracted correspondence, the UN agency agreed to offer me a partial scholarship to cover my books and upkeep. Fortunately, Penn State University admitted me as a postgraduate on a part-time basis. This meant that I had to work as a part-time graduate assistant performing research for the political science department in order to have my tuition waived. I worked as a graduate assistant. During my second semester at Penn State, I enrolled in a political science course devoted to tenets and techniques of foreign policy. A brilliant professor and talented researcher taught the course. However, this teacher had a weird fixation at using the most scathing, derogatory language to lampoon Africans in particular and the Black race in general. We exchanged bitter words. It was my only problem with race at this nearly all-White school. Fewer than three percent of the students were Black."

"Your Penn State professor sounds like one of my middle school history teachers," I joked. "Hearing of your experience is interesting. My friends at rural Penn State also encountered problems with racism in the late 1980s."

Mboga actually had more problems with the Black Americans than the White Americans, especially while he was at predominately Black

Morgan State. The students, and even the Black professors, would ask him questions that displayed their ignorance concerning "Mother Africa." This led Mboga to believe that the enslavement of Africans, effectively perpetuated through the 1960s by so-called White Christians, was the epitome of man's inhumanity to man. He believes that Black Americans have historically been the systematic victims of bigotry, lies, and oppression, but he has noted that the situation has improved since he left the United States.

These experiences set the stage for Mboga to meet Dorothy in 1966. Mboga had been invited by a student group to give a speech about the structure and function of the United Nations. It was there that he met my biological mother. They dated only briefly, but I was conceived and born that same year. At that time, Mboga found Dorothy to be a "highly intelligent and determined girl."

Armed with his bachelor's in economics from Morgan State and his master's degree in political science from Penn State University, Mboga returned to Kenya on February 16, 1968. He had briefly worked for a bank in Philadelphia after leaving Penn State, just before returning to Kenya. Most of Mboga's family were surprised when he suddenly returned to Nairobi one morning with just his three suitcases and a trunk containing his books.

Once the news spread of his return, the whole Mwogeto clan rejoiced. The atmosphere was electric at our Nyakongo village. Women ululated. The men whistled and sang, thanking God and our ancestors for his safe return.

By virtue of his studies and inclination, Mboga's ambition upon arrival in Kenya in 1968 was to join Kenya's Foreign Service as a diplomat. However, because of the rampant tribalism and nepotism, the ruling elite of Kenya denied the young Kisii the opportunity. A single political party had been in complete control of this beautiful, peace-loving country since Kenya gained its independence in 1963. Top jobs in administration, banks, and diplomatic service were almost exclusively reserved for the members of a single ethnic group.

Mboga was flabbergasted. Far less qualified, less educated men were placed in the choice positions. His only alternative was to join Kenya's monstrous civil service and work for the Kenya National Trading Corporation in Nairobi. Later, Mboga managed the western branch in the area of imports and distribution. Although this was an important job in Kenya, Mboga was frustrated that one ethnic group monopolized control over nearly all other key jobs.

Kenyan tribalism and nepotism affected, and still affects, all key political, administrative, financial, and economic institutions. Disillusioned by what he perceived to be a ruling gang of looters, Mboga decided to resign from his job and enter politics in 1974. He ran for Member of National Parliament, or MP, against an incumbent. He did this in spite of the fact that he was relatively young, about thirty-four, for a

Mboga Mageka Omwenga as a young man.

Kenyan politician at that time. His move put him directly on a collision course with the ruling oligarchy. The goal of opposition groups like his has been to use the constitutional process to wrest power from the monolithic one-party political system, to eradicate the atavistic autocracy and corruption in Kenya's multiracial society. Mboga was defeated in the election. The main problem, as he sees it, was not his campaign platform or his charisma, but the corrupt one-party system and tribalism he opposed. He was also one hundred percent honest with the electorate. As his son, I am uplifted just knowing that he ran for office and tried to make a difference. I am fortunate to have found him and to have the opportunity to get to know him.

In the subsequent years, Mboga paid a heavy price for standing up for his political principles, and for criticizing the government. At one point, he narrowly escaped being jailed after being framed with fictitious political crimes. By 1994, the system had hounded him until he lost all of the material wealth he had earned. Choice jobs for which he would be qualified, based on his skills and education, were denied him. Access to entrepreneurial capital has been elusive. His life would likely have been far easier had he returned to the United States after he was defeated at the polls in October 1974. These days, my father is stoic. His greatest wish is that none of his children will ever have to endure such hardships.

I am very proud of my father's perseverance, courage, and high moral character. And thanks to him, I not only have a piece of African land but a link to my African heritage.

CHAPTER FOURTEEN

Enriching Relationships

After reaffirming that the concept of family was important to me, I asked myself, "What do we do now?" Instead of having just the one great family in Pittsburgh I grew up with, I was blessed with a wealth of family. I had a total of three outstanding families in various locations around the world. I considered the possibilities of how I could develop and enrich these abundant relationships, and how those same relationships might expand my horizons.

When an adopted person makes a journey in search of his heritage, typically there is an initial euphoria upon finding the biological parents. Then what is the adopted person supposed to do? At that point, the relationship may take many possible directions. For example, there may be no ongoing relationship; one may just want to satisfy his or her curiosity and then move on. Or, the relationship may be low-key, with sporadic letters and maybe a phone call on a holiday such as Mother's Day. Another possibility is deepening involvement, which was clearly the path I chose with my respective families. However, this path has been wrought with some challenges. Time, distance, and financial resources have been a factor in the relationships. I also had to think about how to address my adoptive family and my friends who were already significant in my life before the reunions with Dorothy and Mboga. Many adopted people set out on their searches without at least thinking about these issues in advance. This can be a big mistake.

After my December 31, 1995, euphoric welcome in Kisii and my initial meeting with my grandmother Kemunto, my "mission was accomplished," at least my initial mission. I had found Mboga, and met him and his children. I had also traveled to my Kenyan family's original village and met my grandmother. I had previously found Dorothy and started building a relationship with her and her other children. This was all far more than I had ever expected. I had closure. I was happy. The additional opportunity, which started when I met Dorothy in 1992, was to build these family relationships and to find a "norm" in terms of how I would interact with each family. I knew that this could take years.

Of course, as with the members of my adoptive family, who I had known my whole life, I could not treat everyone in the new families equally. Relationships are two-way, and require two people exerting effort for them to grow. My relationships with both of my new families have been great, in general. However, I have experienced some challenges with a few people in both of my biological families. Also, finding my biological families has had an effect on my relationship with my adoptive family. In short, new relationships take time. I have found that it took a few years of living through normal—and not so normal—life events, birthdays, Mother's Days, and other holidays before things reached a state of normalcy.

My mother, Joan, eventually struggled a bit with all of the activity surrounding my reunions with my biological parents. This is understandable. Although she was initially supportive in 1992 when I started my quest, Joan grew uncomfortable—maybe even threatened—by 1994, after I made a couple of trips to London to see Dorothy. Joan, born in 1937, with values developed in the conservative 1950s, had always been admittedly somewhat old-fashioned. Joan was raised to be a homemaker, to support the needs of her husband and children. Since she was divorced and had only one child, in many ways I was all she had on this earth. Joan had dedicated her life to raising me, and I am extremely thankful for that.

After I found Dorothy, Joan started to feel that her mother-son relationship with me was threatened. Joan was uncomfortable at first, and might have even been a bit jealous of the high-flying management consultant from London. Joan believed that I might have more in common with Dorothy, and therefore I might not need to spend much time with her, even though she raised me. Dorothy, the baby boomer who went to college in the 1960s, was initially anxious to contact, call, write, and meet Joan. Dorothy wanted to thank Joan for taking care of me when she couldn't. I prevented any interaction, even letters, between Dorothy and Joan up until late 1996. It took a significant amount of time for me to reassure Joan that I still loved her, that she was and always would be my real mother, and that the relationship we always had would not change because I had found Dorothy. Around the end of 1996, I finally began to feel comfortable about facilitating address exchange and letters between Joan and Dorothy. Normally an unintentionally insensitive Sagittarian by nature, I tried to be considerate of Joan's feelings in this matter.

Some of the other members of the Lowry family were affected as well. Most of my cousins did not even know I was adopted until I made contact with my biological parents. The adoption issue had almost never come up. Afterward, one of my cousins was sad, feeling "that Tommie was ours, a Lowry first." Some cousins were concerned that I would reject and replace the Lowry family in my life. However, they soon realized that this quest to know my birth families was important to me and they remained supportive. Overall, the Lowry family continued to give me the same beautiful, unconditional love. I have been told that I still play the same important role in the Lowry family as before, partially because I was the first Lowry to graduate from college, and then also the first to get a master's degree. And I remained a mentor to my younger cousins, always chatting with them about education, drug avoidance, safe sex, and nonviolence.

Just because I then had two newly discovered families in Kenya and England did not mean I was not putting continual joyous investment of time and energy into relationships with my family back in Pittsburgh. And I was convinced that these efforts were noticed and appreciated. For example, my cousin Ricardo Lowry, known affectionately as Bums, asked me to be a groomsman in his wedding in 1997. We had rarely been in contact with each other in the decade leading up to Christmas Eve 1993. On that night, I partied with Bums and my other cousins, Carlos, Billy, and Michael, in the tough North View Heights neighborhood on Pittsburgh's North Side.

Bums and I subsequently became close, even though I only went to Pittsburgh about three times per year. The weekend of his wedding in 1997 was fun. The overall atmosphere for the wedding was really casual. Many guests wore shorts or sneakers to the reception. Everyone had a good time, especially me.

Later, we found out that Bums had an advanced case of multiple sclerosis. He was only twenty-eight years old when he received the diagnosis. At first, we all struggled with him, as we did not understand the condition or what to expect. I went to see him soon after the diagnosis. I also gave him a plane ticket to come to visit me during one of my house party weekends. The personal visit and the plane ticket seemed to mean a lot to him. The trip gave him something else to focus on besides the disease. In no time, he was coping well, along with his great wife and children. Our relationship as cousins grew closer every time I went home to Pittsburgh. His skills as a father have been a great example to me.

My relationship with my cousin Sonja continued to grow as well. She asked me to be the godfather of her second daughter. When Kyra was born in 1998, I immediately flew to Pittsburgh to meet my new goddaughter. I continually told the infant girl, "You are going to have a great life. The world is yours, kid; put it in your pocket. No one is going to mess with you. I love you." When she hugged me back, I perceived she knew that I would look out for her.

I also developed a closer relationship with another Lowry cousin, Christy Cosby, during the 1990s. Christy, a couple of years younger than I, was the second Lowry to graduate from college. Although she was mature and competent, I did try to mentor her when I felt I could be of assistance. However, the relationship was far from one-way. Christy had a great deal of education and experience in the areas of sociology and social work. She was able to provide me with insights on people and relationships that were not always obvious to a direct, blunt person such as me. I knew I could always count on her. Ironically, as older family members noticed our close relationship, they reminded us about how I pushed Christy down the steps when she was three years old and I was five. Neither of us remembers the childhood incident, but Christy's older sister Jackie remembers it vividly. After my misdeed, Christy's older brother Bobby picked me up by the neck and slammed me against the wall and told me to "never touch Christy again." Subconsciously, the incident must have left an impression of some type. I have definitely looked out for Christy over the years.

I know that in terms of my relationships with my family and friends, I have come a long way since that night back in 1993 when I cried in front of my ex-wife. Back then, I was distraught about how weak my ties were with some of my family and friends. After a few years of concerted two-way effort by myself and others, I have seen strong, tangible results.

Overall, my relationships with my English siblings were in good shape. Lotus, the daughter who grew up as the "oldest" in her immediate family is actually almost five years younger than me. She had known that Dorothy had given birth to a son who was given up for adoption since she was a teenager. My relationship with Lotus grew quickly because she had been conceptually aware of me as her "big brother" and had hoped to meet me one day.

To start our brother-sister interaction, Lotus wrote me a long letter in December 1992. Lotus then traveled to the United States in the summer of 1993 and we were able to spend some quality time together in both Houston and Los Angeles. While I was getting used to her "Geordie" accent, typical of northern England, we hung out on Venice Beach and in LA nightclubs and we really bonded. It was great.

Lotus and I also grew closer together during my annual trips to London, which began in 1993. Lotus also met Joan when they both came to visit me in Houston in October 1995. Lotus and Joan are both incredibly nice people, almost too nice sometimes, and I was not surprised that they got along well. During the same time frame, Lotus and I flew away for a few days in San Francisco and visited Dorothy's old Haight-Ashbury stomping grounds. Lotus then helped me host one of my Houston house parties for roughly 150 people, this time for Halloween. Growing close to Lotus was extremely easy because she is a sensitive and caring person. She seems to know what people need before they say it. She is a good judge of character. I really felt like I could rely on her as a sister and a confidante.

The relationship with my English brothers, Atom, Jade, and Derwent, grew more slowly. My English siblings, who have a White English father, all grew up in Newcastle in northern England, not far from Hadrian's Wall. My brothers were not told of my existence until after I made contact with Dorothy in 1992. When the boys first heard about me in August 1992, they were generally excited, surprised, and pleased. Derwent asked Dorothy, "Can I tell everyone about him?" "Of course," answered Dorothy. Sharing this information with her other sons was a big relief. It allowed Dorothy and Lotus to "relax" in the sense that they no longer had to keep a secret.

But knowledge of my existence was a big adjustment for my English brothers. I traveled to London for the first time in December 1993 a few days after Christmas to meet them. We had a good time together and the interaction was warm and easygoing. I was especially touched that the family "delayed Christmas" until I arrived on the 29th. We all exchanged presents, and then I immediately fell asleep on the floor because of exhaustion from jet lag.

We did a lot of interesting things in the subsequent days. We took a family picture on Abbey Road, just like the famous Beatles album cover. We visited London tourist sites, and hung out at the clubs and restaurants in Leicester Square and Covent Garden. We brought in 1994 at a massive "underground" New Year's party—a warehouse rave where we danced to the sounds of London-style Jungle/Drum 'N' Bass music.

In spite of that evening, I didn't feel that I completely bonded with my male siblings until they came to visit me individually in Houston. This gave each of them a chance to see me in my environment, and to

Dorothy with Derwent, Thomas, Lotus, Atom, and Jade in London. December 1993.

live my lifestyle for two weeks each. Specifically, they saw my home and my friends. They were able to live by my hectic "work hard/play hard/ work out hard" schedule. In short, they had to spend time "in my world."

Jade, who is almost ten years younger than I, first related his feelings in a letter in February 1993: "I had mixed feelings when Mum told me that I had another brother. I was shocked and pleased, and at the same time a bit worried because I didn't know how Mum was going to react. I have thought about it quite a lot and I am looking forward to meeting you one day. If we get on well together then that will be great because I like the idea of having another brother. I don't know your feelings about this, but I think they are the same as mine."

Jade flew to Houston to visit me in October 1994 while on his way to Vail, Colorado. He was planning to spend the winter in Vail as a "ski bum" of sorts. His plan was to get a job working in a ski shop and to share an apartment with other young workers who were there for the ski season. I admired his plan. Who couldn't have a great time while snowboarding four or five days per week? When then eighteen-year-old Jade arrived in Houston, I introduced him to an eighteen-year-old girl from India who was a friend of a girl I was dating. The young girl had spent some time living in London, so there was somewhat of a UK bond. It was good to spend time with him for a week, and especially fun to get him into clubs using his fake English ID card. In addition to being with me and seeing my friends and lifestyle, we rented movies that told various stories of the African-American experience. The movies, when supplemented with my college scrapbook and my storytelling were a convenient way to give Jade some insight into my life. I later used the same process with my other English siblings.

After talking with Jade, Atom, and Derwent previously in London about so-called "safer sex," I gave Jade a pamphlet on HIV and other sexually transmitted diseases. While spending time in London in 1993, I inferred that the English level of education on STDs, in general, was then significantly behind that of the United States. I had no specific reason to be concerned about my siblings; I was just trying to play the role of the wise, protective big brother.

Jade ended up doing the "ski bum" thing in Vail for the winters of 1995, 1996, and 1997. I went to visit him all three winters. On my first trip to Vail, my second time ever at a mountain resort, I did okay on skis. Jade then tried to turn me on to snowboarding. Jade is a superb snowboarder but maybe not a great snowboarding teacher. Or maybe he just had a poor pupil. Whatever the case, I couldn't make it down the mountain even one time while properly standing on the snowboard. Even worse, I somehow got separated from Jade during a run. Finally, I decided to sit on my snowboard and ride down on my butt. But snow blew up in my face, and I wrecked—and the board kept going downhill. My goggles were covered with snow. By the time I was able to stop sliding and remove my goggles, the board was gone. I looked for it for about an hour and never found it. I had to pay for it since it was rented. This was a major embarrassment. After that, I stuck to skiing only and subsequently became a skilled skier, and we always had a good time.

Since then, Jade went on to study professional broadcasting. Dorothy believed that my achievements were a good influence to help Jade jumpstart his career.

I noticed by July 1995 that my brother Derwent was more mature and personable than he was when we first met in December 1993. Even though Derwent was relatively young when we met, I immediately could see that he and I were the siblings who were most alike. Initially, he disagreed with me. Ultimately, he agreed wholeheartedly. Derwent, eleven years younger than I, first arrived "in my world" when he landed in Houston in October 1995. Enjoying a bit of the entertainment on Richmond Avenue with my friends, Derwent instantly fit right in. An experienced snooker player in England, seventeen-year-old Derwent destroyed my American friends on the pool table. He even went to visit an elementary school to talk to a fifth-grade class about his life and travels in Europe. Derwent was convinced that he would be a pop music star. I believed him.

Skin color aside, Derwent and I look like brothers. We are both thin and over six feet tall. We share the classic Sagittarian traits of openness and sometimes brutal honesty, as well as a desire to travel the world.

During my December 1994 trip to London, Atom took a day off from work to hang out with me. It was the first time we really spent time together one-on-one. We popped in and out of the shops on Oxford and Regent streets and then went to a number of record shops that sold the twelve-inch Jungle/Drum 'N' Bass records he used as a deejay. It was great to spend time in his world. He was about seven and a half years younger and really into music, but I tried to match his enthusiasm. Although my English siblings grew up in Newcastle, they all seemed to really love living in London.

In March 1996, when he was twenty-one, Atom flew from London to Houston to spend two weeks with me. A few hours later, I had him on another plane, accompanying me on a trip to Dallas. We had a good time, enjoying the Dallas club scene on that first night. We did more club-hopping after returning to Houston. On a separate occasion, Atom was a spectator at one of my basketball league games. He was definitely seeing my work hard/play hard/work out hard lifestyle. Like my other siblings, we bonded while watching African-American movies and looking at my scrapbooks. I was impressed when Atom landed a gig as a deejay one night at a club in Houston. Then I took him with me on a trip to San Francisco. Atom made similar connections on the Jungle/Drum 'N' Bass scene in the Bay Area. One night, I watched him deejay for more than an hour at a club in San Francisco. He was really good, and he definitely kept the crowd dancing, including me.

After three days in the Bay Area, Atom and I were set to fly from San Francisco to Vail to visit Jade. However, we were too tired from the previous night and we missed our flight. Unable at that point to use our airplane tickets to get to Vail, we decided to drive. The long trip started out well. We stopped in Reno, Nevada, to take pictures and to gamble for a half-hour or so. I won sixty dollars playing roulette. Later in the day, however, Atom was pulled over for speeding, even though the speed limit in this desert area was eighty miles per hour. The police were difficult. They suspected Atom wouldn't pay the steep ticket later since he was from England, so they pressured him to produce money on the spot. Atom had no money on him to pay the fine. The police finally let us go after giving Atom a ticket. We later stopped in Salt Lake City and went to the Mormon Temple for a quick photo opportunity.

From then on, the drive was no fun. At 2:30 A.M. Atom was asleep, and I was driving on a dark, narrow, winding, mountain road known as U.S. Route 6. I guess no one saw fit to put an interstate highway through that part of Utah. We made it safely, but we were exhausted when we finally arrived in Vail at sunrise after more than eleven hundred miles and twenty hours of almost continuous driving. I was able to bond with my younger brother Atom during the drive, and Jade was glad to see us. We all skied together during the day and partied all evening. It was a great adventure.

By late 1996 Dorothy grew tired of the London pollution and climate and decided to move to a beautiful area just north of San Francisco. This allowed me to see her more, and the interaction fueled the continued growth of our relationship. Often I was able to schedule business trips to catch my siblings during their trips to California. Shortly after Christmas 1996, I visited with Derwent and Dorothy in California. Although he was considering attending music school, he was clear that his ultimate goal was to be a pop star. I was struck by his conviction. I jokingly asked him if I could be in his entourage once he became famous.

While in California in 1996, I asked during dinner, "Dorothy, it has been years since our reunion. Are you still glad I found you?"

"I am, Thomas, for many reasons. For example, in each dating relationship that I had with men since you were born, I found myself looking to somehow replace what I lost when I gave you up for adoption."

"Oh. I didn't mean to ask a serious question. I was just playing around."

"Well, I am being serious. Looking to somehow replace you using men I dated was, in retrospect, extremely unfair to my partners. Now I have been 'freed' because you found me. And now I have a strong romantic relationship with Paul Herder that began in 1995. I don't think I was truly ready for a strong dating relationship until after my relationship with you, Thomas, had grown solid. Of course, by 1995, this was the case. Before then, I was emotionally crippled and probably unable to have truly successful romantic relationships." Dorothy and Paul have since married, after dating for many happy years.

In addition to my English siblings, another member of Dorothy's family reached out to me. My cousin Vonnie Blazier wrote me a long letter in January 1993, only four months after I first met Dorothy in Houston. Vonnie was the firstborn child of Dorothy's brother Bobby and previously the oldest Blazier grandchild. I "took her place" as the eldest grandchild, but she did not seem to mind at all. At the time, Vonnie was adjusting to the loss of her grandfather and the sickness of her grandmother on her mother's side. She told me that my "presence in the family somehow made it feel better." Vonnie was vaguely aware of my existence years earlier because of some eavesdropping on a conversation between her father and Grandma Maryan. She, like Lotus, had imagined finding me someday. Vonnie graduated at the top of her high school class, scored exceptionally well on her SATs, and had a talent for foreign languages. I was impressed and glad to see the strong intellectual genes in the family.

She was also the owner of an African-American art gallery in Indianapolis, Indiana. This surprised me because she is White, but pleased me as well. She also fancies herself as somewhat of an artist. Through her gallery, she sponsored positive programs in the Black community. Her interest in African-American art and culture was accelerated by the fact that she had lived in Mogadishu, Somalia, in 1980 and 1981. Her father was in the military at the time, and she was following him around the world. This must have been a great experience for a teenager. Our relationship has grown during the late 1990s, and I had the opportunity to meet her siblings and her mother as well. Vonnie and her sister Beth took me to my first Indianapolis 500 auto race in May 1999, and they were waiting on the ground for me when I completed my first skydive that very same weekend.

My great-uncle Bill Blazier, brother of my grandfather George, also reached out to welcome me into his family. I was touched when he included a photo of me in a 1994 Blazier family calendar he created. Lately, I have been an occasional visitor to my octogenarian mentor and great-uncle, who lives in Arizona with his wife Rose.

My relationships with family members in Kenya, after a quick start, had hit a plateau. Lack of communications technology in Kenya, such as telephones and email, was the only reason. After I met my grandmother Kemunto in the Kisii village in December 1995, I returned to Nairobi for a few days before heading home. I subsequently received requests to assist my sister Margaret Kwamboka with her tuition at Kenya Polytechnic and with attendance at a university in the United States. To me, however, attending school abroad was not just a financial challenge. I believed that there were a lot of other hurdles to cross, like getting an acceptable score on the TOEFL (Test of English as a Foreign Language), applying to a university, and getting accepted. I knew that some of these hurdles required money, and I told Margaret that I would help her at each step, to the extent that she showed initiative. I saw no reason to give her money for tuition, even if I had it, when she had not yet completed the aforementioned steps. To facilitate the application process I sent Margaret a large book in 1995 that included all of the information that international students needed to get acceptance and financing at U.S. universities. I hoped Margaret would decide to take the necessary steps, and I was prepared to help.

Although I am way past it now, discussing money and priorities with my family members who lived in Kenya was sometimes tough for me back then mainly because of cultural differences. In my travels, I have noticed that some people in developing countries perceive that all Americans are rich. However, those views may change after worldwide dissemination of video news clips of the human impact of Hurricane Katrina's destruction upon the city of New Orleans in 2005. Even with the United States' huge gross national product, roughly one in four hundred Americans is homeless and some forty-five million have no health insurance. Since these facts have not been as publicized in the mainstream media around the world as our ubiquitous movies and flashy music videos, it is not surprising that others have misconceptions about the wealth of typical Americans.

Perhaps viewing me as a "rich American," my loving Kenyan family may have sometimes expected me to have money to give as gifts or loans. Few people in the west have unlimited money, especially a middle class guy like me, which makes it challenging. Thus, priorities have to be set, which is difficult because different people have different needs. Of course, this dynamic is not uniquely African. It happens in the United States all of the time. It happens within White families. It happens with people who are adopted and with people who are not adopted. However, the dynamic can get especially tricky when you are dealing with cultural differences, a newly reunited family, and money issues all at the same time. The keys to working through it are mutual love and trust, clear open communications, and the setting of priorities.

To find and build initial relationships with my Kenyan family, I traveled to Kenya three times in a twelve-month period. This joyful odyssey, about which I have no regrets, caused me to incur a great deal of credit card debt in the same year in which I bought my first house. I subsequently sent Margaret four hundred dollars to pay the balance of her tuition at Kenya Polytechnic in February 1996. The money order was apparently lost. Margaret told me that she never received the money order, which I found frustrating. I decided right then never to send any significant amount of money or large money orders in the mail to Kenya again. I was told that mail in the Kenyan postal system was sometimes lost because of employee corruption. Since then, I have successfully used money transfer services to send cash reliably.

I have been presented with opportunities to help a few relatives in Kenya with money or loans, or to consider being a dealer of goods that they might want to export into the United States, or to be a partner in their businesses. Of course, I had to first and foremost make sure I could provide Joan with whatever time and economic assistance she needed. Joan was, and continues to be, my priority.

My Kenyan family members are very intelligent and extremely hardworking. They had been supporting themselves long before I arrived on the scene. They lack only the opportunities provided by a strong economy like that of the United States.

Among my Kenyan relatives, I decided for the foreseeable future to focus my very limited resources on my father Mboga, along with siblings Margaret Kwamboka, Christine Bahati, and Machoka Rasugu. Of course, my father Mboga has made it clear that he would never ask me to give him any money. He says, "It is either a loan that I will repay or it is nothing." I understood and respected his position. My mentality, which I came to embrace long before I met my Kenyan and European families, was to try to be neither a borrower nor a lender of money when it came to family and friends. If I gave something to a friend or family member, I made sure that it was an amount that would not cause me resentment if it was not repaid. Although loan repayment is always nice when it happens, I view personal loans to family and friends essentially as gifts. Personal loans to family members are much different than business loans, where payments are on a set schedule, borrowers have their credit reports checked, interest is charged, and a lender can take such actions as repossessing collateral. It does not matter to me whether a friend or family member calls it a "loan" or a "gift." If I get the money back from friends and family, I treat it as a bonus.

I hoped to also provide a positive influence for my siblings, especially Margaret. I dreamed that the stories of my struggles would provide her with inspiration to overcome her own challenges. Although I was far from perfect, I wanted to be a positive role model for her. I believed that meeting me has facilitated positive self-evaluation for Margaret. I reinforced the principles of self-confidence and determination in Margaret, qualities she already had.

Although Christine Bahati and Machoka Rasugu affectionately viewed me as a White *mzungu* man, they still looked up to me and always seemed to look forward to my next visit. They seemed more enthusiastic about studying English so they could communicate with me, the American who knows no Kiswahili. Machoka often bragged to the other children about his "big brother from the United States who flies on airplanes to come to see him." Christine seemed equally enthusiastic about my involvement in her life.

Of course, there were also Kenyan family members living in the United States. I spent the 1996 Thanksgiving holiday with my Kenyan cousins in Dallas. I had dinner with Silas Omwenga Momanyi and Raymond Momanyi. It was good to spend a holiday with members of my new Kenyan family. The gathering was definitely worth the short flight from Houston. I enjoyed it so much that I repeated the tradition the following year for Thanksgiving.

The year 1997 was one of exciting transitions for me. After traveling with fraternity brother Jon Gee to Rio de Janeiro, Brazil, for *Carnaval*, I threw my Houston "goodbye party." A career move took me to Dallas. I was fully settled by June, when I threw my Dallas "housewarming party." Between these two parties, I was a groomsman in three weddings, played on a championship team in a basketball league, and visited Jade in Vail. I timed my 1997 visit to Jade in Vail to coincide with the Black Ski Summit. The folks who attend these trips really know how to ski hard and party hard. It was an amazing experience to see thousands of Black people skiing, partying, and networking. Along with my fraternity, and the National Black MBA Association, I planned to make participation on the ski/party scene a permanent fixture in my life.

In the midst of all of these transitions, I planned my August 1997 trip to Kenya. What really helped was to finally have a relative in Kenya who was tapped into cyberspace. My cousin Denis Omwenga, Uncle Robert Nyamwaro's son, was helpful in terms of relaying my email messages to other family members across Kenya by phone, or through face-to-face discussions. My Kenyan family was impressed when I emailed them to tell them about my 1:59.48 effort, a lifetime best, for the 800-meter run in July 1997. Of course, this was still about eighteen seconds off the world record of a Kenyan-born runner, so I was by no means a professional.

I was really excited about the 1997 trip to Kenya; not only would I get to see my Kenyan family again, but this time two family members from the western world—Grandma Maryan and my sister Lotus—chose to accompany me. First, I planned to meet Grandma Maryan, still a resident of Pittsburgh, in London. I couldn't imagine going to Kenya without stopping through London. Not only was it convenient logistically, but I was able to see my English siblings as well. When I landed, I found that Dorothy, then living in California, had coincidentally just arrived in London on business. I also discovered that Derwent had just returned to London after a long trip to India. This was great—to have all of my English siblings, and my biological mother and grandmother together at one time. It had never happened before.

Lotus organized a great picnic for family and friends in a London park called Hampstead Heath. Later, I was able to see the final version of the short film, written and directed by Lotus, called *Ah Man of Me Dreams!* It is a film about a girl named Janet from Newcastle, England, in search of the ideal man. It was nice to see my name on the credits as "Executive Producer." I guess this is the title you get when you provide some money to help finance the film. I have told each of my younger siblings that I would do at least one major thing to help accelerate their careers. My goal when helping someone is always to provide an "enabler" so the person will, theoretically, not need assistance in the future. I also provided a used computer to facilitate Atom's sound engineering pursuits. As of 1997, younger siblings Jade and Derwent had not cashed in their enabler credit with me. Young siblings Christine and Machoka in Kenya had not cashed in their enabler credit with me, either.

During our time together in London, I again reminded Lotus and Grandma Maryan that traveling to Kenya was not a vacation but an adventure. Then, we took off for Nairobi. After flying all night, we landed in Kenya on Thursday, August 21, 1997. We were met at the airport by Uncle Henderson Magare, Uncle Robert Nyamwaro, Aunt Joyce, and their daughter Stella, a Kenya Airways employee. I was slightly surprised that Mboga was not there, and shocked to learn that no one had spoken to him at all. Although my father did not answer my previous letters about my impending arrival, I had hoped he would make plans to meet me in Nairobi at some point during my visit.

I gave a computer to Henderson Magare with the hope that he would get online access, allowing us to communicate easily via email. My uncle did not need a computer from me. I chose to give it to him because I perceived he could afford to pay an internet service provider for access to services such as email. I was looking to establish better communications, a slightly selfish motive on my part since I felt isolated from my Kenyan family.

On Friday, I was pleased to see my cousin Kefa. He said that he would do his best to help me locate my father Mboga. We did some tourist activities in Nairobi, and spent time with different members of my family. I was especially impressed with the Kenya National Museum and the 1.6 million-year-old fossils of a Homo Erectus boy. We also put in a number of calls to the coastal area in hopes of having someone locate my father. A number of people told me that they would work on this and make sure that I saw Mboga when I returned from safari.

Since we planned on going to the Kisii area to visit Kemunto in the Nyakongo village, it was explained to me that it would not be appropriate for me to visit without there being an appropriate celebratory feast, similar to my previous village visit. I had no problem with this conceptually, even though I don't normally eat red meat items like beef and goat. It was further explained, however, that I needed to finance the "village feast" since the villagers did not have the means to do it. Separate from this cash, I also had to pay, as one would expect, to facilitate transportation of our group to Kisii and back to Nairobi. Additionally, I was now expecting to spend money to facilitate my travel to the coast to see my father. These costs were on top of the cost of airfare and hotels. I was simply running out of money and not anxious to hear any new unbudgeted requests. I felt a bit confused with how the financing of the "village feast" was being handled, but my focus for the Nyakongo visit remained simply to see Kemunto again.

On Sunday I was able to spend a lot of quality time with my Kenyan siblings, including the then-eleven-year-old Christine Bahati and five-year-old Machoka Rasugu. Their English was not very good at that time, but it was much better than my Kiswahili. I hoped, however, that they would work on their English before my next trip. It was normal in Kenya to learn Kiswahili first, and then English later; almost everyone in Nairobi spoke respectable English. If I'd had a wife to help raise him, I would have been interested in discussing the concept of having young Machoka live with me in the United States. This would conceivably give him a strong education and access to a lot of opportunity. Of course, I had no idea how Jane Bosibori and Mboga felt about this idea.

Later that day, I also gave my cousin Denis a personal computer repair book to help him in his career and to thank him for relaying emails to facilitate communications with other family members in Kenya.

I was pleased but not surprised at how well Maryan and Lotus were accepted by my Kenyan family. All of my cousins embraced Lotus as their cousin as well. My Kenyan sister Margaret accepts Lotus as her sister. They are close in age and get along well. My Kenyan family showed love to Maryan, and everyone called her Grandmother. No one that we interacted with in my Kenyan family had an issue with them being White, or with me being multiracial.

We departed Monday for two full days of safari game drives in the Maasai Mara area of Kenya and the Serengeti area of Tanzania. At this time of year, there were hundreds of thousands of wildebeest in the Mara. This attracted a lot of predators. We saw about twenty-five lions, many of them cubs, on our first game drive alone. We took five game drives, seeing every animal possible except cheetah and leopard. Taking the proper nighttime precautions, I was beginning to feel more comfortable with the mosquito and malaria threat. However, my face broke out from the mosquito repellant that I rubbed on it.

Returning to Nairobi, I hoped to hear a credible plan from somebody to intersect with Mboga. Amazingly, no one had any plan, and no one had made any direct contact with Mboga. I was frustrated. I was in Kenya and did not have a plan to see my father. I decided if I wanted to see Mboga, I would have to go to the coast and locate him myself. We all agreed that I would do this Thursday morning, along with Kefa, Uncle Robert Nyamwaro, and Margaret.

Leaving Grandma and Lotus behind, we left Nairobi in darkness at 4:30 A.M. that Thursday. After stopping for tea in a quaint little town called Voi, we eventually arrived in Wundanyi in the Wesu District around 9:15 A.M. I met my Uncle Frederick Monyoncho. Uncle Monyoncho is Mboga's brother and Kemunto's youngest son. The engaging and funny Uncle Monyoncho was the head adminstrator of the Wesu District Hospital. One of his daughters happened to be sick with malaria. Malaria seemed to just be part of the way of life in Eastern Africa. I was told that malaria doesn't usually kill you; you often just feel like you are going to die.

Uncle Monyoncho gave us some pointers on how to locate my father. Mboga was living nearby in a town called Mgambonyi. After asking around, Robert Nyamwaro found some employees of Mboga's timber business. We had missed Mboga by only fifteen minutes.

I was concerned that he had headed out to work and might not return that day. I had no way of knowing his schedule, or knowing if he knew I was in the country since he had not responded to my recent letters.

Discouraged while waiting an hour at Mgambonyi, I started writing a letter to Mboga. My plan was to leave it with Uncle Monyoncho. I took a break from writing to ride back to Uncle Monyoncho's house. When we arrived at Uncle Monyoncho's at 12:30 P.M., Mboga was there waiting for us. In spite of the frustration I had felt earlier, I was happy and relieved to see my father. It would not have been acceptable to leave Kenya without seeing him.

After catching up on the latest happenings in our lives, we discussed prioritizing requests I received from my Kenyan family for financial assistance. It was a positive and constructive conversation. Margaret would continue her work at Kenya Polytechnic on her diploma—the equivalent of an American associate degree—in graphic design and communication until August 1999. In the meantime, she would take initiative on what I perceived as the long process of taking standardized tests and securing admission to a university in the Western world. If Margaret showed initiative at each step, I would help her financially as much as I could. I had already given her books on the admissions process, financial aid, and American universities. She had to take responsibility and make it happen. I guessed she would when the time was right for her.

My first priority after returning to the United States would be getting a computer for Margaret to help with her graphic design work. Finding the computer would take considerable time and money on my end. I'd have to find a good deal to meet her specific user needs as a graphic designer, but I would do my best. During the trip, and in subsequent years, I spent a lot of time communicating with Margaret. I gave her a lot of advice and encouragement related to education, career goals, dating relationships, and life balance.

I encouraged Mboga to pursue his ambition and write a book, possibly semi-fictional, about politics in Kenya. His experiences bucking a one-party Third World political system gave him quite a story to tell. I was willing to help Mboga pitch query letters to publishers.

It was good to see Mboga. I was optimistic he could meet me that subsequent Saturday in Nairobi. I was also pleased to meet Uncle

Monyoncho's wife, Florence, and children, Esther Nzighe, George Nyakundi, Millicent Bosibori, and Norman Rasugu. Norman Rasugu has a large birthmark on his neck that is just like the one on my cheek. He is now special in my eyes, just like I was to my Aunt Cookie, the sister-in-law of my mother Joan, in my childhood, partly because of our similar birthmarks.

Friday morning came too quickly. Kefa and I were both exhausted when we left Nairobi at 5:30 A.M. to head west toward Kisii. Of course, this time Grandma Maryan and Lotus were with us. I was really excited about the meeting of my two biological grandmothers, one a White American and the other a Black African. It made me proud to know that I had descended from such strong women.

We stopped in Nakuru to get a gift for Kemunto. I bought her a colorful blanket to keep her warm. Kefa correctly suggested that I also get a blanket for the other two living grandmothers. I decided against it; I was nearly out of cash and way over budget for the trip already. I was also thinking about the money I had provided in advance for the "village feast."

The welcoming party at Nyakongo was not as big as it had been in December 1995, but it was a very warm reception of about fifty people. We took a lot of good pictures and video footage of my grandmothers Kemunto, Kerubo, and Moraa. In the decades to come, I am sure my descendants will cherish this documentation of their ancestors. We videotaped all of the dialogue between me, my three Kenyan grandmothers, and Maryan. I saw my piece of land again, which I was told was about three acres. It was made clear to me again by the elder family members that I was expected to build a house: "When the villagers see that house, they would be happy."

Kemunto and Maryan were able to meet and embrace each other. I was really impressed but not surprised with how well Maryan fit in with my Kenyan family in the village. It took Kemunto a while this time to remember who I was. Although she was sharp and alert when I visited the village in December 1995, she was old and sick and somewhat cantankerous during this August 1997 trip. Of course, you might be too if you were a hundred years old. Eventually however, she did remember me, her *mzungu* grandchild from the United States. When she figured out it was me, she was upset with the others in the village for not letting her know of my arrival. Of course, they probably told her, and she may have forgotten.

I was so proud and honored to know Kemunto. There were long periods where I just sat and admired her. Also, I wanted to ask her as many questions as possible so I could gain wisdom from her before she passed on. Through Kefa acting as translator, I fired a few questions at my sweet grandmother.

"Grandmother, how old are you?"

"I don't know."

"Do you know approximately?"

"There is no way of knowing"

When my uncle attempts to answer for her, Kemunto cuts him off, "You cannot know, you were not there."

"How old were you when you had your first child?" I asked.

"I don't know. In those days nobody kept track. Do you know your age?" Kemunto asked.

"Yes, I am now thirty years old, born in 1966," I replied.

Kemunto then comprehended that Maryan was my other grandmother. Kemunto embraced Maryan as her "sister" both figuratively and literally. Seeing them hug was a beautiful sight to me. Two sweet, beautiful grandmothers.

"Where is my son Mboga?" Kemunto was getting upset again.

"Tell her that I saw Mboga yesterday at the coast," I said.

Kefa smartly chose not to translate my answer to avoid upsetting my grandmother. The question was subsequently forgotten.

"Do you remember when Mboga went to America?" I asked.

"I cannot remember. I cannot talk about Mboga unless he is here."

I asked Mboga's brother Thomas Ayiera what it was like to grow up in Kemunto's and Omwenga's household. "Those were old days, not like today in Kenya," Thomas Ayiera began. "They just used to dig the farm and feed their mouth with what they got from the farm. They never used to buy anything from the shop. They just used to eat *ugali*, beans, sweet potatoes, and bananas, and they used to feed hand to mouth with what they could get from their mothers."

"Was Kemunto a strict mother?" I asked.

"Kemunto was a kind mother. Of all of the mothers in this village, she was the most kind."

"What kind of father was Omwenga?"

"He was a stubborn man."

"What did Omwenga do for a living?"

"He was a tax collector for the colonial regime and a farmer. He had a general retail shop at Manga Shopping Center, operated by one of his sons. He also had many cows, and that was the key business. Cows."

Since Kemunto was, understandably, old and tired, the other wives came to help speak on her behalf. Moraa, Omwenga's fourth wife, was particularly helpful.

"What was Mboga like when he was young?" I asked.

"Mboga was a very kind man. He didn't have many words to say," said Moraa.

"What were the good qualities of Omwenga?"

"He had a lot of cows, so he was relatively well suited to support a family. I was the fourth and final wife. African men can marry as many wives as they want, as long as they can support them and keep them. They could milk the cows and slaughter the cows."

"How old was my grandfather Omwenga when he died in 1964?"

"He was believed to be about sixty-six years old."

Kemunto wanted to know if I had any children. I answered, "No."

"Why not?"

"I am not married."

"Why? This is unacceptable. This is not acceptable."

Curious about what might have changed since the days of Omwenga and multiple wives, I asked Kemunto, "How many wives should I get?"

"Two."

"Why two?"

"Do you even think you can manage two?"

"Yes. *Hakuna matata.* No problem," I said.

"Looking at you, you can only manage one wife."

"Okay, Grandma, you are right."

"European style is one, so you should only get one."

"Okay, Grandma."

I asked her what it was like living with Omwenga in an environment with four wives. She became upset, "Why are you asking, you don't even have one wife yet!" Kemunto clearly believed that I should get married and have a great-grandchild for her.

Once again, Kemunto wanted to know if I had any children. I answered, "No."

"Why not?"

"I am not married."

"This is unacceptable. You are an old man. I can even see a white hair on your head!"

I laughed at my sweet grandmother's playful comments. At age thirty, I was just getting used to the idea of having one gray hair, and I was in no rush to have children. Most Kisii men at this age are married with many children. It was just a different cultural perspective.

When Kerubo arrived, she explained that the wives took care of each other like sisters, "Whoever cooks, cooks for the entire family. Whoever got firewood would get it for everyone. When one wife had a child, they all shared responsibility. When the wives were breastfeeding at the same time, any of them would grab a crying baby and just feed him. It didn't matter if it was your son, or the son of another wife. Milk was milk. We had no problems at all. Omwenga's father Ayiera Ogeto had seven wives, and things were the same way. Omwenga's mother Kwamboka was Ayiera Ogeto's second wife."

"What kind of man was Omwenga?" I asked.

"Omwenga was a stubborn man, and that made the wives love each other because they had to deal with him together."

"What were Omwenga's good qualities?"

"Intelligence, fairness. He was industrious and just."

Kemunto thanked me for the blanket, and then she became animated because I did not bring a blanket for the other wives, Kerubo and Moraa. How could I forget that these two women cared about me just as if I was a product of their own bloodline? The pressure of my tight cash flow had clearly gotten the best of me. This was an unfortunate mistake on my part since Kerubo and Moraa were the last people interested in getting my money, and I probably hurt their feelings.

I have since learned from my mistake, and the excellent writings of Deepak Chopra have helped. I try to always bring a gift of some type, even if it is a compliment, blessing, or prayer. I now strive to make sure my actions are motivated by love, allowing me to do less and achieve more. This helps me to resist defending my actions or my point of view, and leaves me more open to hearing the views of others.

I asked a number of people for additional insight into the life and personality of my grandfather Omwenga. Omwenga was a clan leader, was widely known in the Kisii district, and was well respected. As elder, he would arbitrate differences between individuals in the group. He was reputed to be talkative, just, and wise. One measure of how a man is viewed in Kenya is if new babies are named after him after the man is dead. The names of those who are wise and respected usually live on with young babies born shortly after their death. There were "many, many babies named after Omwenga" after his death in 1964. For example, Henderson Magare's son Steve also carries the middle name of Omwenga.

During my goodbye speech to everyone in the Nyakongo village, I left a small amount of money as a gift. With Kefa translating, I gave specific public instructions that the money be used for gifts for Kerubo and Moraa. I then made a public apology directly to Kerubo and Moraa for not bringing them a gift in the first place. On a related note, somehow my money for the "village feast" seemed to never have made it to the Nyakongo village. But, overall, it was a good visit to Nyakongo and I was so pleased to see my sweet grandmothers again. Returning from the village the same day, we arrived back in Nairobi around 10 P.M. on Friday. I was exhausted.

Overall, it had been an outstanding trip to Kenya. I had delivered a computer to Henderson Magare to facilitate email communication. We had done a safari trip. I was able to spend time with my Kenyan siblings and Lotus had also gotten to meet them. I had seen Mboga and Kemunto. Maryan and Kemunto were able to meet. All of my trip objectives were met. It had not really been a vacation. It had been a very happy adventure!

On Saturday, my last day in Kenya, we received gifts from Henderson's family. We enjoyed the now-traditional send-off dinner at Robert Nyamwaro's house before the late evening flight. Mboga made it to Nairobi to send us off, leaving me with a memorable speech and his public blessing.

Christine Bahati, Machoka Rasugu, Thomas, Margaret Kwamboka, and Mboga in Nairobi. August 1997.

CHAPTER FIFTEEN

Come Together

I n 1998, I was fortunate enough to continue leading what appeared by all accounts to be a charmed life. Early in the year, I won the Black Engineer of the Year Award in the Technical Sales and Marketing category through Career Communications Group, publishers of *U.S. Black Engineer & Information Technology* magazine. That same summer I was able to spend quality time in London with my siblings. In the fall I traveled to Tokyo, Beijing, and Hong Kong on my first Asian vacation, making friends at each stop. I was even able to briefly rendezvous with Grandma Maryan and my cousin Vonnie for about forty-eight hours in Beijing. We walked together on top of the Great Wall of China as a family. I have been to six continents, with only the continent of Antarctica left to explore—something I hope to do for my fortieth birthday.

In the summer of 1998, I visited Jamaica. The Jamaica trip came sixteen years after initially winning the vacation trip at halftime of the college basketball game back in 1982. The 1998 trip made up for that missed opportunity from my past. I hope I didn't bore my friends with the long version of the 1982 "Jamaica Deferred" story. Of course, we were all intoxicated from the Jamaican rum on the bus ride between Montego Bay and Negril when I told the story, so it was a friendly audience. My Jamaican vacation "ghost" was finally dead. The friends I traveled with loved my story and they seemed to appreciate that my past struggles have helped me to be a better person.

215

One of the members of the traveling party in Jamaica, Todd Hood, became a close friend during 1997 and 1998 while we both lived in Dallas. Todd taught me a great deal about being positive-minded, loving to others, and highly sociable. Whether, we were doing high-speed skiing in Sun Valley, Idaho, or diving headfirst off of cliffs in Jamaica, Todd personified the ideals of being an adventuresome thrill seeker, fun loving and indifferent to social norms. Todd, who is also an Alphaman, introduced me to a number of nice women as well. Inspired by the cliff-diving adventure with Todd in Jamaica, I have since done some skydiving. I also scuba dived at the Great Barrier Reef in Australia and swam alongside barracuda and other ocean predators.

In 1998 I addressed what was discussed during my face-to-face discussion with my father Mboga the year before; I purchased a computer for my sister Margaret to facilitate her graphic design pursuits. With some assistance from Jon Gee, I actually bought it in the Washington, D.C., area when I heard that Uncle Henderson Magare would be visiting there in May 1998. My uncle had traveled from Kenya to the United States to attend his daughter's graduation from Jersey City State College. After the graduation ceremony, he planned to travel south to Washington to see our nation's capital. When I heard of his schedule, I saw a great opportunity to help my sister Margaret. I flew to Washington, D.C., purchased the desktop computer and monitor, and met him so he could carry the equipment back to Kenya. I was very happy to help my sister and fulfill my promise to my father.

Another happy development in 1998 was that I finally put away the ghosts of my near miss at my high school district track championships. Back in 1984, I ran well, but had failed by three-tenths of a second to run the 4:28.9 time needed to qualify for the state championships in the one-mile run. In September 1998, at the age of thirty-one, after training since February, and surviving a car accident and summer flu, I ran a 4:28.61 mile for a lifetime personal best at a meet in Alexandria, Virginia. I finally, figuratively, qualified for the Pennsylvania State Track and Field Championships, just fourteen years too late. I also won the 1998 Eastern Region USA Track and Field Masters Championship for the one-mile run in the process. Earlier in the summer in Chicago, I ran a 4:08.7 for 1500 meters. With great coaching from Dr. Robert Vaughn from the Baylor Sports Medicine Center, I should have run even faster.

That same year, my career received a boost when I accepted a position as Marketing Director with a high-tech, Fortune 50 firm. I was happy to have the increased level of responsibility, and the new position took me from Dallas to another great location, Atlanta, where two of my best friends, Vaughn and Monica Frasier, lived. I hadn't been this excited about going to Atlanta since 1996 when Monica obtained Braves versus Yankees World Series tickets for us, located right behind home plate.

All in all, my work hard/play hard/work out hard lifestyle was going as planned, full speed ahead. Playing hard was especially easy with friends like CJ Bland in Atlanta. In addition to having a high-powered career, he provided strong leadership with the National Black MBA chapter in Atlanta, demonstrating his commitment to economic and intellectual development, and community service. We provided excellent peer counseling and advice for each other. We also cohosted some incredible house parties at our respective homes, attended by hundreds of people around Atlanta. He definitely knew how to play hard, and work hard as well.

In December 1998, armed with thirty-two years of life experience, I finally facilitated the first meeting of my adoptive mother and my biological mother. It had been more than six years since my reunion with Dorothy. I was glad I had taken things slowly, but now everyone agreed it was time for Joan and Dorothy to meet.

Dorothy and Joan met for Christmas Eve lunch at a Grandview Avenue restaurant overlooking Pittsburgh from high atop Mount Washington. It was symbolic. From the restaurant, we had a perfect view across the city of the North Side neighborhoods such as Manchester and Fineview where I grew up. Grandma Maryan, Paul Herder, and I were also there when my two mothers met.

After a period of light conversation, Dorothy said, "The adoption records were sealed. I asked to know how my child was doing after the adoption, but the agency would not share any information."

Joan said, "He was in good hands."

Dorothy said, "I knew that. I always believed that he was, but I just wanted to know. And I never wanted to interfere with your family. I just wanted to know."

Joan repeated her earlier comment, "He was in good hands." She added, "Through all of the struggle and sacrifice, he was always well loved by my extended family and me. My father was extremely proud of Thomas. Always bragging to the point of causing jealousy among

Joan, Thomas, and Dorothy high above downtown Pittsburgh. Christmas Eve 1998.

some of the other grandchildren, but that is the way my father was. He didn't mean to cause jealousy; he was so proud of Thomas. I just wish my mother had lived to have seen how Thomas turned out."

At my prompting, Joan retold the story of how she tried to give me a beating for roaming across the North Side when I was seven years old. However, she tried to leave out the small detail about the fact that she was swinging for my head, not my backside. I didn't let her get away with that omission. Maryan and Dorothy found the story hilarious, and a logical precursor to my behavior as an adult. Maryan declared, "Dorothy did pretty much the same thing to cause me to worry half to death. She left me a note that said, 'I runned [sic] away' when she was about six or seven. We were frantic while looking for her. We started calling everybody and finally I reached the mother of her friend. She had gotten on her bicycle and went to her girlfriend's house. We ultimately retrieved her there."

Thomas asked, "Did you give her a beating?"

"No, I never gave her physical discipline."

"Mom, too bad you didn't have the same philosophy," I said to Joan. "I was getting beatings all the time."

"Oh, he is telling a tale," Joan groaned, in denial of the truth.

"Whatever, Mom," I sighed playfully. "But I know you did it out of love."

"Do you remember those whippings?" Maryan asked.

"Yeah," I smiled.

"You must have been a bad child," Dorothy laughed.

Again I grimaced, and chortled, "Yeah!"

"Why were you so bad?" Dorothy interrogated playfully.

"It wasn't me, it was my environment. See those places over there on the North Side? It was a bad area for a child to grow up in back then." I mused that any excuse was better than admitting the truth that I was rebellious and testing the waters to see how far Joan would let me go before reeling me in. "Some parents fail miserably because they try to be friends with their kids instead of parents. Thankfully, my mom was not confused about her role."

"I taught him to stay out of trouble, to stay out of fights," Joan commented. "But sometimes older kids, young teens, would run him home crying when he was only four or five. I told him that if the kid was bigger that he needed to defend himself, but I didn't want him beating up on kids his age. Many times he would get picked on because of the color of his skin."

"Yeah, Mom, and these were Black people. People who had a problem with the extremely light skin that I had when I was growing up," I added for clarification.

"There is prejudice everywhere. It is a shame," Maryan noted. "My grandson Michael had a Black girlfriend and she was dark skinned. And she became pregnant with his baby. Michael was blonde, so there was a real contrast. So when the baby was born, Michael called me to give me the news of my new great-grandson. Someone said, 'What color is he?' And Michael said 'A perfect shade.' I agreed that it didn't matter because my great-grandson was perfect regardless of the color."

Dorothy wanted to know what I was like when I was an infant.

Joan said, "He was a good baby. He just didn't want to sleep. He wanted to stay awake all day, and then stay awake at night. I said to myself, 'Something's got to break here.' I would have to just leave him in the crib, and let him cry himself to sleep. He would scream his lungs out. Eventually, he would cry himself out and go to sleep."

Maryan said, "Then nothing has changed. When we met up with each other on vacation in Beijing recently, he was exhausted from a day of touring. Then he went out carousing until all hours of the night. He still doesn't want to go to sleep."

I responded, "Yeah. I am afraid that I might miss something."

"Tell me about Thomas' first step," asked Dorothy.

"First step?" Joan asked, a little startled. "At first he was so fat he could barely crawl. At six months, he was hitting about twenty pounds. He didn't lose the baby fat until he was almost four. He was walking at nine or ten months. He cut his teeth faster than any baby the doctor had ever seen. He wasn't about cutting one. He would cut two or three at a time. He soon had a full mouth of teeth and he didn't want that baby food, he wanted real food. And you had to shovel the food in his mouth because he ate it so fast. He crawled earlier than average and walked as soon as he could get his hands up on the coffee table to brace himself. He walked fast, on his toes. I was afraid that he would lose the teeth he had from his frequent falls. I just loved my home life, including raising Thomas. That's me. They call me old-fashioned, but that's all right."

"What were his first words?" Maryan asked.

"His first words were 'Da-Da.' I told him, 'No. No. You say Momma. Momma is the one that takes care of you.' We were at my mother's house that day," Joan continued. "I don't understand how people can have babies and leave their babies in the care of a nanny because of their lifestyle, because they both want to work. They often are living above their means. I don't think it is right. Who is going to be there for the baby's first step? Who is going to be there for the baby's first words? Unless it is an absolute financial necessity, the mother needs to be at home with that child. I adopted Thomas because I love children. I would have adopted more, but with Thomas, my hands were full. It was like having five kids. He could really move. He would be there one minute, and the next minute he would be gone. He would race away on those big, wide feet. I had to order him special baby shoes. But the adoption process was difficult back in the 1960s. The authorities were thorough. They wanted to know your life's history. The whole process took more than two years, but it was worth it. Now I know couples who get babies in only six months. A number of young couples have come to me for advice on adoption because they are aware of my good experience with Thomas."

Dorothy told Joan about going back to visit me at the Zoar home for the first six weeks after I was born. "I wasn't supposed to see him, but I did because I had a friend there," said Dorothy.

"How old was he when you got him?" asked Maryan.

"Six months," replied Joan. "The pediatrician told me his iron was low for a few months after his birth, but I did not get a medical history."

We talked about the octuplets that were born earlier that month to a family in Texas. I commented, "I always wanted to have a twin brother. Can you imagine how great it would be to have two of me?"

"I would have more gray hairs," joked Joan.

Dorothy added to the banter, "Thomas has noticed that I did not have any gray hairs until after we were reunited."

Maryan said, "Every time I would go to England to see Dorothy and the kids when they were growing up, Derwent would purposely ruin the picture. He would make a face, or stick out his tongue, or stick his fingers behind someone's head like a pair of antennae. He was a clown."

I said, "Typical Sagittarian, just like his big brother Thomas."

Maryan said, "Well, I am a Sagittarian and I'm not a clown."

"You think?" I joked. "Tell my mom the stories of your three whirl-wind romances between December 1941 and January 1943." Nothing else was said.

The meeting went well. Joan became acquainted with Dorothy and Maryan, and Dorothy and Maryan became familiar with Joan. We talked about the important, and the unimportant. The lunch lasted for about three hours. Later, talking with each mother separately, I learned that each mother and my grandmother felt comfortable with how the meeting went.

The next day was Christmas. I was glad I had planned for Dorothy and Joan to meet for lunch in the small private setting the previous day. This allowed them to become comfortable with each other in a quiet environment before interacting with a larger audience of family members.

The annual Lowry family Christmas dinner at Aunt Bessie's house was anything but quiet. The house was always jammed with people and noise, which was great. There was my Aunt Elaine who demonstrated her rapier wit. She should have been a part-time comedian. There was constant, loving bickering between the adult cousins. I usually took a lead role in this area. There were also children. Grandpa Bill's great-grandchildren were everywhere, and I couldn't keep up with all of their names since I only saw them once a year. However, I liked playing with them on Christmas Day. Although I knew Dorothy and Maryan were going to be nervous about their acceptance from the Lowry family, I was not worried at all. I knew they would receive a lot of love and acceptance. This was exactly what happened.

Before dinner, we exchanged Christmas presents. Joan received some great presents and was the star of the show. Joan had put in seventeen years of hard work to raise me, setting the foundation that helped me become the person I am today. She deserved praise and presents.

My grandmother Maryan and mother Joan.
Christmas 1998.

I gave a brief speech over dinner to summarize how I was able to find Dorothy and Mboga. Many members of the Lowry family still hadn't heard the story of my reunions with my biological parents.

Only Jackie, the oldest Lowry cousin in my generation, was aware from the beginning that I was adopted. Her view: "He is not adopted. He is just family." The rest of the house agreed unanimously.

I was trying to hold back the tears. I had assumed that Dorothy would be the one crying at this dinner, not me. The love that I was receiving was so overwhelming. Many people don't have one mother around who loves them. I had two, plus three great extended families. I felt so happy and thankful.

Joan turned to Dorothy and said, "The agency had two other children, but God had a special one for me. It was a pleasure to raise this child. I would not trade my experience raising Tommie for anything. I do thank God every day, and this is the truth, for being a mother. And he gave me the right one. I love him with all of my heart. There was no way I was able to reach you to let you know that he was loved."

I was trying to discreetly wipe tears out of my eyes.

"Dorothy called the adoption agency and let them know that she would like to meet Thomas if he ever came looking," Maryan mentioned.

"Yeah, if *he* ever came looking," said Dorothy. "I never wanted to impose myself on him. But if he ever was interested in finding me, I knew I would have been thrilled."

"I am glad he did," Joan confessed.

"Thank you. Obviously, all of the years without him, I grieved losing him. I always worried if he was all right. Was he still alive? Was he happy and healthy?"

"I understand. That is a natural instinct. He was a fat, happy little boy," Joan responded.

"It was such a joy when he contacted me," related Dorothy. "And it just keeps getting better and better because it is such a joy to see his extended family and see how well loved he is."

I was trying to speak, but was too choked up to even get a word out.

Maryan was tearing up as well, but she was at least able to talk coherently, "I will never forget the day when the agency called me and said 'I would like to talk to Dorothy Blazier' and I said 'She's in England. Who is this?' And then the caller gave me the name of the agency and I said, 'Oh, you found him!' And they said we cannot give you any information, we have to talk to Dorothy. So I got their name and number and I called Dorothy right away. I was so excited."

Minutes passed as everyone continued to share his or her thoughts and emotions. My cousin Kim interjected at last, "We want to know how you feel, Tommie. Are you at a loss for words now?"

I was unable to respond.

"If you are happy, then I am happy for you, I truly am," Kim spoke for me.

"I'm-um-uh—" I was too choked up to speak.

Kim continued, "Well, it took me a while to take all of this in. I was in shock. I was really in shock. Because I didn't even know that he had a feeling inside him to even search. And maybe it is a little selfish on my part, and maybe even a little self-centered, but I almost felt threatened, that a part of him was going to go somewhere else."

Dorothy defined her feelings succinctly, "That is why I never wanted to initiate contact."

Kim elaborated, "Because even when he came home to Pittsburgh last Christmas, Tommie didn't seem to want to talk much about his reunions with his biological families. My first reaction was that I felt hurt, though I had no right to feel hurt. However, I really feel now that if he is happy, then we are happy, because he has always been like my little brother."

Jackie added, "I don't feel threatened. As far as I am concerned Tommie is my cousin; he was ever since Joan brought him home. He is part of our family. Dorothy, he is also part of your family. That is how it is, and that is how it will remain until the end of time. He knows that. And he is still a brat." Laughter filled the room.

Normally, I would have retaliated against my "playa hating" cousin for that last comment since she has been doing that for years, but I was still too choked up to speak.

Maryan interjected, "It is good to hear you say this, Jackie, because no one tells the truth about him. He thinks the world is his."

I was being roasted.

Jackie continued, "Adoption never came up, and it never will be an issue. There are still a lot of members of the family that don't even know that Tommie is adopted. He is just family, and that is it. He is Aunt Joan's child and he is spoiled."

Kim mentioned a few of my successes, but it was quickly and right-fully noted that my cousin Christy had just completed her master's in education administration and supervision right before Christmas. She was the second Lowry to get a master's degree, and definitely would not be the last. I was sure that Grandpa Bill was looking on proudly. My yell of congratulations to Christy allowed me to finally break my silence. I wasn't able to speak for myself, but I was able to praise her easily.

Jackie brought the conversation back to me, saying, "Tommie achieved a lot, especially with Aunt Joan being a single parent. The young kids in the family look up to him, and he shouldn't forget that. He must be an example to them."

"He has been a great influence on my other kids," stated Dorothy.

"He has a little brother in Kenya who idolizes him," added Maryan.

"Don't give him too much credit," chimed Jackie. She could always restore somberness to any situation.

Dorothy jumped in, "I was going to say that it is really Joan that deserves the credit. I had to make sure he had a good home. This was something that I could not provide in 1966. And somewhere, there was this generous stranger that took him, and I have always been so grateful to her. And I think she has done such a fabulous job." Her voice trailed off as she fought back her tears.

Joan graciously redefined the situation, "You know Dorothy, God has an appointed time for all things. God may not come exactly when you want him, but He's always right on time. God knew my heart. He knew the love that I could give a child. And I tell Tommie, 'You were not flesh of my flesh, nor bone of my bone. I didn't physically carry you under my heart, but I carried you in my heart.' And I mean that. God played an important role in placing him in the right place. And now, God has allowed Thomas to find you. Those records were supposed to have been sealed. The judge stood there and told me they were to be sealed, but that judge was not God."

"And the judge didn't know Thomas," remarked Dorothy. "Thomas was going to have it his way." I was being roasted some more.

Dorothy continued, "I just feel so fortunate not only that he could come back into my family, but also that you have made me feel so welcome in your family. It is tremendous being here and I am grateful to all of you. Although I couldn't give Thomas a home back in 1966, I just wished that there could have been some window that I could have looked through to know that he was okay. Giving him up for adoption was such a cold, impersonal process. But at the time, I could not have done for him what Joan has done for him."

Joan responded, "I was glad to meet you all yesterday, too. And Dorothy, I understand how you feel as a mother. I often wonder about the one particular baby that I lost to a miscarriage, seven months into the pregnancy. But God has other plans for our lives."

Aunt Bessie put it simply, "God has blessed us!" "Amen" was heard around the room. "Nothing happens by coincidence," Bessie added.

Finally, I was able to speak, "What I was trying to say about ten minutes ago before I started losing it was that I think the reason that I didn't talk much about my relationships with the people in London and Kenya was…"

Dorothy came to my rescue as it became harder for me to speak. "He was trying to protect you. He didn't want his relationships with his Lowry family here in Pittsburgh to change."

Jackie reiterated, "It didn't make a difference. For us other cousins, it didn't matter. And if finding his biological family made him happy, it makes us happy. This is something he had to pursue for himself. Besides, Tommie isn't going to lose us. He is stuck with us."

I tried one last time, "Previously, I just wanted to say that I feel really lucky that I have a great family, the Lowry family here in Pittsburgh. Growing up in the Lowry family was a great thing. That alone puts me ahead of most people. On top of that I feel that I have another great family, including Dorothy, that spans from London to California. And then, in 1995, I made contact with my family in Kenya and have built good relationships with them as well. I feel fortunate to have met my father and grandmother in Kenya, to have visited my Kenyan family's village, and to get information about my proud Kenyan heritage. So, I now have three families who love me on three different continents. I feel extremely fortunate and I want to thank you all that are here today, and all of my family members scattered around the world."

Paraphrasing what my great-uncle Bill Blazier once told me, I remarked to everyone, "My three family trees, which we can trace back to the 1700s and then some, have grown many branches which spread far and wide. As we move into the twenty-first century, it is clear that the three trunks have developed many integrated branches that contain interesting leaves of delightful colors. The beauty of the branches can best be appreciated against a background of the history and cultures of the many racial and ethnic leaves they now contain. African, European, and Native American are now represented in our collective human kaleidoscope. The diversity of my families is further evidenced by the many religious, political, and philosophic preferences that have been documented. Perched on the branches are farmers, doctors, business people, steamboat captains, frontier pioneers, priests, newspaper publishers, educators, champions for social change, and many other contributors to our heritage. As we sit in the protective shade of these trees, let's hold hands and rejoice!"

So there it was. After all of this, Maryan wanted to keep in touch with Joan. After all, they both lived in Pittsburgh and they were really not that far apart in terms of age. The door was open for the relationship between Joan and Dorothy to grow, aided by the fact that Dorothy had moved from London to California. My English sister Lotus had fun with my Kenyan sister Margaret when they met in 1997. I was hoping Margaret would one day attend a university in the United States, which I thought would strengthen her relationships with us Westerners. Many in Kenya were enamored with my grandmother Maryan. Lotus and Joan liked each other when they spent time together in 1995. I had growing relationships with Kenyan cousins Silas Omwenga Momanyi in Dallas, and Richard and Monica Nyamwange in New Jersey. They have shown me so much love and hospitality during my visits there. Similarly, I had recently met Kenyan uncle Andrew Nyaboga and my cousin Brian Rasugu Makwaro in New Jersey.

By 1998, my Kenyan family was more comfortable around White people because they had met Dorothy, Maryan, and Lotus. Similarly, my British siblings were more comfortable around non-White people because of their relationship with me. Lotus had a Nigerian boyfriend for a while, and Atom, Jade, and Derwent have all dated women of color. The bottom line is that we are Earthlings. Thus, the superficial differences of color, nationalism, or language only obscure the truth of that. If we saw ourselves as Earthlings, would we destroy the only home we have, this planet, or exploit members of our own larger family here or abroad? I would like to think that everyone who hears our story would be more comfortable with multiracial friendships, and multiracial relationships and children. New connections are being made, not only by me, but also by my friends and family members. I am just happy to help good people to come together. I truly have a wealth of family.

Epilogue

In 2000, I began a dating relationship with Dominique Walton, a fun, beautiful, physician and MBA known to her friends as "Nikki." Just as my sister Lotus helped inspire me to start writing this book, Nikki provided me with the support I needed to finish the manuscript.

I had learned a lot from my first marriage, and even more in the relationships that followed my divorce before I met Nikki. For most of us, complete happiness eventually includes some relationship with a significant other. Over the long haul, most of us need someone with whom to share career success, financial gains, fun activities, spirituality, family life, and fitness goals. You do not necessarily need to find your "soul mate" to have this area of life in check. The goal is to just be comfortable with what you want for yourself, what you want in the prospective significant other, and with where and how you are looking for your partner. The rest is just a matter of time. Once you get to this point, you can then free your mental energy to focus on other parts of your life such as career, finances, health, and family, whether you are in a relationship or not.

When I decided that I was open to meeting a long-term prospective mate, I made the philosophical commitment to myself to not ask for things I could not give. For example, I could not expect to get a mate who was highly disciplined in terms of her thinking, activities, and goal setting if I was unorganized, undisciplined, and severely lacking in these areas. What we get out of a relationship has a lot to do with what we give to our partner.

Here is a list of some qualities I considered in the women I dated. I prioritized my list with the "must haves" at the top. Determining the ranking and the weight that each item carries is a personal decision. This process can take days or months. That's okay. But I think each item is worth thinking about seriously, and I advise both men and women to start their own similar list.

I looked for someone who:

- Is honest and open.
- Has "chemistry" with me. Both individuals must like each other and progress at a somewhat even pace toward love.
- Has aesthetic good looks (a relatively shallow category).
- Is an exciting, compatible sexual partner.
- Has no sexually transmitted diseases. (Only testing can verify this. Don't be afraid to discuss this. Use a condom and other "safer" practices.)
- Balances life—works hard, plays hard, and works out hard.
- Hangs well with my friends and is a good friend to me.
- Is happy in their career; ambitious with shared life vision.
- Is drug free.
- Keeps their word
- Is a good partner, advisor, and potential parent of children, as applicable.
- Challenges and encourages me in all areas of life.
- Has diverse, practical intelligence.
- Is compatible in terms of thinking and problem solving. (No relationship is trouble-free. Does this person know how to "fight" fairly and calmly, or is it "drama time" for each disagreement?)
- Has financial status, financial future, and financial discipline better than or equal to my own.
- Has a sense of humor.
- Accepts me for what and how I am.
- Has diverse abilities, mindset, friends, activities, music, and other interests. (Watch out for people with only one type of music in their house, one type/race of friend, and so forth.)
- Is disciplined in thinking, activities, decisions, and goal setting.

- Is confident, not possessive.
- Has stable and healthy relationships with their own family and friends.
- Is compatible spiritually in terms of beliefs, activities, and commitment. (This could be about religion, but for some people religion and spirituality are two different things.)
- Is astrologically compatible. (A lower priority, but it makes for interesting reading, especially if you have your complete chart done as a couple.)

Once I had my ranked list in place, and I was willing and able to give everything on my list, my mind and soul were free and open to meet the right person. If I had met someone and after a short time I decided that they did not meet my prioritized needs, I then had a framework for how to deal with that woman. For example, I could have kept her as a workout partner or a peer mentor for my professional career. Or I could have moved her out of my life completely. Whatever choice I made, I eventually learned to communicate my intentions clearly and consistently so that there were no misunderstandings. I expected the same respectful treatment in return from the woman. The framework allowed me to stay in control of my emotions and decisions.

My advice to friends on relationships and many other subjects is, "Don't passively avoid pain…aggressively seek pleasure." When applied to relationships, this means you should put yourself in position to meet the type of people specified by your personal list. This does not mean acting desperately, just proactively. People can join professional organizations or do community service. Go to house parties where the guest list is somewhat filtered. Join a ski club, a scuba diving club, a travel club, or a running club. Actively pursue spiritual beliefs. Learn another language. In short, *be yourself and live up to your own requirements list* and you will soon meet someone who also will live up to your list. The mindset and process described above prepared me to meet Nikki and enabled us to start our dating relationship on solid footing.

In the midst of our happy dating relationship, Nikki and I traveled together to Kenya in December 2000. Since Nikki had already met both Joan and Dorothy, I wanted her to meet Mboga and the rest of my Kenyan family.

After our long flight to Nairobi, Nikki and I were warmly met at Jomo Kenyatta International Airport in Nairobi by Margaret, Uncle Robert Nyamwaro, Uncle Henderson Magare, and about five of my cousins at 11 A.M. Margaret had previously explained on the phone that my father Mboga was staying near the coast, in the Kwale area, and that he was hoping to see me there.

In spite of our jet lag, Nikki and I took a 10 P.M. bus that same evening out of Nairobi for the overnight ride to the coastal city of Mombasa, Kenya's second largest city. Margaret joined us on the bus. This overnight ride was similar to the ride that Margaret took in January 1995 from Mombasa to Nairobi to initially meet me. Being used to smooth, well-lit roads in the United States, the dark, swerving, bumpy ride was difficult for Nikki and me. The seats were small and cramped for my long legs. I could not sleep, but I was relieved when we arrived in Mombasa at 5:30 A.M.

There is a significant Muslim community on the Kenyan coast, and we arrived during the Muslim holy month of Ramadan. Prayers emanating from the loudspeakers at the nearby mosque met our predawn arrival.

By the time the sun rose, we had secured a taxi for our ride to Uncle Monyoncho's new home in Likoni, just south of Mombasa. Mombasa is actually an island. I had not noticed that we had crossed a causeway to the island during the nighttime bus ride. To get to Likoni, our taxi had to ride on a ferry, which I found similar to the way people in Boston get to Martha's Vineyard.

Although I was not surprised, I was really touched by the hospitality my Kenyan family showed Nikki and me, starting with my Uncle Monyoncho, Aunt Florence, and their family. We were welcomed into their home, fed, and treated warmly. They really seemed to like Nikki and made her feel welcome. Aunt Florence even taught Nikki how to cook *ugali*.

It was good to see Mboga. We spent two days together near the coast. I had not spoken to Mboga in over a year, since he had moved and did not have a phone. We were able to reestablish our relationship. Mboga seemed very pleased to meet Nikki. He more than approved of her; he highly recommended her as a potential wife. This was great to hear.

Margaret and my cousin Esther Nzighe joined Nikki and me for an afternoon on the beach. The Mombasa beach area is beautiful. As Ernest Hemingway once said regarding what is now the Kenyan coast, "This cannot be less than natural beauty, the endless sand, the reefs, the lot, are completely unmatched in this world."

Departing Mombasa, Nikki and I flew directly to the Maasai Mara to spend a weekend on a photographic safari. It was Nikki's first experience seeing the incomparable flora and fauna of Africa. We had a great time.

Nikki was thrilled to see lions, cheetahs, elephants, buffaloes, rhinos, hippos, baboons, and hyenas in their natural habitat. She was delighted to see the giraffes, known in Kiswahili as *twigas*. Because my Kenyan family sees the five-foot, eleven-inch Nikki as very tall, graceful, beautiful, and gentle, they had taken to affectionately calling her "Twiga."

I actually had a great time on the safari as well, though I did not expect to be thrilled. It was my third trip to the Maasai Mara National Park, and I expected to not be too excited about seeing the animals again. I had really wanted to climb Mount Kilimanjaro on this trip to Africa. My original plan for the trip called for five days with family, three days to climb Kilimanjaro, and two days in the Maasai Mara. But, I subsequently discovered that it takes one day to get from Nairobi to the base of the mountain, five days to climb the mountain, one day to descend the mountain, and one day to get back to Nairobi. Kilimanjaro would have consumed too much time. I could not do both the Maasai Mara and Kilimanjaro on this trip. I had promised that I would take Nikki to see the animals at the Maasai Mara, and she was keen to go. She was not keen to "risk her life" climbing Kilimanjaro with me. Even though I skipped the mountain climb, I still had a great time with Nikki at the Maasai Mara.

From the Maasai Mara, Nikki and I flew directly to Nairobi on Christmas Eve. We stayed in a Nairobi hotel until December 30. My sister Margaret met us there. We spent the week with her, my aunts, uncles, and many cousins in Nairobi. We had a lot of great cultural exchange about life in Kenya and in America. During the day, we joked and had fun, exchanged a lot of love, and consumed a lot of Kenyan tea and *ugali.*

At night, my cousins Denis, Stephen, Roger, Stella, and Cecilia partied with Margaret, Nikki, and me. We hit Nairobi nightspots, including Carnivore's, the Klub House, and Choices. I am not sure if I was a good influence, but I hoped they could see the value of being able to both work hard and play hard.

Margaret had been experiencing sporadic problems with the computer that I had given her back in 1998. We found a repair person, and I provided some financial assistance to try to get the computer working. I also purchased a wireless mobile phone with an airtime package for Margaret. I figured that this, coupled with the computer and software for graphic design and web page design, would provide Margaret with the tools she would need to jumpstart her business ventures in Kenya.

Although I was optimistic about Margaret's ability to make money doing graphic design and web publishing in Kenya, I hoped she would make more of an effort to attend a university in the United States. Despite our discussions on this subject since 1995, and my previous delivery of books of information on American universities, financial aid, and the TOEFL test, as of December 2000, she had made little progress toward this goal. This lack of progress surprised me, since she was saying that going to an American university was an important goal for her. I did realize, though, that the logistics of the process to become an international student can be overwhelming, especially if you are young and struggling in a developing nation.

Life in Kenya seemed to be even tougher in 2000 than it had been during my previous trip in 1997. I tried to continue to be supportive, providing her with a new set of books on American universities, financial aid, and a study guide for TOEFL test. I promised to pay the cost of the TOEFL test, and to help her with the cost of her applications to the universities. I was hopeful that she would be able to get accepted to a university in the United States. Margaret and her mother Jane Bosibori agreed I had done all that I could. The ball was in Margaret's court. I assumed she would move forward when the time was right for her.

At the conclusion of my trip to Kenya, I was handed this lovely letter by Margaret in the airport just before I went to my gate:

Big Brother Thomas,

It has been great having you around. It is a shame you have to leave now. I wish I could convince you to stay but it seems your mind is set; so all I can do is wish you a safe trip.

Words cannot express my appreciation and how thankful and touched I am by your determination to assist me in all ways. I am very thankful, and I would like you to know that you are my source of inspiration and that I won't let your efforts be wasted. I will put my best foot forward and make the best out of all that you have assisted me with.

I am going to prepare for the TOEFL and apply for university admission. Thanks for bringing me all of the necessary information.

Nikki is a lovely lady. She is calm, bright, and beautiful. The list goes on and on. Take good care of her. Tides and storms will be there in any relationship, but please overcome them and achieve your goals. Be happy, both of you, and let her know that we love her.

Well, I can write a whole book, but this was just a small note to tell you thank you and may God shine his light on you.

Lots of love,

Little Sister Margaret

After traveling overseas with Nikki, and being with her constantly for weeks, I discovered that we did not get on each other's nerves. Better than that, we really enjoyed each other's company. This was the icing on the cake, giving me the final boost of confidence and comfort that I needed to act. I already felt she would be a great mother for future children. She met my "checklist" of qualities that I wanted in a spouse. I expected that having one woman for the rest of my life would enable emotional stability and inner peace, without the external drama I had in the past while dating multiple women.

Furthermore, I reexamined my core motivations: Freedom and flexibility, giving back to disadvantaged youth, financial security, abundance of love/fun/happiness, health and longevity, adventure, inner peace, positive karma, diverse friendships, and intriguing experiences.

I expected Nikki to enhance my efforts to address my core motivations. I finalized my decision to propose to Nikki. Although I expected to be nervous right up until the vows were taken, I was ready to ask her to marry me. My decision was made; however, there was some teasing still to be done.

Nikki, who was thirty-three at the time, had been especially motivated to get married since the early stages of our relationship. She had no children at that point, and she felt the pressure of her ticking "biological clock." That pressure quickly spilled over to me. Although I loved Nikki and had hoped to one day marry her, I did not want her ticking biological clock to cause me any undue pressure. So, we avoided the marriage discussion with a "moratorium" for months, until late 2000, right before the trip to Kenya. When the issue crept back up on the table, I told her that I would propose to her by June 27, 2001, or she could break up with me. This "deadline" helped diffuse the issue a bit, giving her assurance that I would not keep her hanging on indefinitely waiting for a proposal from me. After an additional gentle push from Nikki, the proposal "deadline" was moved up to May 27, 2001.

Meanwhile, I had already been shopping for a pear-shaped diamond ring on a platinum setting.

Many opportunities for me to propose passed. On the Maasai Mara trip to see the wildlife, we could not find the elusive, nocturnal leopard, known as *chui* in Kiswahili. I told Nikki that if she could locate a *chui* while on safari, the "deadline" would get moved in to February 27, 2001. However, Nikki was unable to find the so-called "platinum *chui*." Christmas in Nairobi came and went. No ring. New Year's Eve found us in London. No ring. Our one-year celebration of dating as a couple passed after we returned to America. No ring. Nikki's thirty-fourth birthday passed. No ring.

As we flew to the Heavenly ski resort above Lake Tahoe for Valentine's Day weekend, I told her the "deadline" was still May 27. Nikki was a bit discouraged about her engagement prospects. I subsequently told her that she would have three separate opportunities to take one month each off the "deadline." Specifically, if she did not ask me to carry any of her luggage or rented ski gear, I would take one month off the "deadline." This was designed to encourage her to not overpack. Since it was her first-ever ski trip, if she successfully got on and off the ski lift after only two tries, I would take one month off the "deadline." If, by the end of the trip, she could ski an entire green trail—the designation for an easy ski run—without falling, I would take one month off the "deadline." In other words, she had the opportunity to move the "deadline" up to February 27.

On Thursday, her first day of skiing, she successfully negotiated the ski lift, pulling in the "deadline" to April 27. I joked that there would be a number of high visibility opportunities before the end of April for me to give her the ring, such as a planned trip to Europe, as well as the holidays of St. Patrick's Day and Easter. I was still teasing her until the last moment to maximize her surprise.

On Friday morning, I awoke early, telling Nikki I wanted to get in "first tracks," skier jargon for being the first person to ski through the fresh snow that had fallen the night before. It was a set up. I needed an excuse to leave the room early without her.

At 8:30 A.M., I went to the office of a mountain photography company. They position photographers each day at scenic points on the resort's mountains. If you elect, you can pose for a picture on the mountain. At the end of the day, you can go to their office to view the pictures. If you like them you can buy them. I found the photographer who was to be located at the top of the Heavenly tram on the California side of the resort. I told her my plan. Then I took a lift up the mountain and still enjoyed some first tracks.

Just after 9 A.M., I met Nikki at the bottom of the tram. I had told her that her lessons on the beginner slope did not give her a good opportunity to see Lake Tahoe. I suggested that we grab some breakfast at the restaurant at the top of the tram, catch the morning view, and then she could take the tram back down to her morning lesson on the bunny slope.

On the previous day, I had checked out different scenic points on the mountain, and I had talked to a few photographers about the sunlight at different times of day. I knew that 9:45 A.M. would be the perfect time to get a great picture on the top of the mountain on the California side with the lake in the background and no shadows. The planning and logistics were meticulous.

While we were having breakfast, Nikki asked, "Do you have the camera?"

"Uh, I have to look for it," I replied vaguely. I did have it on me as a backup, but I knew the photographer would be there when we arrived outside.

"Look, Nikki," I said as we walked back outside, "there is a sign saying that we can get our picture taken here at the top." The photographer put us in a variety of poses. Nikki had no idea what was going on.

"Get on one knee," the photographer asked. Nikki still didn't get it.

"Do you want me on my left knee or my right?" I asked.

"Get on your left knee," the photographer directed, "She can sit on your right leg."

We took some more pictures, and then Nikki stood up. I acted like my leg was hurt and that I was having trouble getting up.

"Would you help me?" I asked. She looked confused and tried to help me up. I was already down on one knee. I opened up the box, exposing the ring inside. I continued, "Would you help me enjoy the rest of my life by joining me in marriage?" She started crying and answered, "Yes!" I then noticed that I had mistakenly opened the box upside down, but she easily grasped the idea. She jumped on the ground, and on me, kissing me, hugging me, and crying. Just to be sure, I asked her again, "Do you want to marry me?" Again, while still crying she answered, "Yes! Yes!" She was totally surprised.

Thomas proposes to Nikki at the Heavenly Valley Resort, high above Lake Tahoe on the California side. February 2001. [Courtesy of SharpShooter Imaging, Heavenly Valley Resort]

I put the ring on her finger. The photographer pulled out a backpack that I had given her earlier that morning. The backpack contained a bottle of champagne and two glasses. We took some more pictures and continued kissing and celebrating.

Finally, I asked Nikki, "Are you going to your ski lesson?"

"No, I am going to call my mother and tell her the good news!"

"Okay," I said, "I am going to ski. Meet me for lunch at noon. We will go to the restaurant at the top of the mountain."

Later, when we walked into the cafeteria for lunch, Nikki suspected nothing. She was still excited about the proposal. In the cafeteria, there was a group of resort employees holding a sign with her name on it. They told her to follow them. They led us out the back of the restaurant and into a wooded area. After climbing down some snow-covered rocks and going through some trees, we walked up to an elegant table with two chairs set up for a romantic lunch. Nikki was amazed. We enjoyed a secluded four-course lunch outside on the snowy mountain and enjoyed, once again, a great view of Lake Tahoe.

After the romantic lunch, I asked Nikki, "Are you going to take an afternoon ski lesson?"

"No, I am too happy! I am going to call some of my friends."

"Okay," I said, "I am going to ski over to the Nevada side of the Heavenly resort. I will meet you at 4 P.M. at the photography office to buy the proposal pictures."

When we returned to the condo at 5 P.M., wine, cheese and crackers, and chocolate were waiting in the room. Of course, there was a card from me congratulating Nikki on her engagement.

Coincidentally, my sister Lotus was married the very next weekend in England. Nikki and I attended as the newly engaged couple. I gained a great brother-in-law, John Miles, a native Londoner. Dorothy and Maryan were quite excited about the potential prospect of grandchildren and great-grandchildren, respectively. Lotus and John, and Nikki and I, hoped to quickly grant their wish.

Atom was by then a manager at a music store in San Francisco. He was making his mark on some weekends as a Drum 'N' Bass deejay in the Bay Area.

Perhaps inspired by his big brother from America, Jade completed a B.A. honors degree in Professional Broadcasting at Ravensbourne College in London in 2001.

Derwent subsequently completed his BSc (Honors) in Herbal Medicine at the University of Westminster. He was multitasking, like his oldest brother, juggling both a musical career and herbal medicine. He recently moved to Paris, where he is doing solo music gigs and planning an album.

Thanks to assistance from me, and from Kenyan cousins Richard and Monica Nyamwange in New Jersey, my sister Margaret was accepted at and entered East Stroudsburg University in Pennsylvania. She received a 3.4 GPA in her first semester. She continued to excel and eventually graduated in 2005 with a bachelor of science in media communication and technology. She is now pursuing a master's degree as well. Our sibling relationship has grown very strong, and we talk frequently. Perhaps Christine Bahati and Machoka Rasugu will also consider educational and career opportunities in the West. Christine Bahati currently seems to be interested in nursing.

On the subject of encouraging education, the Leaders of Tomorrow high school mentoring program that I chaired for the Atlanta Chapter of the National Black MBA Association grew to nearly one hundred students by 2001. We offered free monthly workshops on a variety of topics to get the students ready for college. We also added an SAT Preparation Course. The lag that American minorities have experienced in wealth, health care, and political power needs to be addressed. Some African-Americans have called for reparations from the U.S. government as compensation for four hundred years of inequity and discrimination on the North American continent. I personally want to focus on the future, so I have focused my individual efforts on programs like Leaders of Tomorrow, which has helped so many young African-Americans find a brighter future. I teach, first and foremost, that individuals, especially African-Americans with major hurdles to overcome, must hold themselves personally responsible. People must take persistent action and be self-reliant and produce results in spite of the obstacles. Individuals, regardless of race, cannot allow themselves to fall into the mentality of the victim. Secondly, from a public policy perspective, the key is education. As Malcolm X said, "Education is our passport to the future, for tomorrow belongs to the people who prepare for it today."

We can make a big improvement in this area by implementing school vouchers, but let me be clear. I do not support school vouchers that allow public money to be diverted to private schools. Public tax dollars getting diverted to religious-based private schools does not sound like a separation of church and state to me. My school voucher plan would be limited to public schools only in a given city or county or school district. This way, public schools would be forced to compete with each other, and public schools that excel would be rewarded for demonstrating the desired behaviors. The rewards should include a larger budget for the school to spend, and better pay for teachers and administrators. Schools and their students would be measured based on items such as grades, attendance, graduation rates, performance on state and national standardized tests, etc. Private schools should always be an option for individuals who can afford it, but public tax dollars should not be used. By the way, the Thomas Brooks of the 1970s on the North Side of Pittsburgh probably could not have afforded private school, even with vouchers. Strengthening public schools with competition and vouchers is the answer.

Doing our part to generate intellectual and financial wealth in the minority community, my good friend CJ Bland and I launched www.MinorityProfessionalNetwork.com in 2001. Minority Professional Network, Inc. (MPN), provides the premiere "Career, Economic and Lifestyle Connection™" for progressive minority professionals.

In October 2001, in front of roughly two hundred friends and family members from all over the world, Nikki and I were married in Atlanta.

Kenya, England, and every part of the United States were well represented as we began our life together. I was nervous, but it was probably the best decision I have ever made. A good time was had by all at the reception.

Multicultural family members from around the globe witness the Nikki and Thomas wedding. October 2001. [Courtesy of Bass Photography]

Subsequently, Nikki became pregnant. Our first son, Joshua Omwenga, was born in 2002, roughly ten years after my reunion with Dorothy. Our first daughter, Kendall Kemunto, was born in 2005, roughly ten years after my reunion with Mboga. Now that I have children of my own, I have even more appreciation for the job that Joan did as a single mother.

After they read this narrative of heritage and reunion, I hope that all of our children, and their children, can learn from my few achievements and from my many mistakes.

We have been blessed with a wonderful son named Joshua and a delightful daughter named Kendall. February 2006.

Be Featured in Our Next Book

Alpha Multimedia, Inc., is developing a new book and e-book that will chronicle the adoption-related stories of numerous individuals around the world. Tentatively titled *The Joy of Search: Stories of Adoption, Reunion, and Inspiration,* the book gives you a chance to tell your story to the world. Adoption and reunion have affected people's lives in many ways. It is likely that your adoption-related story has affected you, and your family and friends.

Submit online: (recommended method)
www.AlphaMultimedia.com/JoyofSearch.htm

Submissions by mail: Send the completed form to
Alpha Multimedia, Inc.
P.O. Box 722034 • Houston, TX 77272, USA

Your Name: _____

Address: _____

City: _____

State/Province:_____ Postal Code: _____

Country: _____

Email: _____

Phone: _____

URL: _____

Answer the questions below, and write as much as you like. Attach a separate document to provide your answers.

- What are the detailed circumstances related to the adoption?
- Why did it occur?
- How has your life changed since the adoption?
- Has there been a reunion between the child and parent(s)?
- If so, has the reunion changed the lives of those involved?
- What is unique and/or inspirational about your story?

Give the Gift of

A Wealth of Family

An Adopted Son's International Quest for Heritage, Reunion, and Enrichment

to Your Family, Friends, and Colleagues

CHECK YOUR LEADING BOOKSTORE OR ORDER HERE

❑ **YES**, I want _____ copies of *A Wealth of Family* at $17.95 each, plus $4.95 for USA shipping for the first book and $3.00 for USA shipping for each additional product. (Texas residents please add $1.48 sales tax based on 8.25% rate per book).

International Shipping: $14.00 for first book or CD-ROM and $7.00 for each additional product. Foreign orders must be accompanied by a postal money order in U.S. funds. Allow at least twenty days for delivery.

My check or money order for $_____ is enclosed.

Please charge my: ❑ Visa ❑ MasterCard
❑ Discover ❑ American Express

Author autographing requested for entire order quantity: ❑ Yes ❑ No

Name _____

Organization _____

Address _____

City/State/Postal Code _____

Country _____

Phone_____ Email _____

Card # _____

Exp. Date_____ Signature _____

Please make your check payable and return this form to:

Alpha Multimedia, Inc.
P.O. Box 722034 • Houston, TX 77272-2034 • USA

Online orders: **www.AlphaMultimedia.com/order.htm**

Order toll-free by phone: **1-800-431-1579**

About the Author

Thomas Brooks

Thomas Brooks has published several articles and spoken frequently on the radio and in other forums. In 1998, Brooks won a national award through Career Communications Group in the "Technical Sales and Marketing" category. In 2001 he cofounded an online business, www.MinorityProfessionalNetwork.com, which provides a global Career, Economic and Lifestyle Connection™. Brooks lives with his wife and children outside of Houston, Texas, USA.